Tima T. Moldogaziev, Gene A. Brewer,
J. Edward Kellough (eds.)

PUBLIC POLICY AND POLITICS IN GEORGIA

Lessons from Post-Soviet Transition

With a foreword by Dan Durning

Bibliografische Information der Deutschen Nationalbibliothek
Die Deutsche Nationalbibliothek verzeichnet diese Publikation in der Deutschen Nationalbibliografie; detaillierte bibliografische Daten sind im Internet über http://dnb.d-nb.de abrufbar.

Bibliographic information published by the Deutsche Nationalbibliothek
Die Deutsche Nationalbibliothek lists this publication in the Deutsche Nationalbibliografie; detailed bibliographic data are available in the Internet at http://dnb.d-nb.de.

ISBN-13: 978-3-8382-1535-8
© *ibidem*-Verlag, Stuttgart 2021
Alle Rechte vorbehalten

Das Werk einschließlich aller seiner Teile ist urheberrechtlich geschützt. Jede Verwertung außerhalb der engen Grenzen des Urheberrechtsgesetzes ist ohne Zustimmung des Verlages unzulässig und strafbar. Dies gilt insbesondere für Vervielfältigungen, Übersetzungen, Mikroverfilmungen und elektronische Speicherformen sowie die Einspeicherung und Verarbeitung in elektronischen Systemen.

All rights reserved. No part of this publication may be reproduced, stored in or introduced into a retrieval system, or transmitted, in any form, or by any means (electronical, mechanical, photocopying, recording or otherwise) without the prior written permission of the publisher. Any person who does any unauthorized act in relation to this publication may be liable to criminal prosecution and civil claims for damages.

Printed in the EU

Soviet and Post-Soviet Politics and Society (SPPS) Vol. 228
ISSN 1614-3515

General Editor: Andreas Umland,
Institute for Euro-Atlantic Cooperation, Kyiv, umland@stanfordalumni.org

Commissioning Editor: Max Jakob Horstmann,
London, mjh@ibidem.eu

EDITORIAL COMMITTEE*

DOMESTIC & COMPARATIVE POLITICS
Prof. **Ellen Bos,** *Andrássy University of Budapest*
Dr. **Gergana Dimova,** *University of Winchester*
Dr. **Andrey Kazantsev,** *MGIMO (U) MID RF, Moscow*
Prof. **Heiko Pleines,** *University of Bremen*
Prof. **Richard Sakwa,** *University of Kent at Canterbury*
Dr. **Sarah Whitmore,** *Oxford Brookes University*
Dr. **Harald Wydra,** *University of Cambridge*
SOCIETY, CLASS & ETHNICITY
Col. **David Glantz,** *"Journal of Slavic Military Studies"*
Dr. **Marlène Laruelle,** *George Washington University*
Dr. **Stephen Shulman,** *Southern Illinois University*
Prof. **Stefan Troebst,** *University of Leipzig*
POLITICAL ECONOMY & PUBLIC POLICY
Dr. **Andreas Goldthau,** *Central European University*
Dr. **Robert Kravchuk,** *University of North Carolina*
Dr. **David Lane,** *University of Cambridge*
Dr. **Carol Leonard,** *Higher School of Economics, Moscow*
Dr. **Maria Popova,** *McGill University, Montreal*

FOREIGN POLICY & INTERNATIONAL AFFAIRS
Dr. **Peter Duncan,** *University College London*
Prof. **Andreas Heinemann-Grüder,** *University of Bonn*
Prof. **Gerhard Mangott,** *University of Innsbruck*
Dr. **Diana Schmidt-Pfister,** *University of Konstanz*
Dr. **Lisbeth Tarlow,** *Harvard University, Cambridge*
Dr. **Christian Wipperfürth,** *N-Ost Network, Berlin*
Dr. **William Zimmermann,** *University of Michigan*
HISTORY, CULTURE & THOUGHT
Dr. **Catherine Andreyev,** *University of Oxford*
Prof. **Mark Bassin,** *Södertörn University*
Prof. **Karsten Brüggemann,** *Tallinn University*
Dr. **Alexander Etkind,** *University of Cambridge*
Dr. **Gasan Gusejnov,** *Moscow State University*
Prof. **Leonid Luks,** *Catholic University of Eichstaett*
Dr. **Olga Malinova,** *Russian Academy of Sciences*
Dr. **Richard Mole,** *University College London*
Prof. **Andrei Rogatchevski,** *University of Tromsø*
Dr. **Mark Tauger,** *West Virginia University*

ADVISORY BOARD*

Prof. **Dominique Arel,** *University of Ottawa*
Prof. **Jörg Baberowski,** *Humboldt University of Berlin*
Prof. **Margarita Balmaceda,** *Seton Hall University*
Dr. **John Barber,** *University of Cambridge*
Prof. **Timm Beichelt,** *European University Viadrina*
Dr. **Katrin Boeckh,** *University of Munich*
Prof. em. **Archie Brown,** *University of Oxford*
Dr. **Vyacheslav Bryukhovetsky,** *Kyiv-Mohyla Academy*
Prof. **Timothy Colton,** *Harvard University, Cambridge*
Prof. **Paul D'Anieri,** *University of Florida*
Dr. **Heike Dörrenbächer,** *Friedrich Naumann Foundation*
Dr. **John Dunlop,** *Hoover Institution, Stanford, California*
Dr. **Sabine Fischer,** *SWP, Berlin*
Dr. **Geir Flikke,** *NUPI, Oslo*
Prof. **David Galbreath,** *University of Aberdeen*
Prof. **Alexander Galkin,** *Russian Academy of Sciences*
Prof. **Frank Golczewski,** *University of Hamburg*
Dr. **Nikolas Gvosdev,** *Naval War College, Newport, RI*
Prof. **Mark von Hagen,** *Arizona State University*
Dr. **Guido Hausmann,** *University of Munich*
Prof. **Dale Herspring,** *Kansas State University*
Dr. **Stefani Hoffman,** *Hebrew University of Jerusalem*
Prof. **Mikhail Ilyin,** *MGIMO (U) MID RF, Moscow*
Prof. **Vladimir Kantor,** *Higher School of Economics*
Dr. **Ivan Katchanovski,** *University of Ottawa*
Prof. em. **Andrzej Korbonski,** *University of California*
Dr. **Iris Kempe,** *"Caucasus Analytical Digest"*
Prof. **Herbert Küpper,** *Institut für Ostrecht Regensburg*
Dr. **Rainer Lindner,** *CEEER, Berlin*
Dr. **Vladimir Malakhov,** *Russian Academy of Sciences*

Dr. **Luke March,** *University of Edinburgh*
Prof. **Michael McFaul,** *Stanford University, Palo Alto*
Prof. **Birgit Menzel,** *University of Mainz-Germersheim*
Prof. **Valery Mikhailenko,** *The Urals State University*
Prof. **Emil Pain,** *Higher School of Economics, Moscow*
Dr. **Oleg Podvintsev,** *Russian Academy of Sciences*
Prof. **Olga Popova,** *St. Petersburg State University*
Dr. **Alex Pravda,** *University of Oxford*
Dr. **Erik van Ree,** *University of Amsterdam*
Dr. **Joachim Rogall,** *Robert Bosch Foundation Stuttgart*
Prof. **Peter Rutland,** *Wesleyan University, Middletown*
Prof. **Marat Salikov,** *The Urals State Law Academy*
Dr. **Gwendolyn Sasse,** *University of Oxford*
Prof. **Jutta Scherrer,** *EHESS, Paris*
Prof. **Robert Service,** *University of Oxford*
Mr. **James Sherr,** *RIIA Chatham House London*
Dr. **Oxana Shevel,** *Tufts University, Medford*
Prof. **Eberhard Schneider,** *University of Siegen*
Prof. **Olexander Shnyrkov,** *Shevchenko University, Kyiv*
Prof. **Hans-Henning Schröder,** *SWP, Berlin*
Prof. **Yuri Shapoval,** *Ukrainian Academy of Sciences*
Prof. **Viktor Shnirelman,** *Russian Academy of Sciences*
Dr. **Lisa Sundstrom,** *University of British Columbia*
Dr. **Philip Walters,** *"Religion, State and Society", Oxford*
Dr. **Zenon Wasyliw,** *Ithaca College, New York State*
Dr. **Lucan Way,** *University of Toronto*
Dr. **Markus Wehner,** *"Frankfurter Allgemeine Zeitung"*
Dr. **Andrew Wilson,** *University College London*
Prof. **Jan Zielonka,** *University of Oxford*
Prof. **Andrei Zorin,** *University of Oxford*

* While the Editorial Committee and Advisory Board support the General Editor in the choice and improvement of manuscripts for publication, responsibility for remaining errors and misinterpretations in the series' volumes lies with the books' authors.

Soviet and Post-Soviet Politics and Society (SPPS)
ISSN 1614-3515

Founded in 2004 and refereed since 2007, SPPS makes available affordable English-, German-, and Russian-language studies on the history of the countries of the former Soviet bloc from the late Tsarist period to today. It publishes between 5 and 20 volumes per year and focuses on issues in transitions to and from democracy such as economic crisis, identity formation, civil society development, and constitutional reform in CEE and the NIS. SPPS also aims to highlight so far understudied themes in East European studies such as right-wing radicalism, religious life, higher education, or human rights protection. The authors and titles of all previously published volumes are listed at the end of this book. For a full description of the series and reviews of its books, see www.ibidem-verlag.de/red/spps.

Editorial correspondence & manuscripts should be sent to: Dr. Andreas Umland, Institute for Euro-Atlantic Cooperation, vul. Volodymyrska 42, off. 21, UA-01030 Kyiv, Ukraine

Business correspondence & review copy requests should be sent to: *ibidem* Press, Leuschnerstr. 40, 30457 Hannover, Germany; tel.: +49 511 2622200; fax: +49 511 2622201; spps@ibidem.eu.

Authors, reviewers, referees, and editors for (as well as all other persons sympathetic to) SPPS are invited to join its networks at www.facebook.com/group.php?gid=52638198614
www.linkedin.com/groups?about=&gid=103012
www.xing.com/net/spps-ibidem-verlag/

Recent Volumes

219 Dmitry Travin, Vladimir Gel'man, Otar Marganiya
The Russian Path
Ideas, Interests, Institutions, Illusions
With a foreword by Vladimir Ryzhkov
ISBN 978-3-8382-1421-4

220 Gergana Dimova
Political Uncertainty
A Comparative Exploration
With a foreword by Todor Yalamov and Rumena Filipova
ISBN 978-3-8382-1385-9

221 Torben Waschke
Russland in Transition
Geopolitik zwischen Raum, Identität und Machtinteressen
Mit einem Vorwort von Andreas Dittmann
ISBN 978-3-8382-1480-1

222 Steven Jobbitt, Zsolt Bottlik, Marton Berki (Eds.)
Power and Identity in the Post-Soviet Realm
Geographies of Ethnicity and Nationality after 1991
ISBN 978-3-8382-1399-6

223 Daria Buteiko
Erinnerungsort: Ort des Gedenkens, der Erholung oder der Einkehr?
Kommunismus-Erinnerung an einem historischen Ort am Beispiel der Gedenkstätte Berliner Mauer sowie des Soloveckij-Klosters und -Museumsparks
Mit einem Vorwort von Sigrit Jacobeit
ISBN 978-3-8382-1367-5

224 Olga Bertelsen (Ed.)
Russian Active Measures
Yesterday, Today, Tomorrow
With a foreword by Jan Goldman
ISBN 978-3-8382-1529-7

225 David Mandel
"Optimizing" Higher Education in Russia
University Teachers and their Union "Universitetskaya solidarnost'"
ISBN 978-3-8382-1519-8

226 Daria Isachenko, Mykhailo Minakov, Gwendolyn Sasse (Eds.)
Post-Soviet Secessionism
Nation-Building and State-Failure after Communism
ISBN 978-3-8382-1538-9

227 Jakob Hauter (Ed.)
Civil War? Interstate War? Hybrid War?
Dimensions and Interpretations of the Donbas Conflict in 2014–2020
With a foreword by Andrew Wilson
ISBN 978-3-8382-1383-5

Acknowledgements

We extend our heartfelt appreciation and acknowledgement to many colleagues and friends that made this edited book possible. We recognize with deep gratitude the University of Georgia (U.S.) Research Program in Public Policy for the Republic of Georgia, funded by the U.S. Department of State from 2017 through the spring of 2019. We thank the U.S. Embassy in Georgia, and in particular Embassy employees Jeffrey K. Reneau and Nino Gagua for their kind support during the program period and after its completion. Their assistance and guidance were vital.

We are grateful to our partners in Georgia who made this program possible. The Georgian Institute of Public Affairs in Tbilisi (GIPA) was our host institution in Georgia. We thank Dr. Maka Ioseliani, the GIPA Rector; Dr. Natia Tchigvaria, Director of the PhD Program in Social Sciences; and Davit Akhvlediani, the MPA Program Coordinator.

We also extend our thanks to Dr. Rusty Brooks of the University of Georgia (U.S.) Carl Vinson Institute of Government, for his support with program development and liaison with the U.S. Department of State. Similarly, we thank the Departments of Political Science and Public Administration and Policy in the School of Public and International Affairs (SPIA) at the University of Georgia, for providing a critical administrative platform for the program. Dr. Brad Wright, Professor and Chair of the Department of Public Administration and Policy, assisted in developing project components, leading program workshops, and mentoring research projects of program participants. We thank him individually and thank all the faculty and staff in SPIA who were directly involved with our efforts.

The chapters in this book are a sample of research projects completed by scholars in Georgia as part of the University of Georgia Research Program in Public Policy. We thank all the participants for their attentiveness in our classes and their work on varied research projects. We trust that they developed useful skills through participation in our program. We can affirm that we learned much from them.

Guidance and leadership from the Commissioning Editor at *Ibidem Press* Jakob Horstmann and the editorial team was critical to the success of this book. We also deeply appreciate the feedback from an anonymous reviewer, who provided constructive suggestions on submitted manuscript materials. Finally, we thank Andreas Umland, the editor of the *Soviet and Post-Soviet Politics and Society Series* for including this book in the series.

Dedication

Georgia is a hidden jewel nestled in the Caucasus region of south-central Eurasia. Her captivating physical beauty and panoramic landscapes have inspired generations of Georgians to repel hostile forces and preserve their beloved country. Georgia's rich culture is unsurpassed, and the Georgian people are known for their world-class hospitality and strong family values. Above all, Georgia is a country on the move–searching for an even brighter, more prosperous future in the years ahead. I therefore dedicate this book to the coming age of Georgian splendor.
Gene A. Brewer, Athens, Georgia (USA), September 2020

To my long-time friends from Georgia who first introduced me to this beautiful country: Vaso Jaiani and Levan Samadashvili
J. Edward Kellough, Athens, Georgia (USA), September 2020

To my friends in the country of Georgia and the state of Georgia
Tima T. Moldogaziev, University Park, Pennsylvania, September 2020

Preface

Supporting the Development of Public Policy and Administration Education in Georgia: The University of Georgia's Partnership in Tbilisi

Efforts of the University of Georgia (UGA) to help two Georgian institutions of higher education develop Western-style public policy and administration education programs began with a small step in September 1998. "University of Georgia" in the above sentence refers to the American university located in Athens in the state of Georgia. The "Georgian institutions of higher education" were degree-granting institutions operating over 6,000 miles away in Tbilisi, the capital of the country of Georgia in the South Caucasus region.

The small step was a visit I made to Tbilisi as a faculty member from UGA's Carl Vinson Institute of Government, a public service unit of UGA that had recently created a center to develop joint programs and partnerships with non-U.S. universities, mainly those in countries that had left the Soviet Union and had started the process of building democracies. The Carl Vinson Institute had just completed its first such project in Ukraine, where it had a partnership with Uzhgorod State University (USU) that introduced the study of public administration and public policy to interested faculty members and helped several of them develop relevant courses they could teach. The Carl Vinson Institute also encouraged USU to create a center to offer training programs for local government managers in the Transcarpathian Oblast, the region in which the university–now named Uzhgorod National University–is located. For that purpose, USU set up the Institute for Public Administration and Regional Development that exists to this day.

The 1998 exploratory trip to Tbilisi came after we learned about a possible partner institution for future joint projects. It was the Georgian International Training Center for Environmental Management and Planning (GITC). This private university had been created jointly in 1990 with the help of the Georgian Academy of Sciences and UGA's College of Agricultural and Environmental Sciences to offer undergraduate and graduate degrees in agribusiness management, environmental management, and modern immunology. GITC rose and operated with the assistance of two grants to UGA from the United States Information Agency (USIA). Grant funds were used partly to pay for faculty exchanges but mainly to finance the study of a dozen GITC students at UGA for a semester or more.

U.S. government funding of the joint program had ended in 1997, but GITC had continued to offer its degree programs. In 1997 it had awarded fifty Bachelor of Science degrees, and in 1998 the number of conferred degrees reached 59. From 1993 to 1997, graduate students had earned 64 Master of Arts degrees from GITC. Despite its previous successes, however, the future of the program was uncertain, I was told, because not only had USIA funding ended, but also GITC's rector, a dynamic and well-connected businessman, had died unexpectedly in 1996, leaving it rudderless.

During the exploratory trip to Tbilisi, I met with the leaders of the GITC, including Valeri Melikidze, an Academy of Science member whom GITC had appointed to lead its side of the partnership with UGA. Prof. Melikidze's terminal degree was in human geography, and he had a good record of carrying out applied policy-related research. Representing UGA, I proposed a partnership like the one the Carl Vinson Institute had had with Uzhgorod State University that focused on helping GITC develop the capacity to add new programs in public administration education and outreach. GITC's leadership found the partnership proposal to be acceptable.

Our new partnership came at a good time. The USIA had issued a call for proposals for grants to finance partnerships between universities in the United States and those in countries that were "Newly Independent States." In coordination with Prof. Melikidze, I wrote a grant proposal for the USIA's "NIS Colleges and Universities Partnerships Program." The grant proposal, entitled "Building New Public Administration Education and Outreach Programs at the International Training Center in Tbilisi, Georgia," stated that it would "strengthen education in Georgia on public administration and public policy in a democratic context." It proposed to do so by helping GITC faculty members — present and newly added — to develop expertise in public administration subjects so they could teach them and provide training related to them.

While putting together the grant proposal, I learned that the USIA, with an office in the American Embassy in Tbilisi, had been investing heavily in another project to improve public administration education to Georgia. Beginning in 1995, it had funded activities of the National Academy of Public Administration (NAPA), a prestigious group in the United States that had helped create the Georgian Institute of Public Administration (GIPA). This nonprofit educational institution offered a Master of Public Administration (MPA) degree in Tbilisi. NAPA not only helped to develop education and training materials for the new program, but it also supplied its faculty members: visiting American professors taught most of the courses in the one-year MPA program. This English-language program graduated about thirty students each year. In our partnership grant application, we made it clear that GITC would not be competing with GIPA, but that it would expand the opportunities for Georgian students to study public policy and administration through courses taught in Georgian.

Despite concerns at the USIA about the shaky financial situation of the Georgian International Training Institute, in the middle of 1999, it approved a grant of about $250,000 for the UGA-GITC partnership. The joint project began in earnest in January 2000 with semester-long visits of Prof. Melikidze and three other GITC faculty members to UGA. These visitors, and others who came to UGA in the years that followed, had an opportunity to attend policy and public administration courses taught by UGA's Department of Political Science faculty members, confer with them and other UGA faculty members on syllabi and course materials, and sample the Carl Vinson Institute's extensive local government training programs. Although UGA's Department of Political Science was not involved in administering the grant, many of its faculty members voluntarily participated in project activities.

In May 2000, when two Carl Vinson Institute faculty members traveled to Tbilisi, one for a one-month visit and the other for two months, they found that GITC was defunct, but that its leaders were attempting to find the funding needed to resume operations. The UGA faculty members contacted Giorgi Margvelashvili, GIPA's rector, and Mzia Mikeladze, GIPA's dean, to offer their services to that institution. Both Rector Margvelashvili and Dean Mikeladze had been appointed in 2000 to replace the Institute's previous leaders. These new leaders of GIPA had big plans for its development, and they made use of visiting UGA faculty members to support GIPA's activities.

By the middle of 2001, after UGA had hosted three more would-be GITC faculty members during the Spring semester, it became clear that the Georgian International Training Center was dead, and UGA asked the USIA to designate GIPA as its grant partner. The request was approved, and UGA shifted its efforts to working with its new partner, which was developing both a new Georgian-language degree for local government managers and a program to provide local government training. Educating and training local government officials had become an urgent priority because Georgia had recently elected about 30,000 local government leaders who previously were appointed.

After GIPA received funds in 2002 from the Urban Institute to finance its planned Local Government Manager master's degree program and to provide related training, UGA faculty members helped GIPA prepare to teach the academic and applied courses that were part of the new program. Among its activities, UGA hosted semester-long visits of a young man and two young women who were preparing to teach courses in the new degree program. Also, when in Tbilisi, UGA professors helped several GIPA faculty members hone their training skills and prepare training materials. In addition, UGA facilitated the ten-day visit of Tamara Sulukhia, the woman appointed to head GIPA's Local Government Manager programs, who traveled to UGA to learn about its training programs for local governments.

Also, during 2002, GIPA Rector George Margvelashvili visited UGA for two weeks to talk to UGA administrators about issues of higher education management. Under his leadership, the Georgian Institute of Public Administration had changed its name to the Georgian Institute of Public Affairs, reflecting its new degree program in Local Government Management and another new graduate program it had added in journalism (the Caucasus School of Journalism and Media Management). These new academic programs were the first of many that Rector Margvelashvili and Maka Ioseliani, who became GIPA's Dean in 2003, would initiate in the coming years. (In November 2013, a year after stepping down as GIPA's rector, Margvelashvili was elected President of Georgia, serving a term in office that lasted until December 2019.)

The UGA-GIPA partnership grant program ended in 2004. Its project activities had included fourteen trips to Tbilisi by eight UGA faculty members who spent a total of 53 weeks there and ten semester-long visits by Georgian faculty members to UGA, a total of 150 weeks. However, the expiration of the partnership grant did not mean the termination of UGA's work with GIPA. Instead, UGA was offered the opportunity to continue the partnership for three additional years.

The opportunity arose because the National Academy of Public Administration had decided to discontinue its cooperative work with GIPA, primarily because of a dispute between the two about a personnel decision made by Rector Margvelashvili. After NAPA halted its partnership activities, the U.S. Department of State's Bureau of Educational and Cultural Affairs (BECA) invited UGA to submit a proposal for a three-year project that would take over NAPA's work with GIPA while also undertaking other activities to enhance GIPA's ability to sustain its operations when grant funds to pay visiting U.S. faculty members were no longer available. (BECA took on the responsibilities of the U.S. Information Agency when that organization was abolished.) In response to the invitation from BECA, UGA submitted a grant proposal with the title "Transition to a Sustainable Model of Public Administration Education." It was approved along with a $300,000 grant.

Grant funds continued to finance the three-week courses taught by visiting American faculty members at GIPA, with the number decreasing each year. They also paid for an institutional assessment of GIPA and strategic planning activities, plus for the continued visits of GIPA faculty and staff members at UGA, though in smaller numbers and for shorter times. In addition, the grant purchased equipment, including computers, for GIPA's use and provided small research grants for GIPA faculty members.

After the grant activities had begun, GIPA's primary strategy for sustainability became clear: it intended to generate the revenue it needed to operate by offering new self-financing degree and non-degree programs. Pursuing that strategy, GIPA initiated a continuing education MPA degree program for employed students unable to attend its more intensive standard program. Also, it started certificate programs in law and other topics, training in rural development, a new master's degree in International affairs, and a new Ph.D. in Public Administration.

When the second grant ended in March 2007, UGA's formal partnership program with GIPA was over, but in the years that have followed, some UGA faculty members have periodically taught courses at GIPA and have worked cooperatively on other ventures. GIPA has continued its growth. Its present offerings include nine bachelor's degrees in disciplines that include political science, sociology, applied psychology, business administration, and economics; ten masters degrees, including, in addition to public administration, public policy, international law, and business administration; and a Ph.D. in Social Sciences. It offers more than two dozen certificate programs, operates a radio station, and publishes an academic journal with Troy University, the *Journal of Politics and Democratization*. GIPA is now rated among the best universities in Georgia.

In 2017, UGA was awarded a new grant from the U.S. Department of State to provide training in social science research methods for faculty members and PhD students in Georgian universities. Because faculty members at UGA had experience traveling to Tbilisi and working with GIPA in the past, Maka Ioseliani, now serving as GIPA's Rector, agreed that GIPA would serve as a local host for the new program and provided classroom space, computer labs, and logistical support. The chapters in this book are based on papers developed by Georgian scholars who participated in this new training program offered in 2017 and 2018.

Dan Durning

Contents

Acknowledgements i

Dedication ii

Preface by *Dan Durning* iii

1 Lessons for Policy, Administration, and Politics from Georgia
   J. E. Kellough, G. A. Brewer, T. T. Moldogaziev 3

Part I: Georgian Independence and Democracy in the South Caucasus Region

2 Georgians' Political Knowledge and Attitudes towards the West and Russia
   Anna Menagharishvili 15

3 Russian Soft Power in Georgia
   Marika Mkheidze 33

4 Analyzing the Potential Causes of Ethno-Political Conflicts in the South Caucasus
   Nino Okhanashvili 67

5 Voter Turnout of Ethnic Azerbaijani Women in Georgia
   Aytan Hajieva 97

Part II: Public Policy and Administration in Georgia

6 Low Performance Issues in Public Elementary Schools in Georgia: Implications for Policy-Makers
   Ana Laitadze 117

7 Georgian Higher Education Policy and Ethnic Minority Performance
   Giorgi Tchumburidze 137

8   Roadmap to Employability: The Relationship between Generic Skills and Employment
    Elene Jimsheleishvili 155

9   How Do Mining Activities in Georgia Affect Local Public Health?
    Natia Tchigvaria 185

Part III: Georgia in the Context of Post-Soviet Transitions

10 Centralized versus Decentralized Human Resource Practices: The Cases of Georgia and Estonia
    Sabina Alakbarova 207

11 Legal Institutions, Financial Liberalization and Financial Development in Transition Economies
    Ulrich Eydam, Irakli Gabriadze 224

12 Estimation of the Government Spending Multiplier for Countries in Transition
    Lasha Arevadze 260

13 Geographical and Globalization Patterns in Georgian Trade
    Davit Akhvlediani 292

Contributors 306

1
Lessons for Policy, Administration, and Politics from Georgia

J. Edward Kellough, Ph.D.
Gene A. Brewer, Ph.D.
Tima T. Moldogaziev, Ph.D.

This edited book presents original studies on issues pertinent to public policy, public administration, and politics from and about Georgia, all written by Georgian scholars. The research focuses on Georgia's struggle for independence and democracy in the South Caucasus region, public administration and policy, and Georgia's rightful place in comparative public sector governance studies. The lessons from Georgia are important in the twenty-first century because Georgia itself is increasingly important to study as a relatively successful post-Soviet transition story and because an understanding of Georgia can offer insights that are useful for other transitional and developing cases of interest. Most immediately, many of the governance implications of these studies are relevant to the broader Caucasus region and other post-Communist countries.

Though the chapters in the book focus primarily on Georgia's short history of post-Soviet independence and its ongoing struggle for political and economic freedom in the Caucasus region and beyond, Georgia is not a newly formed state. Rather, its recorded history dates back more than 2,500 years, and its capital city, Tbilisi, is more than 1,500 years old. Georgian culture is a rich tapestry of art, music, literature, religion, food, winemaking, and more. The Georgian language is one of the oldest in the world and consists of at least eighteen different dialects and a distinctive alphabet. Georgia was the second country in the world to adopt Christianity in the Fourth Century, and the Georgian Orthodox Church has been a state-sanctioned religion for much of Georgia's history—serving as a stabilizing influence for the country.

Geographically, Georgia is at the crossroads of Eastern Europe and Western Asia; Russia sits on her northern border and the Middle East lies due south. The Black Sea forms the country's western border. Georgia is thus situated at the confluence of several strong cultures and has experienced centuries of regional turmoil and contested borders. Much of Georgia's home territory was fought over by the Persian, Roman, Byzantine, Arab, Mongol, and Ottoman armies from at least the First Century B.C. through the Eighteenth Century, and more recently, Georgia was in the Soviet orbit and is still in a tug of war with Russia for control of its borderlands.

Georgia was once a destination on the Silk Road and its strategic position has accrued numerous benefits over the years, but it has also created turbulence and insecurity. While the Georgian culture has survived and even thrived through the years, Georgians have not had a unified, independent state for very much of their history. The zenith of Georgia's power as an independent kingdom came in the Eleventh and Twelfth Centuries. In 1783, the Treaty of Georgievsk allowed the Russians to take over the kingdom as its protectorate. Shortly afterward, the Russian empire began annexing Georgian territory and ruling over Georgia's regions. That form of governance lasted until recently. As the Soviet Union was collapsing, Georgia held an independence referendum and declared independence on April 9, 1991. Georgia then elected the first President of independent Georgia, who has been followed by five others. Georgia thus became a presidential republic with a single-chamber parliament comprised of members of several political parties. The judicial branch, which was weak during the Soviet era, is now being strengthened and reformed. Local governments outside Tbilisi have little formal power and even fewer resources, but they often act independently. Thus began Georgia's great experiment with independence and democracy, which provides lessons for other post-Soviet countries in transition.

At the same time, Georgia is important to understand because its transition from a post-Soviet system and away from Russia's sphere of influence has not been without pitfalls. The civil war in the early days of independence, separatist conflicts in the Abkhaz and Ossetian autonomous regions, which resulted in frozen conflicts and an internal displacement of people, and persistent attempts by Russian President Vladimir Putin's administration to hold a tight grip on Georgia's post-Soviet trajectory provide others with a rich set of lessons to learn from (Lanskoy and Areshidze, 2008; O'Beachain, 2011). Yet, among former Soviet states, Georgia's economy has shown notable growth with significant foreign direct investment. Specifically, from 1995-2018 the Georgian economy grew every year, except for 2009 because of a Russian military incursion into the country, with an average growth rate of 5.5%. Meanwhile, from 1997-2018 foreign direct investment averaged 8.3% of Georgia's GDP. Most of this growth came after the painstaking reforms of former Georgian President Mikheil Saakashvili, who fundamentally restructured formal and informal governance institutions in the country, often with what has been described as authoritarian undertones (Mitchell, 2009; Cheterian, 2008; Lanskoy and Areshidze, 2008).

Central and local government administrations in Georgia in post-Saakashvili years continue to press forward with reforms, albeit with a more measured tone toward Russia. As a result of reforms, recent assessments rank Georgia among the most successful examples of countries tackling public sector corruption, on par with European Union (EU) member states from the Baltic and Central European regions, countries that also completed their own transitions from Communist governance systems (Aliyev, 2014; Light, 2014; Ivanov, 2013; Common, 2011). As Georgia's economy expands and governance institutions strengthen further, its role in the Caucasus—and even more broadly in Eastern Europe and Central Asia—is likely to grow significantly.

Meanwhile, the independent nation state of Georgia has sought to forge its own path in international relations. While somewhat unsuccessful, Georgia has actively pursued EU and NATO membership in a westward-looking foreign policy (Meyer, 2017; Diesen, 2015). Though such membership may remain unattainable in the near future, economic and political ties with European member states continue to grow. The visa free regime with Schengen states is certainly a result of such improvement in ties (Loda, 2019). Additionally, since the breakup of the Soviet Union, the United

States has worked to strengthen diplomatic relations with Georgia. This is illustrated by presidential and vice-presidential visits from the U.S. to Georgia, educational programs sponsored by the U.S. Department of State, and the 2009 U.S.-Georgia Charter on Strategic Partnership that documents the importance of the relationship (Mitchell and Cooley, 2010). The future of Georgia's relations with the West, and how successful they may be, could be an important facet of international relations in the twenty-first century.

Beyond the intrinsic value of studying Georgia itself, understanding Georgian politics and public policy processes is important for what it reveals about other cases around the world. Whether considering the 15 sovereign states that emerged from the breakup of the Soviet Union, the seven states that formed from the division of Yugoslavia, or transitions from command-and-control systems more broadly defined, there are many important questions that scholars and policy makers must face. Much can be learned for future emergent countries by examining the first three decades a state has experienced under a more capitalistic economic system and new democratic regime. To policymakers in a newly formed government, these chapters offer both a sense of what could be expected in a new nation's future as well as which policy approaches have the most potential. Whether handling relations with a strong neighbor (such as Georgia with Russia), equitably integrating sizable ethnic minorities into society, politics, and the economy (such as Azeris and Armenians in Georgia), or finding its place in the world economy by increasing trade and remittances, certain emergent states will likely find strong parallels with Georgia.

Some of the greatest similarities and applications of lessons from Georgia will naturally be found with other former Soviet states. These countries must weigh what it means for domestic and international policy and politics to be neighbors with Russia (as well as China for countries in Central Asia). Many of these countries also have large ethnic minorities, at least in part because of years of Soviet dysfunctional border making and divisive politics toward various nationalities. Often, the minority citizens that now find themselves in dozens of newly independent countries communicate with other groups by speaking the Russian language instead of their own national languages, which can pose questions for political incorporation and communication, and even susceptibility to Russia's influence (Brubaker, 2011; Pavlenko, 2008). These nations in transition also have had to sort out their position in the global economy, deciding questions such as whether to look to their former Communist compatriots for cultural, economic, political, and trade partners, or to search elsewhere. As we address such questions in Georgia, we also may gain relative insight that would apply not only to the other post-Soviet countries but also the Eastern and Southeastern European nations in general. For all of these reasons, we believe the studies in this volume are of great value not only to the reader who is interested in Georgia itself but to anyone interested in the policies and politics of post-Communist transition.

The chapters in the edited book take a variety of methodological approaches, which are driven by their respective research questions. The key here is that rather than U.S. (or Western) scholars studying Georgia or the Caucasus region, it is scholars from Georgia itself who author the studies. Unlike scholarship from overseas that seeks to understand how events in Georgia relate to them, often from an ethnocentric perspective and with limited understanding of local dynamics, scholars from Georgia have first-hand experiences regarding what works or does not work in the country or the region. In the development of this volume, we refrained from inserting our ideas about the complex relationships that exist and our prescriptions for how the country or region should be studied. The very incidences where parsimonious approaches by Georgian scholars could offer clear explanations for the political or public policy phenomena and outcomes should not be brushed aside. Also, the definitions of politics and policy utilized by the authors of this edited book are primarily at the micro or meso-levels of analysis, which are very different from the macro- or international themes that are prevalent in scholarship about the region that emanates from the West. Very often, when discussing Russian, European Union, or the US role in Georgia or the Caucasus region, we forget about the bread and butter issues that are more pertinent to Georgians in their own daily lives than to outsiders looking in.

The co-editors of the book worked with Georgian scholars on key components of what it means to conduct research in social sciences broadly defined. After several rounds of revisions and resubmissions of research, as well as a subsequent research conference in Tbilisi, Georgia, we ensured that all chapters in the proposed book are high-quality studies on important political and policy topics in Georgia and the post-Communist region. Our objective was not to claim ownership of work by Georgian scholars, but rather to assist in developing a sustainable base of scholars and a national research capacity for conducting governance research in Georgia.

Mapping Book Chapters

The studies in this book are organized thematically. Part I of the book focuses on Georgian independence and democracy in the South Caucasus region. As an independent nation state, the views of ordinary citizens and how they exercise their political rights are essential to national politics, and Georgia's struggle for autonomy and independence in the region is of utmost importance to most Georgians. In Chapter two of the volume, Anna Menagharishvili studies mass views about Russia, the EU, and NATO among Georgian citizens. She finds that better-informed citizens tend to share political elites' favorable views on forming a military alliance with NATO; however, better-informed ethnic minorities, who primarily speak Russian, tend to oppose a NATO alliance. This cleavage in public opinion extends to other issues relevant to Georgia's effort to break free from Russian influence and form Western ties.

Chapters three and four consider how Russia's desire for autonomy and regional influence affects Georgian politics and national security. In Chapter three, Marika Mkheidze explores the extent to which Russia exercises 'soft power' in Georgia through mechanisms like propaganda, and she illustrates how such propaganda can influence citizens' policy attitudes. This chapter builds on the previous chapter by laying bare the forms and effects of Russian propaganda. In Chapter three, Nino Okhanashvili explains how Russian desire to maintain influence in the South Caucasus region has been a key precipitator of ethnic conflicts in Georgia and

Armenia. She employs well-known theories of international relations and evidence collected from expert interviews and secondary sources to establish that Russia has hegemonic ambitions in the region. She concludes that Russia is seeking to advance its own goals and to maintain or expand its former sphere of influence by stoking ethnic conflicts in the region. Russia's hegemonic aims have largely framed Georgian foreign policy and national security in the early post-Soviet period.

Finally, in Chapter five, Aytan Hajiyeva focuses on the fundamental right to vote and examines the question of why ethnic Azeri women have a particularly low voter turnout rate. Since high turnout that is uniform across groups is desirable in democratic processes, this is a particularly important puzzle for an emergent democracy that is normalizing its electoral system, and it can be explained to a large degree by gaps in education and language abilities of women in the predominantly Muslim ethnic group.

Part II of this edited book turns to important policy and administration themes in Georgia. Starting with primary-level education in Chapter six, Ana Laitadze examines student performance in schools sampled from various regions of Georgia. Studying grade distributions, she shows that, while the effect is nonlinear, smaller class sizes tend to lead to better student performance. Pivoting into higher education, Giorgi Tchumburidze further analyzes the impact of Georgia's innovative "1+4 program" in Chapter seven, which was designed as a way to increase higher education enrollments among ethnic minorities who do not speak Georgian. While quantitative work does not yet show evidence of more bachelor's degrees among ethnic minorities in the program's short history, student interviews show satisfaction, encouragement, and positive signals to neighbors that may raise the impact in the immediate future.

In Chapter eight, Elene Jimsheleishvili considers what all of this means for the workforce in the face of high unemployment in Georgia. She shows that better-educated workers who have certain skills are more likely to be employed. From primary school through the workforce, then, these chapters offer several ideas on which public policies (and where those policies) would be successful.

Finally, in Chapter nine, Natia Tchigvaria considers the implications of weakly enforced environmental regulations by contrasting public health statistics across Georgian municipalities. Focusing on mining, she shows that if a municipality contains a mine that releases toxins, certain kinds of diseases (typically cardio-vascular) are, on average, significantly elevated. As nations consider their environmental practices, these findings are worth considering.

Part III chapters place Georgia in a comparative context relative to countries within and outside of post-Soviet transitions. In Chapter ten, Sabina Alakbarova considers human resource management in public administration, contrasting the cases of Georgia and Estonia. While there can be arguments for centralized versus decentralized hiring practices in both countries, decentralization policies appear to be helpful for keeping turnover rates among public servants low. In Chapter eleven, Ulrich Eydam and Irakli Gabriadze examine the states that were either Soviet Union member states or its satellites and investigate the development of financial institutions. They show that legal institutions that define and guarantee property rights are key to developing quality financial institutions in these emergent economies.

In Chapter twelve, Lasha Arevadze considers the impact of government spending in the Commonwealth of Independent States. He computes the multiplier effect of government spending and shows that it does have an expansionary effect on macroeconomic growth that is comparable to other developing countries, though the effect can vary somewhat by fiscal circumstances. Finally, in Chapter thirteen, Davit Akhvlediani models patterns in Georgia's trade and shows that a Gravity Model is a useful framework for understanding Georgia's relations with its trade partners.

References

Aliyev, Huseyn. 2014. "The Effects of the Saakashvili Era Reforms on Informal Practices in the Republic of Georgia." *Studies of Transition States and Societies* 6(1): 19-33.

Baimenov, A., and Liebert, S. 2019. "Governance in the post-Soviet Era: Challenges and Opportunities." *Public Administration Review* 79(2): 281-285.

Brubaker, Rogers. 2011. "Nationalizing States Revisited: Projects and Processes of Nationalization in post-Soviet States." *Ethnic and Racial Studies* 34(11): 1785-1814.

Cheterian, Vicken. 2008. "Georgia's Rose Revolution: Change or Repetition? Tension between State-building and Modernization Projects." *Nationalities Papers* 36(4): 689-712.

Common, Richard. 2011. "International Trends in HRM in the Public Sector: Reform Attempts in the Republic of Georgia." *International Journal of Public Sector Management* 24(5): 421-434.

Diesen, Glenn. 2015. *EU and NATO relations with Russia: After the Collapse of the Soviet Union*. Ashgate Publishing.

Ivanov, A. 2013. Anti-corruption Policy and Legal Regulations for Counteracting Corruption in Georgia. *Law and Modern States* 4: 50–56.

Lanskoy, Miriam, and Areshidze, Giorgi. 2008. "Georgia's Year of Turmoil." *Journal of Democracy* 19(4): 154-168.

Light, M. 2014. "Police Reforms in the Republic of Georgia: the Convergence of Domestic and Foreign Policy in an Anti-corruption Drive." *Policing and Society* 24(3): 318-345.

Loda, Chiara. 2019. "Georgia, the European Union, and the Visa-Free Travel Regime: Between European Identity and Strategic Pragmatism." *Nationalities Papers* 47(1): 72-86.

Mayer, Sebastian. 2017. "The EU and NATO in Georgia: Complementary and Overlapping Security Strategies in a Precarious Environment." *European Security* 26(3): 435-453.

Mitchell, Lincoln A. 2009. "Compromising Democracy: State Building in Saakashvili's Georgia." *Central Asian Survey* 28(2): 171-183.

Mitchell, Lincoln A., and Cooley, Alexander A. 2010. "After the August War: A New Strategy for US Engagement with Georgia." *The Harriman Review* 17(3-4): 2-72.

Ó Beacháin, Donnacha. 2012. "Snapshots from Abkhazia 2001-2012," In Metin Sönmez eds., *Reflections on Abkhazia 1992-2012*. London: Abkhazworld.

Pavlenko, Aneta. 2008. „Multilingualism in post-Soviet Countries: Language Revival, Language Removal, and Sociolinguistic Theory." *International Journal of Bilingual Education and Bilingualism* 11(3-4): 275-314.

Part I

Georgian Independence and Democracy in the South Caucasus Region

Part 1

2
Georgians' Political Knowledge and Attitudes towards the West and Russia[1]

Anna Menagharishvili

The political landscape of Georgia, a country nested between Turkey and Russia, has drastically changed since the dissolution of the Soviet Union, of which it was a constituent part. Georgia's 1991 declaration of independence marked the transition of the country from Soviet rule to democratic governance. With little experience as an independent state, Georgia quickly became a transitional country. This transition period can be described as "democratizing backwards," which refers to a situation where democratic institutions were put in place; yet, they were created before the rule of law and civil society (Rose & Shin, 2001). Now, Georgia had to quickly forget its totalitarian past and become a democratically minded country. After the collapse of the Soviet Union, almost no one thought the process of transition to democracy would be such a difficult, long, and painful one. Even in the very first years it became clear that democratic institutions alone couldn't create active, engaged and responsible citizens. The country faced serious challenges before identifying the direction it would go and the political path it would follow.

As Georgia is forging its own path, one of the main issues it faces is deciding which countries it should form international alliances with. Georgia is in a difficult geographical location because it represents the corridor between Europe and Asia, which raises further questions about which path Georgia will follow. With regard to economic and security relations, a natural path would be to ally more closely with Russia, which was the leading power in the Soviet Union. The other path is to turn to the West for international

---

[1] The author would like to thank Professor Axel Gosseries from the Catholic University of Louvain.

alliances—reaching out to the United States or, more likely, the more proximate European Union (EU) member states. Georgia's leadership has largely focused on allying with the West. But what does the mass public think about this issue?

Understanding whether Georgian citizens favor allying with Russia or with the West is useful for two reasons. First, it helps to explain how democratic citizens form their opinions in general. Second, it helps to discern the probability of long-term popular support for the political elite's preferred policy of allying with the West. In fact, an even more specific research question is: How does political knowledge affect individuals' attitudes in forming a preference for one alliance or another?

To answer this question, this chapter proceeds as follows. First, prior literature about how political knowledge matters to understanding public opinion is reviewed. Second, the background on Georgia's relations with Russia and the West is discussed to set terms of the issue to be studied. Third, the theory and hypotheses are described. Fourth, a data analysis is undertaken in order to show how Georgians' knowledge has affected their attitudes about alliances. Finally, the implications of the study are discussed.

Political Knowledge and Political Attitudes

On foreign relations (or any issue), why is political knowledge so important to public opinion? According to numerous studies, citizens who know a vast amount of information are considered to be central players in democratic theory and this is a crucial element of democracy (Dahl, 1973). Political scientists like Almond and Verba (1963) mention that civic competencies and abilities are important for democracy (also Verba, 1961; Verba et al., 1978; Verba et al., 1995). Citizens should have some knowledge about general politics in order to exercise their power through elections or other democratic means.

There have been serious debates among scholars about what the concept of political knowledge means; it is hard to define and also hard to measure. Delli Carpini and Keeter (1996, 10) define political knowledge as "the range of factual information about politics that is stored in long-term memory." Scholars also refer to knowledge about the political system in general (Milner, 2007) or to political circumstances, which are mostly related to election campaigns (Prior and Lupia, 2008). Some scholars suggest that political knowledge should be measured using individuals' recall of events and people in the political sphere (Garramone and Atkin, 1986), or on factual knowledge about major political figures (Dow, 2009). Other scholars identify the main components of citizens' political knowledge as civic knowledge and policy knowledge (Andersen et al., 2002), while some refer to knowledge of both national and international affairs (Mondak, 2000).

Politically knowledgeable people seem to engage differently in thinking about and doing politics than less knowledgeable people. They may process information differently. Research has shown that political knowledge is linked to more politically stable opinions, more to left wing opinions than to right-wing ones, and unwillingness to accept irrelevant and propagandistic information. Furthermore, relevant political knowledge allows individuals to translate their preferences into meaningful policy demands, and high levels of political knowledge can affect voting behavior by helping voters realize which candidates and parties offer policies that are consistent with their personal values (Delli Carpini and Keeter, 1996).

In terms of how people form attitudes, Zaller (1992) argues that opinions are based on the information they process, which they have to receive and accept as valid. As they hear this information, people form "considerations" in response to elite discourse in the mass media. This discourse consists of multiple, frequently conflicting streams of persuasive messages. In fact, these processes require cognitive and intellectual engagement. The greater an individual's level of political awareness, the more likely he or she will receive these messages. It should be noted, however, that greater political knowledge may increase the chance that a person will think critically and accept the received information or not. Hence, the least knowledgeable people are likely to have uninformed and random opinions, while the most knowledgeable people often have rigid opinions and are difficult to change.

Context of the Issue: The Choice between Russia and the West

Before considering how citizens choose their preference for Russia or the West, it is essential to consider the recent history of Georgian foreign relations, with particular attention to the relationship with Russia. Georgia has a challenging geopolitical location. Its relationship to Russia has been very complicated historically. It was part of the Russian Empire from 1801 to 1917. During that period, Russia not only took away Georgia's political independence but also the independence of the church. Shortly after the establishment of the Soviet Union, Georgia became a member state and remained so until 1991. Relations with Russia flared with the war in Abkhazia in 1992-1993. This repeated itself in 2008 after Russian military incursion into Georgia and continued occupation of 20 per cent of the country, including South Ossetia. Russia continues its "creeping occupation" by frequently manipulating the frozen conflict at its own pleasure.

Due to major events that have happened in Georgia since independence, the task of establishing civil society was further delayed. Unlike in Western countries, in post-Soviet countries there are not only social and economic differences, but the perceptions and behavior of people are different (Pietrzyk-Reeves, 2008; Howard, 2003; Rose & Shin, 2001; Makarovič and Tomšič, 2010). Other researchers indicate that in former Soviet countries the population is cynical and apathetic (Howard, 2003; 2011; Rose & Shin, 2001). People exhibit low levels of trust in state institutions, and they are less involved in volunteer activities. People have difficulty in reducing post-communist thinking and exercising the liberties offered by a democratic regime, such as active participation in the decision-making process and taking democratic responsibilities. Of course, no society merely receives various resources from the state. Political processes and participation in politics largely depend on the relationship between people and the state. Post-Soviet citizens' attitudes about state decisions often include political distrust, cynicism, and apathy. The same pattern applies to the Georgian population.

In the context of these complexities and challenges, Georgia is currently moving toward the West and seeking to join the European Union. After signing the Association Agreement and Visa Liberalization, the country has taken on necessary social and political reforms in order to do this. In fact, Georgian politicians from the government and opposition alike make a virtue of their links to Europe, and few major political actors would question Georgia's European trajectory. At the same time, the European Union and NATO have invested significant efforts and resources in Georgia. Is the Georgian public following the politicians' lead on this issue? How does opinion vary among Georgian citizens and what might that mean for long-term support of the pro-Western foreign policy?

Theoretical Framework

As mentioned before, Georgia's foreign policy is primarily oriented towards the West. One important question is which members of the public are more likely to support this policy and is their support related to their level of political knowledge? It seems likely that those who know more about politics are more likely to support allying with the West than those who know less about politics. Whether it is Russia's ongoing "creeping occupation" or the EU's investments into Georgia, these political processes affect the population in various ways, especially when it comes to shaping pro-Western attitudes.

The average Georgian probably favors political autonomy and opposes military aggression by outside powers, and likely opposes Russian influence. He or she would oppose allying with Russia because it has limited Georgia's political autonomy and occupied parts of the country in recent years. As a person becomes more politically knowledgeable, they will likely become more aware of how Russia has threatened Georgians' autonomy, state sovereignty, and peace. As they become more aware of these facts, Georgians' preferences for allies will likely shift to the West. More knowledgeable people follow the news more closely to learn more about politics. They will learn not only these facts about Russia, but also the arguments made by the government as to why allying with the West is a good idea.

On this point, Zaller (1992) argues that the information people receive can be important. More knowledgeable people receive more information. In Georgian-speaking regions, by and large, this should mean that the most knowledgeable people are the most aware of Russia's adversarial past with Georgia. On the other hand, in Georgia, there are densely populated regions where ethnic Azeris and Armenians live, mainly the Marneuli and Akhaltsikhe regions. These people have lived in those regions for centuries, do not command the mastery of a Georgian language, and have differing religious and cultural traditions from most other Georgians. For these reasons, they are likely to feel nonintegrated with ethnic Georgians on a number of issues. They mostly communicate with each other in Russian and receive political information from Russian language media, meaning they see Georgia's future from this alternate, often distorted perspective. Hence, in Russian-speaking regions flooded with propaganda from Russia, the most knowledgeable people are likely consuming more news and propaganda from Russia, which means they would likely form a pro-Russian disposition. Therefore, in those regions, we could expect to find reduced support for the West and increased support for Russia. In contrast, regions that are not dominated by the Russian language and dependent on Russian media ought to have stronger preferences for Western alliances than citizens in the country overall. Hence, it is essential to condition the effect of knowledge on how well a citizen knows the Russian language.

Based on this framework, we state the formal hypothesis. Overall, Georgian citizens with greater political knowledge should be more favorable towards the EU and the West, and less favorable towards Russia, relative to citizens who are less politically knowledgeable. These effects will be more pronounced for citizens primarily speak Georgian. Among those who are fluent in Russian, however, the effects will be reversed: citizens with higher political knowledge should be less favorable towards the EU and the West, and more favorable towards Russia, relative to citizens who are less politically knowledgeable.

Data and Variables

This study analyzes data from the Caucasus Barometer Survey (2017), which is mostly about socio-economic issues and political attitudes. This survey recruited respondents using multi-stage cluster sampling with preliminary stratification. 2,379 residents of Georgia completed the survey, of which 54% were women, and 46% were males. 45% of respondents live in the rural areas of Georgia, 29% in the urban areas, and 27% in the capital city. The age distribution of individuals participating in the study is as follows: 18 to 35 years was 33%, 36 to 55 years was 34%, and 56+ was 33%. As for ethnic groups, the majority of survey participants were ethnic Georgian at 84%, 9% were ethic Azerbaijani, 5% ethnic Armenians, and the remaining 2% were from another ethnicity (including Russian).

There are two general ways to measure political knowledge: The first is testing people with factual questions; and second is using other people's evaluations of how knowledgeable a person seems to be when discussing issues. This study will measure political knowledge by using the survey interviewer's evaluation of the respondent's knowledge. Specifically, interviewers were asked to rate on an ordinal scale how many questions they thought the respondent did not understand.

This primary predictor variable, which is the knowledge of the respondents about social, political and economic issues, is measured with the following question—interviewers were asked how often did they felt respondents did not understand the questions asked: 42% of respondents were described as never misunderstanding a question, 33% were confused on 10 or fewer questions, 18% were confused on some questions but not that many (10-20 questions), 5% were described as misunderstanding many questions but still understanding a majority of what was asked, and only 1% of respondents were described as being confused throughout most of the interview.

As a potential conditioning variable, the effect of knowledge might be linked to language barriers. After the Soviet Union collapsed, the Russian language and Russian propaganda are still tools through which Russia continues to influence the Georgian population. In this survey, 48% of the respondents have an intermediate knowledge of Russian, 23% are advanced in Russian, and only 8% of the survey participants do not have basic knowledge of the Russian language. This variable may moderate the effect of knowledge on attitudes.

The primary dependent variables in this study include what the Georgian population actually thinks about whom the country should establish close international relations with. Respondents were asked to what extent they would support Georgian membership in the European Union, in NATO, and in the Eurasian Economic Union led by Russia. Figure 2.1 shows the results on these three questions.

Figure 2.1 Overall Support for Alliances with Western and with Russian-Aligned Institutions

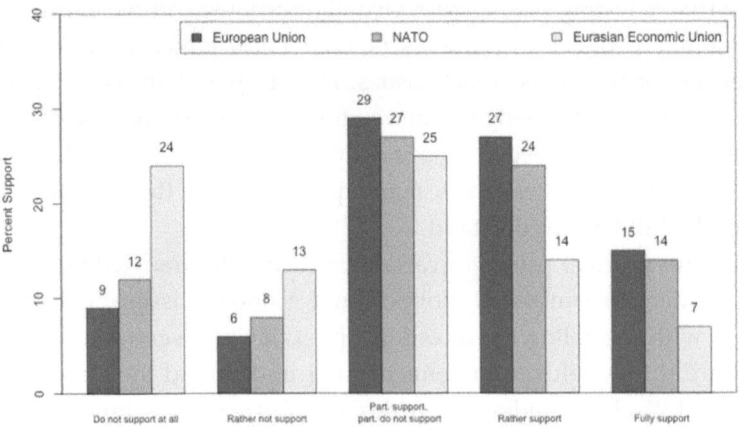

As shown in Figure 2.1, a plurality of the respondents (29%, 27% and 25%) in all three cases partially support and partially do not support membership in those alliances, which might mean they do not have enough information and knowledge to have a strong opinion about the stated choices. The options of "rather support" and "fully support" are much more popular for the European Union and NATO than they are for the Eurasian Economic Union. Hence, we can see that overall levels of support for Western alliances are higher among Georgians on the whole than for a Russian-oriented alliance. But does political knowledge affect whether a respondent expresses greater support for an alliance with the EU, NATO, or the Eurasian Economic Union? This question can be addressed with regression analysis.

Empirical Analysis

In order to understand which factors have a strong influence on citizen support for joining each of the three alliances (the European Union, NATO, and the Eurasian Economic Union), multiple linear regression models are run on each. The main predictor variable in each model is how unknowledgeable or confused the interviewer thought the respondent was (which is the opposite of being knowledgeable). The interaction effect between confusion and knowledge of the Russian language is entered in each model as the product of those variables. Age in years and ethnicity (coded as a dummy variable in which 1 = Georgian ethnicity) are entered as control variables.

Table 2.1 Linear Regression of Support for EU Membership (5-Point Scale)

Parameter	Estimate	Std. Error	t value	Pr (>|t|)
Intercept	4.1670	0.2384	17.47	0.000
Confusion	-0.0826	0.0987	-0.83	0.403
Know Russian	0.0061	0.0694	0.88	0.930
Age	-0.0100	0.0014	-7.30	0.000
Georgian ethnicity	0.0208	0.0811	0.26	0.798
Confusion*Know Russian	-0.0274	0.0332	-0.85	0.409

Notes: N = 2,037. R^2 = 0.0456.

Table 2.1 shows the model of support for Georgia becoming a member of the European Union. The effect of confusion is not significant; nor is the interaction of confusion with knowledge of

Russian language. This means that, despite the fact that many Georgians know the Russian language well, language does not seem to affect their opinions about establishing closer ties with the European Union. The effect of age, as expected, is negative and statistically significant. Younger people are more aware of the threats coming from Russia and prefer to ally with the West. The effect of Georgian ethnicity is not significant, which means that whether or not respondents are ethnic Georgians does not affect their support for joining the EU once all other factors are held constant.

Table 2.2 Linear Regression of Support for NATO Membership (5-Point Scale)

Parameter	Estimate	Std. Error	t value	Pr (>|t|)
Intercept	4.2816	0.2620	16.33	0.0028
Confusion	-0.3225	0.1080	-2.98	0.0028
Know Russian	-0.1762	0.0760	-2.17	0.0206
Age	-0.0110	0.0045	-7.39	0.0000
Georgian ethnicity	0.2856	0.0905	3.15	0.0016
Confusion*Know Russian	0.0714	0.0364	1.95	0.0503

Notes: N = 2,021. R^2 = 0.0457.

Table 2.2 shows the model of support for Georgia becoming a member of NATO. The effect of confusion is negative and significant, which is consistent with expectations. The more knowledge someone has, the more likely he or she is to support Georgia joining NATO. Additionally, the interaction of confusion with knowledge of Russian is positive and significant, which is also consistent with expectations. This means that the effect of knowledge is weaker among Georgian citizens who know Russian well. In addition, as those who are fluent in Russian become more politically knowledgeable, there is less change in their support for Georgia forming strong relations with a military alliance like NATO. Moreover, the main effect of knowing the Russian language itself presents the result for a respondent with no survey confusion. This coefficient is negative and significant, which means that those who speak better Russian are less likely to support NATO membership, on average and with all other variables held constant. The effect of age is negative and statistically significant, which is again consistent with expectations: the younger generation is more supportive towards allying with NATO. The effect of ethnicity is positive and significant which highlights the fact that ethnic Georgians oppose the Russian occupation and prefer to cope with Russian military aggression with the support of a strong security alliance like NATO.

Table 2.3 Linear Regression of Support for Eurasian Economic Union Membership (5-Point Scale)

Parameter	Estimate	Std. Error	t value	Pr (>|t|)
Intercept	2.5749	0.2641	9.74	0.0000
Confusion	0.2078	0.1099	1.89	0.0589
Know Russian	0.0416	0.0774	0.53	0.5914
Age	0.0077	0.0015	5.08	0.0000
Georgian ethnicity	-0.2476	0.0462	-5.36	0.0000
Confusion*Know Russian	-0.0068	0.0371	-0.18	0.8540

Notes: N = 1,920. R^2 = 0.0638.

Table 2.3 shows the model of support for Georgia becoming a member of the Eurasian Economic Union. The effect of confusion is positive and significant, which was hypothesized: the more knowledge someone holds, the less likely they are to support Georgia joining an alliance like the Eurasian Economic Union, on average and with all other variables held constant. However, the interaction of confusion with knowledge of Russian is not significant. The effect of age is positive and significant which was expected: the older a citizen is the more likely they will support joining the EEU on average and with all other variables held constant. The effect of ethnicity is negative and significant as hypothesized: if a person is ethnic Georgian, they are less likely to support Georgia joining the EEU on average and with all other variables held constant.

Does Ethnicity Affect This Relationship?

The one case in which Russian fluency conditioned the effect of political knowledge on attitudes about alliances was for opinions about joining NATO. As mentioned earlier, the primary Russian-speaking populations that consume Russian-language information are ethnic Azerbaijanis and ethnic Armenians. Do the results differ across Russian-speaking ethnic groups? To consider this possibility, another regression analysis of support for NATO membership was estimated, again with respondents' confusion level as the main predictor. Confusion was interacted with three ethnicity variables: an Azerbaijani indicator, an Armenian indicator, and an indicator for "other" ethnicity (not Azerbaijani, Armenian, or Georgian). Hence, being ethnic Georgian is the reference ethnicity value in this model, and the main effect for confusion is the effect for those who are ethnically Georgian. Age in years is a control variable.

Table 2.4   Linear Regression of Support for NATO Membership (5-Point Scale)

Parameter	Estimate	Std. Error	t value	Pr (>|t|)
Intercept	4.0894	0.0943	43.33	0.0000
Confusion	-0.1377	0.0346	-3.90	0.0001
Azerbaijanis	-0.6683	0.3371	-1.98	0.0476
Armenians	-1.0946	0.3662	-2.99	0.0028
Others	-0.4696	0.5169	-0.90	0.3637
Age	-0.0111	0.0014	-7.45	0.0000
Confusion*Azerbaijanis	0.2489	0.1412	1.76	0.0780
Confusion*Armenians	0.2524	0.1513	1.67	0.0955
Confusion*Others	0.1338	0.2527	0.53	0.5967

Notes: N = 2,021. R^2 = 0.0427.

Table 2.4 shows the model of support for Georgia becoming a member of NATO by ethnicity. The effect of confusion is negative and significant, as expected, which means that for an ethnic Georgian, the more confused they are, the less they want Georgia to become closer with an alliance like NATO. Meanwhile, the main effects for the indicators for ethnic Azerbaijanis and Armenians are negative, which was expected: the lack of fluency in the official state language and looking towards the future through the lens of the Russian news media shapes that opinion. The effect of age is negative and significant meaning that younger respondents want Georgia to join NATO more than older respondents. Most importantly, the interaction of confusion with the Azerbaijani indicator is positive and significant, and the interaction of confusion with the Armenian indicator is also positive and significant. The importance of this is striking: More knowledgeable Azerbaijanis and Armenians have most likely been consuming Russian-language news and thus propaganda. In fact, the interaction term is so large that it overtakes the main effect in the model. On one hand, when ethnic Georgians are more knowledgeable, they become *more* supportive of NATO.

On the other hand, when ethnic Azerbaijanis or Armenians become more knowledgeable, they become *less* supportive of NATO. Language explains this difference.

To illustrate this effect, Figure 2.2 displays predicted levels of support for joining NATO by ethnicity and level of confusion for a person of the average age from the survey. To show the effect of confusion, the predicted level of support is shown for someone who is maximally confused (scoring 5 on the confusion scale) and for someone who is not-at-all confused (scoring 1 on the confusion scale). Higher predicted values indicate greater support for NATO on the 1-5 scale.

Figure 2.2 Predicted Levels of NATO Support by Ethnicity and Level of Confusion

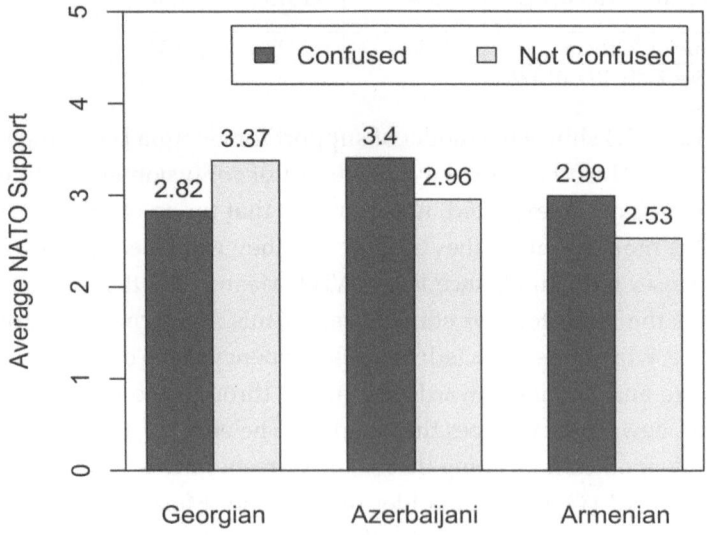

As we can see in Figure 2.2, ethnic Georgians who are not confused are more supportive of joining NATO than confused or unknowledgeable ethnic Georgians. The average NATO support score from least knowledgeable to most knowledgeable rises from 2.82 to 3.37 on a five-point scale. By contrast, the effect runs the other way for ethnic Azerbaijanis. Confused or unknowledgeable ethnic Azerbaijanis support NATO membership as shown by their mean score of 3.40 out of 5. However, non-confused or knowledgeable ethnic Azerbaijanis support NATO less with an average score of 2.96. Similarly, among ethnic Armenians, those who are unknowledgeable support NATO membership as shown by their mean score of 2.99 out of 5, while the most knowledgeable only support NATO membership with a score of 2.53. So while ethnic Georgians (who are fluent in the state language) become more supportive of NATO with more information, while ethnic Azerbaijanis and Armenians (who primarily speak Russian) become less supportive of NATO with more information. This confirms that the source of information matters.

Conclusion

This chapter shows that more knowledgeable Georgians are more likely to support NATO membership and less likely to support EEU membership. For NATO, this effect is conditioned by the person's Russian language ability. These findings are relevant for state public officials in order to better understand how citizens form their attitudes and develop support for state foreign policy. The findings are relevant for interested officials from the West and elsewhere to better analyze whom Russian propaganda can reach. On questions related to economic alliances like the EU or EEU, there appears to be little effect that Russian propaganda can have. For military or national security questions, as seen in the case of Georgia joining NATO, knowledge and the language people learn with is very important.

We can see that both ethnic Azerbaijanis and ethnic Armenians, two predominantly Russian-speaking groups (in addition to their respective native tongues), become less supportive of NATO with greater political knowledge. This suggests that Russian-language news and propaganda is likely having an effect. Whether a citizen speaks Georgian or Russian primarily, the kind of information they receive is a strong conditioning factor to their opinions. Moving forward, politicians and news outlets may want to bear this in mind as they determine which audiences they are reaching and what messages those audiences are receiving. Finally, this study and its findings suggest that improved language education can foster the political participation and integration of ethnic minorities in contemporary Georgia.

References

Almond, G. A., and Verba, S. 1963. *The Civic Culture: Political Attitudes and Democracy in Five Nations.* Princeton, NJ: Princeton University Press.

Andersen, Robert, Heath, Anthony, and Sinnott, Richard. 2002. "Political Knowledge and Electoral Choice." *British Elections and Parties Review* 12(1): 11-27.

Berent, M. K., and Krosnick, J. A. 1995. The Relation between Political Attitude Importance and Knowledge Structure. In M. Lodge & K. McGraw eds., *Political Judgment: Structure and Process.* Ann Arbor, MI: University of Michigan Press.

Bennett, Stephen Earl. 1988. "'Know-Nothings' Revisited: The Meaning of Political Ignorance Today." *Social Science Quarterly* 69(2): 476–490.

Cassel, Carol A., and Lo, Celia C. 1997. "Theories of Political Literacy." *Political Behavior* 19(4): 317–335.

Caucasus Research Resource Centers. 2017. "Caucasus Barometer". Retrieved from http://www.crrccenters.org/caucasusbarometer/.

Dahl, Robert A.1973. *Polyarchy: Participation and opposition.* New Haven, CT: Yale University Press.

Delli Carpini, Michael X., and Keeter, Scott. 1991. "Stability and Change in the U.S. Public's Knowledge of Politics." *Public Opinion Quarterly* 55(4): 583-612.

Dow, Jay K. 2009. "Gender Differences in Political Knowledge: Distinguishing Characteristics-based and Returns-based Differences." *Political Behavior* 31(1): 117-136.

Garramone, Gina M., and Atkin. 1986, Charles K. "Mass Communication and Political Socialization: Specifying the Effects." *Public Opinion Quarterly* 50(1): 76-86.

Graber, Doris A. 1996. "Wrong Questions, Wrong Answers: Measuring Political Knowledge." Conference paper, *Midwest Political Science Association,* Chicago, IL.

Howard, M. M. 2003. *The Weakness of Civil Society in Post-Communist Europe.* Cambridge, the UK: Cambridge University Press.

Howard, M. M. 2011. "Civil Society in Post-Communist Europe." In M. Edwards eds., *The Oxford Handbook of Civil Society.* Oxford, the UK: Oxford University Press.

Luskin, Robert C. 1987. "Measuring Political Sophistication." *American Journal of Political Science* 31(4): 856–899.

Makarovič, Matej, and Tomšič, Matevž. 2010. "Democrats, Authoritarians and Nostalgics: Slovenian Attitudes toward Democracy." *Innovative Issues and Approaches in Social Sciences* 8(3): 8-30.

McGuire, W. J. 1986. "The Myth of Massive Media Impact: Savagings and Salvagings." In G. Comstock eds., *Public Communication and Behavior*. San Diego, CA: Academic Press.

Mehrens, William A., and Lehmann, Irvin J. 1984. *Measurement and Evaluation in Education and Psychology*. 3rd ed., New York, NY: Holt, Rinehart and Winston.

Meinhold, J. L. and Malkus, A. J. 2005. "Adolescent Environmental Behaviors: Can Knowledge, Attitudes, and Self-Efficacy Make a Difference?" *Environment and Behavior* 37(4): 511–532.

Milner, H. 2007. "The Political Knowledge and Political Participation of Young Canadians and Americans." Conference Paper, *Annual Meeting of the Canadian Political Science Association*, Saskatoon, Canada.

Mondak, Jeffery J. 2000. "Reconsidering the Measurement of Political Knowledge." *Political Analysis* 8(1): 57-82.

Neuman, W. Russell, Just, Marion R., and Crigler, Ann N. 1992. *Common Knowledge: News and the Construction of Political Meaning*. Chicago, IL: University of Chicago Press.

Pietrzyk-Reeves, Dorota. 2008. "Weak Civic Engagement? Post-Communist Participation and Democratic Consolidation." *Polish Sociological Review* 161(1): 73-87.

Prior, Markus, and Lupia, Arthur. 2008. "Money, Time, and Political Knowledge: Distinguishing Quick Recall and Political Learning Skills." *American Journal of Political Science* 52(1): 169-183.

Rose, Richard, and Shin, Doh Chull. 2005. "Democratization Backwards: The Problem of Third-Wave Democracies." *British Journal of Political Science* 31(2): 331-354.

Verba, S. 1961. *Small Groups and Political Behavior*. Princeton, NJ: Princeton University Press.

Verba, S., Nie, N. H., and Kim, J. O. 1978. *Participation and Political Equality: A Seven-Nation Comparison*. Cambridge, the UK: Cambridge University Press.

Verba, Sidney, Schlozman, Kay Lehman, and Brady, Henry E. 1995. *Voice and Equality: Civic Voluntarism in American Politics*. Cambridge, MA: Harvard University Press.

Zaller, John R. 1992. *The Nature and Origins of Mass Opinion*. New York, NY: Cambridge University Press.

Appendix

List of the variables used in the chapter.

P22. Using a scale of 1to 5, where code "1" means no support and code "5" means your full support, to what extent would you support /country's/ membership in NATO? [NATOSUPP]

P25. Using a scale of 1to 5, where code "1" means no support and code "5" means your full support, to what extent would you support /country's/ membership in European Union? [EUSUPP].

P28_GEO. Using a scale of 1to 5, where code "1" means no support and code "5" means your full support, to what extent would you support Georgia's membership in Eurasian Economic Union led by the Russian Federation? [EEUSUPNG].

D7. Please tell me which one of these levels best describes your ability in the following:
Russian No Knowledge 1; Advanced 4.
English No Knowledge 1; Advanced 4.
Other Foreign language No Knowledge 1; Advanced 4.
Computer No Knowledge 1; Advanced 4.

W3. How often did you feel that the respondent did not understand the questions you asked? [FRQUNDST]
Never 1
Just for a few questions (fewer than ten) 2
For some questions, but not that many (approximately between 10 and 20 questions) 3
For a substantial number of questions, but less than half the interview 4
Throughout most of the interview, or through the entire interview 5

3
Russian Soft Power in Georgia

Marika Mkheidze

In this chapter, I consider the case study of how Russia has worked to exercise soft power in Georgia. The term *soft power* was coined by Joseph S. Nye in late 1980s to depict the ability of a state to make "others to want the outcomes that you want" or "the ability to achieve goals through attraction rather than coercion" (2005, 5), as opposed to "the ability to get others to act in ways that are contrary to their initial preferences and strategies" (2011, 11). Pursuant to Nye, soft (or persuasive) power encompasses attraction and emulation "associated with intangible power resources such as culture, ideology, and institutions" (Nye, 2009, 63). Due to certain limitations of the opposing concept of *hard power* (i.e. the cost of sustaining an army, the short duration of the outcome, increased international scrutiny, and fear of opposing a stronger power), soft power is being applied by an increasing number of states (Wagner, 2014). Yet scholars argue that the most effective mechanism is *smart power*, "the capacity... to combine elements of hard and soft power in ways that are mutually reinforcing" (Wagner, 2014). In this regard, soft power may be seen as a tool to prepare grounds for exercising hard power and limiting the negative effects of compulsion, including "conflict and lack of voluntariness to consent" (Gallarotti, 2011).

Russia aims to challenge the current international order (Laruelle, 2015). As a revisionist force, Russia wishes to ensure that its neighbors, former "captive nations of the Soviet empire" who are now referred as "close abroad," exercise limited independence in their foreign and internal affairs, and it wants to diminish the powers of Atlantic Alliance and European Union (particularly its role as rule-settler in energy policy) (Lucas, 2014). However, Russia keeps in mind that its military and economic strengths are far behind those of its main perceived rival, the United States, without whom "Europe would be far more vulnerable to Russian pressure" (Lucas,

2014). Namely, in 2014, the US allocated 610 billion USD (3.5% of GDP) for military purposes, whereas Russian military spending was 84.5 billion USD (4.5% of its GDP) (Stockholm International Peace Research Institute, 2015).

The Russian *soft power* concept is rather new. Notwithstanding the fact that propagandist tools were widely utilized by the Soviet establishment, implementation of soft power was initiated in the 2000s, after the creation of the relevant institution, Rossotrudnichestvo. Based on Vladimir Putin's definition of the term, this concept encompasses informal interaction with the outside world rather than mere creation of an attractive image of Russia (Burlinova, 2015). This tactic is part of a wider strategy that aims at "protecting rights of compatriots." The latter is a part of the set of policies developed by Russia toward the Russian speaking minorities in the former Soviet states (Conley et al., 2011, 7). By creating the concept of *Russkiy Mir* (Russian World), Russia attempted to build a Russian supra state populated with *compatriots*. The latter term is broader than a mere citizen and covers even those foreign citizens who admire the Russian language (Conley et al., 2011).

The main messages of propagandist actions are directed towards presenting Western civilization as a corrupt, immoral space in the eyes of the target audience and emphasizing common historic, cultural and political interests of Russia and target countries. The results of propaganda often produce strong support among the residents of the so-called spheres of influence and attempt to influence the course of the government via the residents and voters. Based on these developments, research is needed to better understand the rationale and tools of Russian soft power in Georgia.

To this end, I pose the following research questions:

1. What is the extent of Russian soft power in Georgia?
2. What are the dimensions of soft power exercised by Russia in Georgia?
3. Which tools are used to exert influence through soft power?
4. How can Russian soft power potentially influence public opinion on Georgia's proposed European and Euro-Atlantic integration?

To answer these questions, the methodologies utilized in this study are twofold. First, I apply the results of a media content analysis undertaken by the Media Development Foundation in 2014-2017 to the context of the Georgian case. The said information was applied to identify main trends in the narratives of TV programs and the editorial content of newspapers and magazines. It also aimed to detect anti-Western and pro-Russian publications and sentiments. Content analysis also included other reports of international and regional organizations as well as scholarly and political articles. My second method is to analyze the results of public opinion surveys conducted by the National Democratic Institute (the NDI) throughout the years 2012-2018. The said survey was used to identify the main trends in foreign policy-related sentiments among the citizens of Georgia. The outcomes were analyzed in a manner that would ensure identifying the link between the reinforced anti-Western propaganda facilitated by the pro-Russian actors in Georgia with the slight decline in popular sympathy towards following the Euro-Atlantic integration path.

My analysis of the methods employed by and on behalf of the Russian Federation in Georgia provides evidence of a somewhat modified theory of soft power. Namely, instead of a traditional win-win strategy, this version of soft power employs tactics based on the idea of pluralism. That is, the tactic is to create as many competing narratives as possible to create a sense that there is no objective truth. In the remainder of this chapter, I first describe the theoretical background of this study based on past literature. Second, I explain the impact that Russian soft power has in the world today. Third, I explain the means through with Russia exercises soft power in Georgia. Fourth, I explain the impact that Russian propaganda has had on public opinion. Finally, I offer conclusions from this case study.

Theoretical Framework

This chapter is based on the theory developed by Joseph Nye that suggests a new paradigm for defining the strength of the state in international relations and proposes that emphasis has shifted from military force to technology, education, and economic growth. Nye also accentuates the declining importance of national security due to the increased concerns related to economic and ecological security. While not completely dismissing the importance of military power as a self-help instrument, he suggests that the increased cost of use of force causes countries to concentrate more on communications, organizational and institutional tools, and the manipulation of interdependence. In these terms, the strategies used by countries to achieve the desired balance-of-power have evolved. New challenges faced by traditional superpowers, including the spread of new technologies, have diminished their ability to control the environment. Increased interdependence has caused states to use communication as a weapon (Nye, 1990).

This chapter will investigate the dimensions of soft power described by Nye: willingness of countries to follow a single state and a country's ability to persuade other countries "to want what it wants." Nye's framework will be utilized to determine whether Russian actions fall within a classical understanding of soft power or traditional Soviet-style propaganda. Particular emphasis is placed on the premise that soft power can virtually replace hard power by increasing the attractiveness of the aggressor country, which restricts the follower states' ability to contradict or even harm the interests of the country exercising soft power (Nye, 1990). The theoretical framework of soft power is largely linked to the theory of Neoliberalism, under which the concept of complex interdependence was created. Three pillars of complex interdependence between states are: increased contact channels between societies, reluctance of governments to use military force, and decreasing importance of security in international relations. Classic soft power is closely intertwined with both the theory of complex interdependence, developed by Keohane and Nye (1977), and the Liberal theory. These theories envision an almost complete abandonment of military force (Gomichon, 2013).

The level and content of propagandist messages in Georgia, as well as the channels (including the media, Orthodox Church, and political parties) spreading such messages are of utmost importance in terms of defining the link between foreign policy-related attitudes among Georgians and the activities of pro-Russian forces in Georgia (Avalishvili, Lomtadze, and Kevkhishvili, 2016). Hence, the evolution of Russian efforts in Georgia starting from 2007 and up to 2016 provides an interesting picture. The effects of homegrown (e.g., Georgian media and political parties), Russian (e.g., Russian media), and international (e.g., Euro-skeptic European parties supporting Putin's nationalistic politics) channels of Russian soft power provide a more complete picture of the means of influencing the mindsets of Georgians (Tugushi et al., 2016).

This chapter also seeks to analyze the rationale behind using soft power in Georgia. According to certain authors, Russian soft power as "a security tool for Russia in Georgia," is used for the strategic purposes of preserving the post-Soviet regional agenda and concentrates on de-legitimizing Western institutions. It also attempts to persuade its former zone of influence that Russian guidance is merely a form of protection. Unlike the Western model of soft power that concentrates on knowledge transfer and change promotion, Russian soft power attempts to reinforce the "Euro-skeptic attitudes and conservative beliefs of existing constituencies" (Makarychev, 2016). Furthermore, the failed attempts of Russia to present itself as a trustworthy partner among Western audiences, as well as relevant nation branding and public diplomacy theories of Russia's us-versus-them mentality will also be addressed to understand the motives driving Russian soft power (Avgerinos, 2009).

The Importance of Understanding Russian Soft Power

The importance of understanding Russian soft power is apparent when examining major events in the relations between Russia and former Communist states — like Moldova, Ukraine, Latvia, Kazakhstan, Belarus, or Georgia. Russia is a revisionist country that aims to rewrite history and inspire uncertainty about the present among its target states by painting Euro-Atlantic institutions as a potential threat to its borders (Ganieva, 2018). Hence, installing pro-Russian governments in the "near abroad" (i.e. post-Soviet space) is an effective tool for ensuring that Russia's sphere of influence is unaffected by pro-Western sentiments.

In the 2008 Russian-Georgian five-day war, Russia launched military action against Georgia under the pretext of protecting residents of Georgia's breakaway region of Samachablo (also called South Ossetia). Many residents of this disputed territory had acquired Russian passports as a result of large-scale *passportization* throughout 2002-2008 (Socor, 2019). The presence of these passport holders helped pave the way for the military invasion of Georgia, since Russia's use of force in South Ossetia was justified as defense of "the dignity and honor of the Russian citizens" (*The Economist*, 2008). However, Russia not only deployed its troops in the territory of Samachablo, but also broke deeper into Georgia. The ceasefire agreement between Russia and Georgia was signed only as a result of intervention from the international community (CNN Library, 2008). However, the creeping occupation has continued since, namely upon launching the "demarcation" process on the territory of Georgia, with the use of metal-wire fences. Since then, Russia illegally changed the occupation line further into Georgian territory (Shakila, 2019). The passportization scenario was applied later on, in the process of annexing Crimea (Socor, 2019). Thus, Russia's revisionist plans on the former USSR territory became clear even for those sceptics who refused to see expansionist threats in the country's actions. According to one reputable foreign affairs journal, "Russia's willingness to violate Ukraine's territorial sovereignty is the gravest challenge to the European order in over half a century" (Krastev, 2014). Thus, Russia's actions in Georgia are not unique.

The combination of a wide range of non-military tools, including disinformation, psychological influence, and attacking the image of reputable information systems can be more effective in influencing the behavior of countries than conventional weapon systems.[1] Russian propaganda has largely been utilized during conflicts throughout the last decade. Informational warfare is directed

---

[1] Drawn from an extract from the speech of General Viktor Samsonov, Chief of the Russian General Staff delivered on December 23, 1996, available at https://static.aminer.org/pdf/PDF/000/261/818/cyber_warfare_peacekeeping.pdf, page 6. Last accessed on January 4, 2018.

towards discrediting opponents in the eyes of the West and assuring the Russian people that its government's actions are justified. Hence, information warfare has become one of the greatest challenges of the modern world, and it was utilized by Russia throughout most of the Russian-Ukrainian conflict in 2014-2015 (Veebel, 2015). In that conflict, Russia violated the territorial integrity of Ukraine by occupying the Crimean Peninsula and sending troops to support Eastern Ukrainian separatists. Similarly, in the Russian-Georgian war, Russia invoked its "right" to protect Russian citizens (i.e., residents of Georgia who acquired Russian passports several years before in 2006) and eventually occupied part of the Tskhinvali region. In both of these instances, invasions were preceded by lengthy Russian propaganda.

Hence, it is clear that Russian soft power threatens political sovereignty of Georgia, since its ultimate goal is to establish proxy governments that are effectively controlled by Russian politicians. Russian propaganda also aims at eliminating Georgia's European and Euro-Atlantic aspirations. Ultimately, Russian soft power can be regarded as a first step of its *smart power* that leads to violating the territorial integrity of Georgia. Hence, threats coming from the northern neighbor should not be underestimated.

Even though Rossotrudnichestvo (the main tool of Russian Propaganda) is hardly competent, the threats coming from Russian propaganda and soft power should not be underestimated (Bai, 2015). Social media accounts of Russian government-backed trolls were utilized both prior to the United Kingdom's Brexit vote in 2016 and before the US Presidential elections in 2016. As a result, the anti-Muslim and phony-patriotic statements made prior to, respectively, the US presidential elections and the Brexit referendum reached over 126 million US through Facebook alone users (according to Facebook's General Counsel) and arguably have affected the outcomes of the British referendum (Romm, 2017; Watts and Weisburd, 2016).

Russian soft power is active in Georgia as well. In the NDI survey, the growth of Russian influence in Georgia was noticeable to 44% of the participants. Evidence of an increased Russian impact in Georgia since 2013 was reportedly noticed by the participants of focus groups as well. The members of the focus groups also referred to the increased amount of anti-Western and pro-Russian messages in the media as well as changed rhetoric of public officials. Hence, the "Reset of Relationship Policy" adopted by the new government was perceived as a signal of activation by the Russian propagandist machine and officials.

The exercise of soft power in the former USSR countries, where sentiments towards the former Empire are still vivid, may turn out to be more effective than the military interventions. Even violation of Ukraine's territorial integrity that was largely regarded as an attempt to politically, culturally, and militarily resist the West, rather than an opportunistic hard power grab, was preceded by a strong propaganda campaign in Crimea region. After the outbreak of the Ukrainian crisis and following the murder of Russian opposition leader Boris Nemtsov, reputable British and American media outlets started noticing the effects of the Kremlin's low-key propaganda (Koshkin, 2015). Namely, it was argued that the PR approach adopted by high-level Russian officials utilized the notion of pluralism to create competing narratives, which led to chaos and provided the Kremlin with the necessary cover to act undetected (*The Guardian*, 2015).

The Russian approach to soft power is different from the standard approach. Generally, soft power effects are positive for both the addresser and addressee of the influence (e.g., educational, exchange, and diplomatic activities). The definition of soft power offered by President Putin in February 2012 does not necessarily imply establishing an attractive image, but rather on informational work with the surrounding world (Koshkin and Smertina, 2016). The soft power strategy pursued by Russia is based on the idea that there is no such thing as objective truth. In other words, the aim was "to muddy the water to a point where the audience simply gave up on the search for truth" (Pomeranstev, 2014). Respective power ensures that relevant stakeholders are persuaded that certain action is right. For Russia, soft power is closely intertwined with national propaganda. Namely, the essence of soft power is presenting a nation as a model for replication by other countries, by accentuating its cultural and political values as well as successful foreign policy.

However, the approach taken by the Russian Federation in attempting to exert soft power over nations within its perceived sphere of interest simply relies on discrediting others using new technologies in information warfare. However, "hackers and trolls might help you discredit the opponent, but they cannot create a positive image of your country, when it is a poor, unfree state with rampant corruption, backward education and a weak healthcare system" (*Democracy Digest,* 2017).

Means of Russian Soft Power

The tools employed by the Kremlin in Georgia are a mixture of classical soft power and traditional propaganda. In this section, I specifically focus on three of these tools: Georgia's church and civil society, narratives in Georgian political discourse, and Russian propaganda in the media. In general, Russian activity is mainly aimed at the countries in the Baltic states and the Commonwealth of Independent States (CIS) that have significant numbers of Russian-speaking people (Conley et al., 2011). The type of messages spread by the Russian propaganda establishment varies depending on the target country. In Romania, for example, Russian-backed media tools aim to weaken democratic institutions and suggest that Romania's joining the EU would be a mistake (EURACTIV.com, 2019). The main messages spread in the Czech Republic and Slovakia criticize US energy policy and present Western civilization as a neocolonial power that instigates conflicts in various parts of the world based on its selfish interests (*The Spectator,* 2017). Russian propaganda blamed the government of Finland for child abductions, whereas the Swedish government has been accused of promoting sexual decadence (Lucas and Pomeranzev, 2016). The rhetoric used in the Baltic countries allegedly reveals the discrimination experienced by Russian minorities there (Lucas and Pomeranzev, 2016). These baseless allegations are mainly spread via the main propagandist channel Первый Балтийский канал (First Baltic Channel), Regnum.ru, and Baltnews, where information is presented in native Estonian, Latvian and Lithuanian languages.

Russia's effort in Georgia employs a variety of tools. Geopolitical realists believe the Kremlin's actions towards the country in the South Caucasus resemble the characteristics of activities undertaken by the classic superpower that seeks to gain control over the region (Makarychev, 2016). Russian propaganda in Georgian discourse is based on three main pillars that emanate from efforts to (a) establish a belief of threat (threat of war, threat of loss of territories, or threat of loss of identity) among the audiences, (b) cause distrust towards partners and Western institutions by promoting the idea that Russia is the only option in fighting against the threats, and (c) argue that authoritative, Soviet-style governance is necessary (Kintsurashvili, 2018).

Namely, according to the pro-Russian narrative, Georgia not only launched a war against Russia in August 2008, but also was pushed to do so by the US. Thus, keeping close ties with the US and Europe might lead the country to yet another military action involving Russia. As already noted above, propagandist messages also attempt to convince Georgians that European integration and cooperation with NATO through joint military trainings will provoke Russia to take aggressive steps against Georgia. Yet another narrative spread by the Kremlin propagandist machine portrays Turkey as a possible threat to the territorial integrity of Georgia by suggesting that the Kars Peace Agreement will expire in 2021 thus enabling Turkey to invade the Adjara region of Georgia. This narrative portrays Russia as the only force able to deal effectively with the alleged Turkish threat (Myth Detector, 2017; Kintsurashvili, 2018).[2]

Another vast portion of the disinformation focuses on the possible threat of bio-subversion by suggesting that outbreak of seasonal flu in Georgia is closely tied with the Richard Lugar Public Health Research Center in Tbilisi. Namely, according to the widely spread conspiracy theory, the center develops lethal viruses that

---

2   The Treaty of Kars was signed on October 13, 1921 between Turkey, on one side, and Armenian, Azerbaijani, and Georgian Soviet Socialist Republics, on the other, in Kars. According to the treaty, Turkey transferred a part of Adjara, including Batumi, as well as Gyumri, to the Soviet Union, receiving Kars, Artvin and Ardahan in exchange.

affect the well being of Georgians (Agenda.ge, 2018). The said narrative is also advanced in Abkhazia. According to the so-called Secretary of the Security Council of the occupied region, Mukhamed Kilba, "biological weapons are manufactured in the biological laboratory in Georgia which is located close to Abkhazia's border. We consider that mass poisonings of children in Tkvarcheli in 2013, as well as swine flu cases of which have been detected here, are related to the activities of that laboratory" (Kilba, 2017).

Kremlin propaganda in Georgian discourse promotes the fear of loss of Georgia's religious, ethnic, and cultural identity. The Russian narrative reinforces the idea of Georgia's being the beacon of Orthodox Christianity and culture in the relevant region, thus inspiring a sense of superiority in a nation plagued by wars and economic hardships. Furthermore, whilst demonizing Georgia's strategic partners by insinuating that European and Euro-Atlantic integration will come at the high price of losing identity, this narrative presents Russia as a defender of Christianity and supporter of conservative values. Propaganda attempts to present NATO and the USA as expansionist forces that not only attack countries based on their strategic importance, but also provoked Georgia to instigate war with Russia.

As an alternative, Russia is depicted as a force for good, fighting for peace in the countries oppressed by NATO and the US, and the enemy of terrorism. Propagandist messages attempt to reinforce Euroscepticism by suggesting that Georgia's EU integration is impossible and the breakup of the EU is inevitable, as evidenced by Brexit. Furthermore, propaganda insinuates that visa liberalization granted by the European Union to Georgia would not benefit citizens of the country because it comes with the precondition that Georgia would accept migrants from Syria, increasing the risk of terrorism and the need to assimilate the Georgian nation (Kintsurashvili, 2018). Furthermore, the Government of Georgia and many non-governmental organizations promoting human rights in Georgia make decisions based on the instructions provided by western institutions that do not serve the interests of the Georgian people.

Russian politicians largely share the idea that Georgia's EU Association Agreement (signed in 2014) entails Russia's further relegation in Europe. It shall be noted that Russia has repeatedly failed to offer arguments that would have been totally appealing to Georgians. Notwithstanding the Kremlin's claim that Georgians are reluctant to follow the European and Euro-Atlantic integration path and are simply drawn by the US in that direction, Moscow's actions against the South Caucasian state (including the recognition of Abkhazia and South Ossetia as sovereign states) has diminished its influence over Georgia (Makarychev, 2016).

The Georgian Orthodox Church, Civil Society, and the Pro-Russian Narrative

The main messages spread in Georgia include allegations regarding the threat to Georgian culture and traditions coming from European integration. The religious ties between Georgia and Russia are being exploited. Namely, the tools of leverage actively employed by the Russian Federation when exercising soft power in Georgia include the narrative concerning "Two Brotherly Churches." Russian religious diplomacy that supports the idea of retaining warm relations with the Georgian Orthodox Church whilst following the conservative agenda that has been used by the Russian political leadership to block Georgia's western integration. For instance, the LGBT issue is used to distance Georgia from the West. In 2014, an anti-discrimination law, which prohibits discrimination on the basis of sexual orientation, was actively protested by pro-Russian groups in Georgia. They claimed that such a ban was tantamount to promoting non-heterosexual relations.

The Georgian Orthodox Church itself is quite controversial as well. Georgian Patriarch Ilya II has demonstrated his sympathies for Stalin and praises Putin, but he makes prominent pro-Western statements and criticizes Russia's politics in Abkhazia and South Ossetia. Except for the occasional funding allocated by the Russian Orthodox Church to religious youth camps as well as limited theological university ties, there is little evidence of the Russian church's direct interference in Georgia. However, in 2013, representatives of the Georgian Orthodox Church stated that the West is even "worse than Russia" and that the Russian invasion in 2008 was a form of a "heavenly intervention" directed against Georgia's western integration (Cecire, 2015). It should be noted that the messages spread by the Georgian Orthodox Church, as the most trusted institution in Georgia, are significantly important in shaping public attitudes.

Another tool of influence in Georgia can be found in Russian-backed representatives from the civil society. These representatives actively engage in spreading misinformation through channels. The Caucasian Dialogue program, co-managed by the Tbilisi-based Caucasian House and the Gorchakov Foundation, promoted the idea that Russia's military actions against Georgia represented a reaction to Tbilisi's anti-Russian policy. This notion maintains that if Georgia refrained from irritating the Kremlin, Georgia's territorial integrity could have been restored. Russian aggression, in the opinion of the said organization, was triggered by the Saakashvili government and, without him, normal business relations could have been restored with Russia. Furthermore, a number of Georgia-based NGOs foster the idea of Georgia's complete integration with Eurasian projects. These NGOs include the Society of Irakly II as well as Eurasian Choice-Georgia, which maintain close links with the advocates of the Russian World. Said organizations support the idea of close natural dependence of Georgia on Russia. Such groups spread Russian influence by appealing to Georgian social conservatism, economic vulnerability, and angst against previous government abuses, whilst using local Georgian media that are not noticeable to the international community. While protesting in Tbilisi streets against "losing Georgian values" and holding suspiciously well-funded campaign rallies ahead of elections, they provide evidence that Russian influence in Georgia has grown (Cecire, 2015).

One of the cornerstones of Russian propaganda in Georgia is conducted over several local web portals that have close ties with pro-Russian NGOs. Namely, these are Sakinform, "Georgia and the World", and Iverioni. They are partners of a strong pro-Russian NGO known as the Eurasian Institute. Though the institute does not disclose its financial sources, another NGO, the famous Russian ideologist Alexander Dougin's International Eurasian Movement, has disclosed that the institute is its official partner (*Liberal*, 2016). Meanwhile, a civil movement named Georgian Dasi, which openly supports Russia, started disseminating anti-Turkish messages after Turkey downed a Russian warplane. The leader of the Georgian Dasi announced the establishment of the Russian liaison office in Georgia on December 14, 2015 and noted that "via opening this office we start the lobbying of Russia in Georgia" (*Liberal*, 2016). These civil society members and movements maintain close ties with the Georgian Orthodox Church and often justify their actions as protecting Christian values (that are allegedly shared by Georgia and Russia) from the destructive nature of liberal, Western forces.

Russian Propaganda in Georgian Political Discourse

With a democracy score of 4.68, Georgia is a nation with a transitional government, or hybrid regime (Freedom House, 2018). Notwithstanding the slight improvement in the overall democracy score since 2012, when the previous ruling party, the United National Movement (UNM) was defeated in parliamentary elections, Georgia's democratic transformation is still largely stalled due to the "half-hearted democratic reforms" implemented by the ruling elites (Freedom House, 2018). The Georgian Dream Coalition (GD), created in 2012, achieved an overwhelming victory in the 2016 Parliamentary elections. In an attempt to retain and increase its political influence, GD largely capitalized on the general negative image of the previous UNM-led government. Representatives of the GD blamed Saakashvili's regime for taking ill-thought steps that provoked the Russian Federation to launch the Russian-Georgian War of 2008 (RT, 2012). This speculation was reiterated by the former Prime Minister of Georgia, Georgian Dream Founder Oligarch Bidzina Ivanishvili, who made his fortune in Russia (Civil.ge, 2018). This was also stated by President of Georgia Salome Zurabishvili, who participated in the 2018 presidential elections as an independent candidate but was backed by the GD (Agenda.ge, 2018).

Blaming the UNM-led regime for provoking the Russian Federation to start war (or, in the case of Mrs. Zurabishvili, openly blaming Saakashvili for starting the war) can be attributed to the ruling party's desire to maintain and aggravate negative public attitudes towards their main perceived political rivals (UNM and later other opposition parties that were established after the United National Movement split). However, political statements of this nature also might affect Georgia's standing in the case brought by Georgia against Russia in International Court of Justice. That case concerns the conflict of August 2008, and these statements provide the Russian Federation with exculpatory evidence in ongoing hearings (GRASS FactCheck, 2018). In that case, the Georgian side claims that the Russian Federation "has violated its obligations under CERD during three distinct phases of its interventions in South Ossetia and Abkhazia," in the period from 1990 to August 2008. According to Georgia, "the Russian Federation, through its State organs, State agents, and other persons and entities exercising governmental authority, and through the South Ossetian and Abkhaz separatist forces and other agents acting on the instructions of, and under the direction and control of the Russian Federation, is responsible for serious violations of its fundamental obligations under CERD, including Articles 2, 3, 4, 5 and 6."[3]

However, in the objection documents filed to the International Court of Justice, the Russian Federation used a quote from Salome Zurabishvili's book to justify its military intervention in Georgia. Namely, in the book, Salome Zurabishvili (former Foreign Minister of Georgia and current President) insinuates that in the second half of 2007 and the first half of 2008 Georgia pursued a military build-up strategy. It shall be noted that Zurabishvili's statements of this type are especially threatening to the position of Georgia in the International Court of Justice since she has become the president. Namely, a president's media statements might entail legal obligations for a state, based on the precedent the International Court of Justice set in the 1974 case of *Australia v. France* (GRASS FactCheck, 2018).

---

3   International Court of Justice; Application of the International Convention on the Elimination of All Forms of Racial Discrimination (Georgia v. Russian Federation); overview of the case; available at: https://www.icj-cij.org/en/case/140.

Such remarks may also be used as a propaganda instrument to deepen pro-Russian sentiments among Georgian citizens. Such statements are in line with the messages spread by Russian high-ranking officials and echo the pro-Kremlin propaganda statements made by various marginalized and openly pro-Russian media outlets and political parties. Furthermore, notwithstanding the fact that the current government of Georgia remains committed to join the EU and NATO, remarks of members of Georgian Dream's former ruling coalition (2012-2016) regarding the country's foreign policy choices caused some confusion. A survey conducted in 2015 by the Media Development Foundation among youth found that only 10.6% of respondents believed that messages from various branches of power on Euro-Atlantic integration were consistent, whereas 40.2% felt that various government representatives were making contradictory statements (Media Development Foundation, 2015). Whilst supporting close ties and normalization of relations with Russia, the Georgian Dream Coalition became a "safe heaven" for politicians who contested Georgia's integration with NATO, justified Russia's actions in Syria, and emphasized the benefits of negotiating with Russia (Media Development Foundation, 2017).

After the parliamentary elections of 2016, statements made by the representatives of the ruling party became noticeably pro-Western. Representatives of the ruling party support Russian rhetoric only in terms of transferring the blame for starting the 2008 war onto Georgia (Kintsurashvili, 2018, 23). Nevertheless, other political parties continue supporting Russian propaganda by reinforcing fears amongst Georgians, such as NATO joint military training in Georgia as a threat of provoking Russia or the threat of Turkish invasion upon expiration of Kars Agreement. For example, the Alliance of Patriots of Georgia is a party that gained six seats in the Parliament of Georgia for the first time in 2016. This is a right-wing populist party that is affiliated with Russia, positions itself as anti-liberal, affiliates with ethno-nationalistic groups known for Anti-Western sentiments, and opposes Georgia's integration into NATO. Meanwhile, pro-Kremlin political parties led by former Parliament Speaker Nino Burjanadze won only one seat in the Supreme

Council of Adjara (Dzvelishvili and Kupreishvili 2015, 17). Messages spread by openly pro-Kremlin and right-wing populist political parties reiterated that western countries hampered a direct dialogue between Georgia and Russia. Said political parties support the disinformation, which insinuates that in order to achieve EU-Georgia visa liberalization (which, starting from 2016, allows citizens of Georgia to travel to the Schengen Zone without visas for up to 90 days), Georgia must accept migrants, which would pose a demographic threat. The topic of the West's fighting against Orthodox Christianity and imposing homosexuality was also part of the discourse of almost every political party.

Alongside with above-mentioned statements, the GD-led government attempted to reset Georgian-Russian relations starting in 2012, when the GD-led government revised Mikheil Saakashvili's policy towards Russia with the goal of eliminating the perceived threat of war. The normalization policy involved re-establishing direct dialogue between Georgia and Russia through creating a round-table format between the Special Representative of the Prime Minister of Georgia for Relations with Russia (a position established by the former PM Bidzina Ivanishvili) and the Russian Minister of Foreign Affairs. The goal of this dialogue was to restore economic, cultural, and humanitarian relations between the countries. The "reset policy" also included freeing several individuals accused of spying for Russia without pre-conditions and without demanding that Russia release any Georgians serving similar sentences. Furthermore, in 2012 Georgia started broadcasting certain Russian news channels, which had been shut off in August 2008 by the former government under the leadership of Saakashvili (Jamnews Tbilisi, 2018).

Russian Propaganda in the Media

Recent developments in Georgia's media landscape contributed to dropping the country's score on the International Research and Exchanges Board's (IREX) Media Sustainability Index from 2.34 to 2.31 in 2018. A legal battle over the ownership of top-rated opposition TV channel Rustavi 2 was perceived as an attempt by the government to gain influence over its editorial policy that openly criticized Georgian Dream (including its effort to "reset policy" and improve relations with Russia) (Amnesty International, 2017). Former Prime Minister and then-unofficial leader of the Georgian Dream, Bidzina Ivanishvili, made harsh remarks regarding the complicity of Rustavi 2 managers with the opposition party United National Movement, and he linked the country's economic problems with the channel's editorial policy. Subsequently, the decision of the Supreme Court of Georgia to reinstate the ownership rights over Rustavi 2 TV Channel, a popular and outspoken government critic, to its former co-owner were harshly criticized by the international community as an attempt to limit public access to opposition views.

The merger of the other three major private TV Channels with government-friendly editorial policies — Imedi, Maestro TV, and Georgian Dream Station (GDS) — was perceived as a step towards consolidating the media powers supporting the current ruling party. TV Union Obieqtivi is affiliated with the right-wing Alliance of Patriots of Georgia (one of the political parties openly fighting against liberal values in Georgia) and is far from being a top-rated TV channel, but it obtained the greatest share of its revenues from donations (81%). That station is actively engaged in promoting hate speech. The European Commission Against Racism and Intolerance (ECRI) of the Council of Europe opposes awarding state service contracts for dissemination of information and advertisement to media outlets like Obieqtivi TV, whose editorial policy supported intolerance among the population. However, the government continued to award contracts to Obieqtivi in 2016 and 2017 (ECRI, 2016).

The impact of fringe media outlets on public opinion is limited. Russian media (such as Sputnik, RT, NTV, and Russia 1) merely represent a source of narratives for the local pro-Russian media. Such narratives can also be channeled by local mainstream and local media. Thus, the national media are increasingly engaged in spreading Kremlin narratives. The increasingly oligarchic nature of the media space in Georgia enables pro-Russian forces to influence editorial policies of the national and local media, which are under control of these groups (Media Development Foundation, 2017).

Effects of Russian Propaganda on Public Opinion

The above-mentioned factors contributed to a decline of pro-Western sentiments among Georgians. Figure 3.1 shows the results of surveys conducted on behalf of NDI from 2013-2017.[4] The horizontal axis represents the time of the survey, and the vertical axis reports the percentage of Georgians responding with a certain answer. The black dotted line with diamond points represents the percentage of survey respondents who support joining the European Union, while the solid gray line with square points represents the percentage of survey respondents who support joining the Russia-backed Eurasian Economic Union. While support for the EU is always higher than support for the Eurasian Economic Union, we can see that there are trends favorable to it at the EU's expense. The all-time low of EU support was 47% in August 2015, and this has rebounded somewhat. However, in December 2017, support for joining the Eurasian Economic Union hit its all-time high of 29%. This trend could be on account of the information that the public is receiving.

---

4   Figure 3.1 is created using the relevant findings of the public opinion polls conducted in Georgia with the financial support of the National Democratic Institute. The source is available at: https://www.ndi.org/georgia-polls; Library of NDI Georgia Public Opinion Research. NOTE: the absent percentage indicates population that did not know the answer or refused to answer.

MARIKA MKHEIDZE

Figure 3.1 Support for Joining the European Union and the Eurasian Economic Union

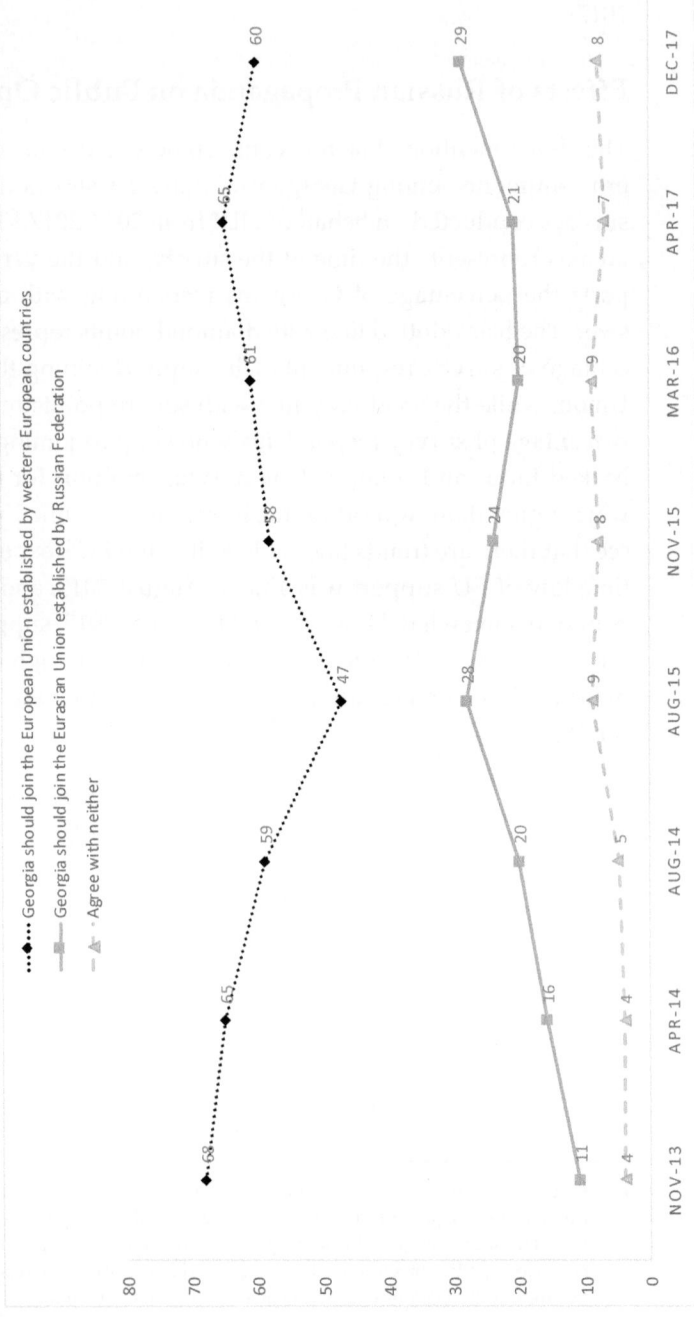

Figure 3.2 shows that the decline of popular support for the Georgian government's stated goal of joining the EU and NATO was also noticeable during that period.[5] In this bar graph, black bars represent survey respondents' opinions regarding the Georgian government's stated goal to join the EU, while gray bars represent respondents' opinions about the government's stated goal to join NATO. The horizontal axis notes at each time point which bars represent approval versus disapproval of the respective goals. The percentage holding each opinion is also numerically labelled at the top of each bar. The support of Georgians for their government's aspiration to join the EU and NATO plummeted between 2013-2016. The trend was particularly noticeable with regards to NATO, which dropped from an all-time high of 81% to an all-time low of 61%. For the EU, support dropped from 85% to 68%. Since then, support for each has rebounded considerably. The results show the mild but existent impact of pro-Russian propagandist messages during this time frame that instigate fear of war with Russia and losing Georgian traditional values to European liberal forces because of Georgia's European and Euro-Atlantic integration.

---

5. Figure 3.2 is created using the relevant findings of the public opinion polls conducted in Georgia with the financial support of the National Democratic Institute. The source is available at: https://www.ndi.org/georgia-polls; Library of NDI Georgia Public Opinion Research. NOTE: the absent percentage indicates population that did not know the answer or refused to answer.

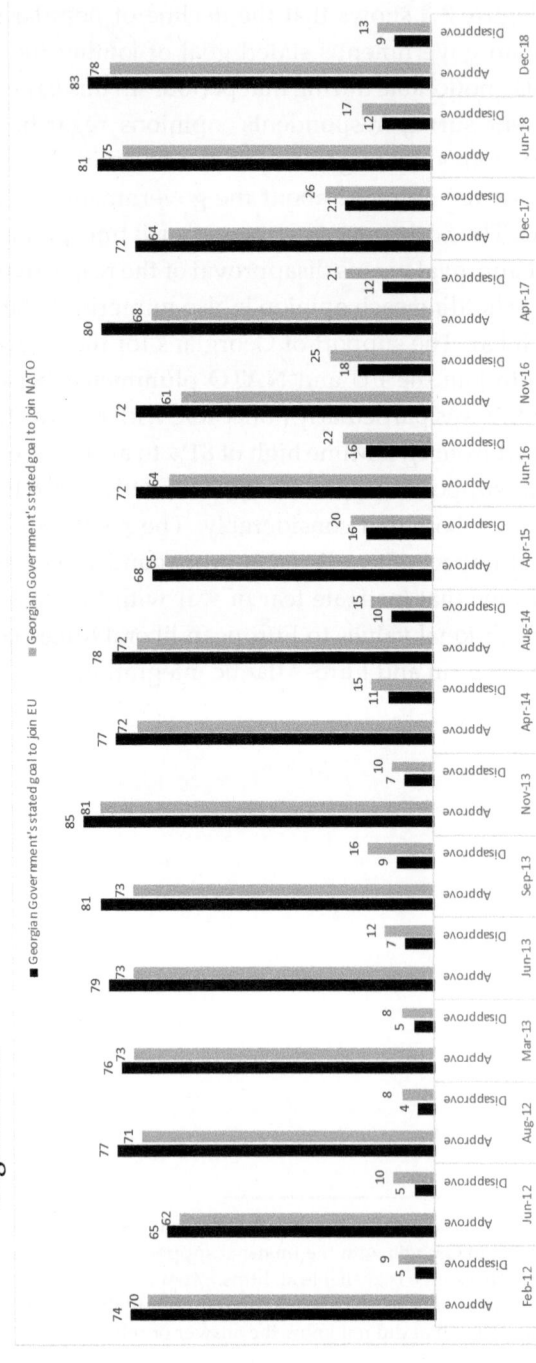

Figure 3.2 Support for the Government's Stated Goals to Join the European Union and the North Atlantic Treaty Organization

Figure 3.3 speaks to the sentiment of Georgians regarding maintaining neighborly relations with Russia during the period from 2014-2016.[6] This graph reflects the findings of public opinion polls conducted in Georgia with the financial support of the National Democratic Institute over the years regarding attitudes of Georgians towards the European and Euro-Atlantic integration of the country vs. improving relations with Russia. The horizontal axis represents time, and the vertical axis represents the percentage of respondents supporting each option. The dark dotted line represents the percentage feeling that Georgia would benefit most from European integration, while the light dashed line represents those who believe that better relations with Russia would best serve the country. As the line graph shows, those willing to abandon Euro integration in favor of establishing better relations with Russia increased by 11 percentage points (from 20% to 31%) over this time frame. Simultaneously, support for European integration dropped five percentage points over this period (from 58% to 53%). These sentiments are closely linked to the Kremlin narrative that, upon severing ties with the EU and NATO, good-neighborly relations with Russia would be possible.

---

[6] The data for Figure 3.3 are from the Library of NDI Georgia Public Opinion Research; available at: https://www.ndi.org/georgia-polls.

Figure 3.3 Benefits from European integration as opposed to neighborly relations with Russia

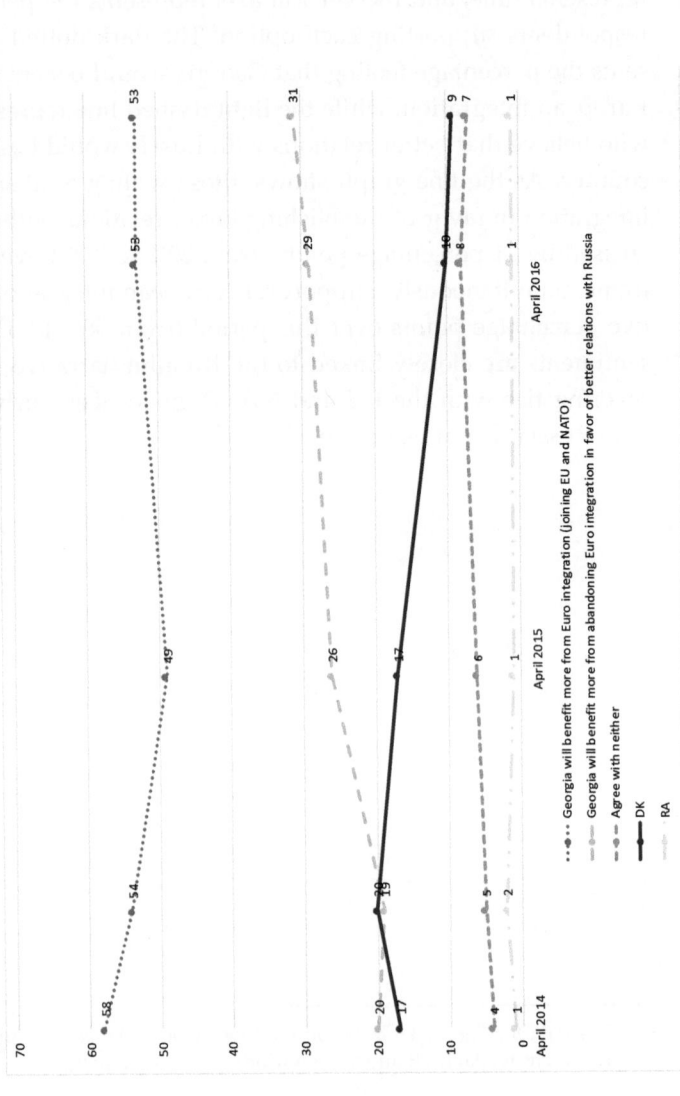

There are two details that we shall pay attention to when summarizing Figure 3.3. First and foremost, Kremlin propaganda seems to be trying to present itself as an alternative to the two largest coalitions (the EU and NATO) and seems to have succeeded in doing so over the time frame that this question has been posed to Georgians.[7] The question itself implies that Georgia cannot have it all, by pursuing its Euro-Atlantic aspirations while retaining positive or even neutral relations with Russian Federation. The second point that shall be noted based on the analysis of the surveys is the fact that over the years the said question was asked (2012-2016), up to 9% of population did not know how to answer or refused to answer. This implies that a portion of Georgians that have not yet made up their minds can easily succumb to the propagandist messages spread by pro-Russian forces and potentially join the ranks of those who consider that abandoning European aspirations will be more beneficial to the country (Iancu, Fortuna, and Barna, 2016, 52).

Figure 3.4 Attitudes of the Georgian Population towards Russia

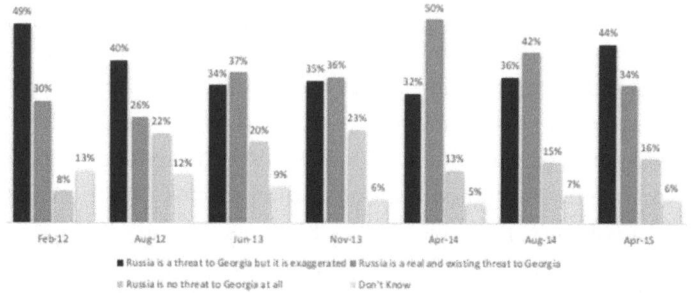

As for the impact of messages that reinforce and spread the idea of Russia's invincibility, Figure 3.4 shows a compilation of findings of thematic opinion polls conducted in Georgia and

---

7. Many authors have argued that there is no real choice. On the one hand the EU has economic, social, and human rights-related benefits. By contrast, Russia has financial struggles (Russell, 2018), is unable and unwilling to promote high human rights standards (Human Rights Watch, 2019), and sees Georgia not as a partner, but rather as part of its sphere of influence as Russian remains an "imperial parasite which feeds itself from the spaces of putrefaction and zones of destabilization" (Tavadze,2014, 128).

funded by the National Democratic Institute throughout years 2012-2015.[8] The horizontal axis denotes the time of each survey. For each wave there are four bars for the possible responses, with the darkest bar signifying those who feel Russia is a threat but it is exaggerated, the next bar indicating that Russia is a real threat, the third bar indicating Russia is no threat, and the lightest bar representing those who don't know. The percentage choosing each response is also written at the top of each bar. The darkest bar, indicating that the threat from Russia is not unlimited, took a dip in the middle of the series, but rebounded by April 2015. Hence, the public appears to be able to assess the threats coming from Russia quite realistically, without succumbing to the pro-Kremlin narrative regarding Russia's unlimited strength and capacity.

Conclusion

The pro-Kremlin propagandist machine employs various tools to influence Georgian public opinion in an attempt to divert the country from its selected path of European and Euro-Atlantic integration. Alongside with instigating fears for territorial integrity, prospects of economic development, and the health and welfare of the Georgian population, Russian soft power attempts to present western civilization as a destructive power. Said power, according to discourse among the above listed politicians and media outlets, attempts to strip the maligned nations of their values, traditions and religion. In contrast, Kremlin politics towards Georgia is depicted as a demonstration of tough love from a big brother that tries to salvage the family member from a disastrous path that he has embarked upon.

These public opinion surveys demonstrate that Russian efforts have been somewhat successful in Georgia. European countries were Georgia's historical family, but these ties were lost after the Soviets invaded Georgia in 1921. Whilst the majority of Georgians still remain committed to rejoining their historical family, the

---

[8] Figure 3.4 was created using the data available at: Library of NDI Georgia Public Opinion Research; available at: https://www.ndi.org/georgia-polls.

trends in the data are favorable to Russia's preferences. The Kremlin's excessive use of trolls throughout social media, its influence through traditional media outlets, and its strong support for anti-Western and nationalistic movements, NGOs, and political parties all pose a realistic threat that Russia may be able to exercise increased influence the coming period.

The existence of pluralistic media and a diverse political party spectrum in Georgia, paired with increasing opportunities for Georgians to travel and study in Europe and the US, are strong tools for raising general public awareness. Such awareness can mitigate the risks associated with Russian disinformation. However, in light of recent attempts of the Russian propagandist machine to interfere with the domestic and foreign affairs of countries in Europe and elsewhere, Russia should be regarded as a threat that cannot and will not be completely discarded. The only effective response to this threat will be a common opposition approach adopted by the EU, the US, and countries aspiring to become part of the pro-Western unions.

References

Agenda.ge. 2018. "Georgian Health Official Says Russia's Allegations about Lugar Lab in Tbilisi Are False." Last accessed on April 8, 2019 at http://agenda.ge/en/news/2018/2072.

Agenda.ge. 2018. "Georgian Dream Endorses Salome Zourabichvili's Candidacy in Presidential Elections." Last accessed on April 9, 2019 at http://agenda.ge/en/news/2018/1875.

Amnesty International. 2017. "TV Channel Ownership Dispute Threatens Media Freedom in Georgia." Last accessed on April 8, 2019 at https://www.amnesty.org/download/Documents/EUR5658332017ENGLISH.pdf.

Avalishvili, L., Lomtadze, G., and Kevkhishvili, A. 2016. "Kremlin's Information War: Why Georgia Should Develop State Policy on Countering Propaganda." Last accessed on August 2, 2017 at https://idfi.ge/en/informational-war-of-kremlin-against-georgia-the-necessity-of-having-state-policy-against-propaganda.

Avgerinos, K. 2009. "Russia's Public Diplomacy Effort: What the Kremlin is Doing and Why It's Not Working." Last accessed on August 3, 2017, from http://jpia.princeton.edu/sites/jpia/files/2009-6.pdf.

Bai, E. 2015. "Sorry, but Soft Power is Not a Part of the Russian Tradition." *Russia Direct*. Last accessed on January 3, 2018 at: http://www.russia-direct.org/opinion/sorry-soft-power-not-part-russian-tradition.

Burlinova, N. 2015. "Russian Soft Power is Just Like Western Soft Power, But with a Twist." *Russia Direct*. Last Accessed on March 14,2016 at: http://www.russia-direct.org/opinion/russian-soft-power-just-western-soft-power-twist.

Cecire, M. 2015. "The Kremlin Pulls on Georgia, It's Time for the West to Stop Taking Tbilisi for Granted." *Foreign Policy*. Last accessed on March 12, 2019 at http://foreignpolicy.com/2015/03/09/the-kremlin-pulls-on-georgia/.

Civil.ge. 2018. "Salome Zurabishvili's August War Remarks Draw Criticism from Political Parties." Last accessed on April 9, 2019 https://civil.ge/archives/248876.

Conley, H.A., Gerber, T. P., Moore, L., and David, M. 2011. *Russian Soft power in the 21st Century, An Examination of Russian Compatriot Policy in Estonia*. A report of the CSIS Europe Program.

CNN Library. 2019. "2008 Georgia Russia Conflict Fast Facts." Last accessed on June 19, 2019 at https://edition.cnn.com/2014/03/13/world/europe/2008-georgia-russia-conflict/index.html.

Democracy Digest. 2017. "Russia's Information Warfare: Propaganda is Not Soft Power." Last accessed on June 19, 2019 at https://www.demdigest.org/oft-power-v-propaganda/.

Dzvelishvili, Nata, and Kupreishvili, Tazo. 2015. "Russian Influence on Georgian NGOs and Media." Tbilisi: Damoukidebloba. Last accessed on April 9, 2019 at https://idfi.ge/public/upload/russanimpactongeorgianmediadaNGO.pdf.

The Economist. 2008. "Medvedev on Russia's Interests: Moscow's Guiding Principles?" Last accessed on June 19, 2019 at: https://www.economist.com/certain-ideas-of-europe/2008/09/01/medvedev-on-russias-interests.

ECRI. 2016. "ECRI Report on Georgia, Fifth Monitoring Cycle." Last accessed on April 17, 2019 at https://rm.coe.int/fourth-report-on-georgia/16808b5773.

EURACTIV.com with AFP. 2017. "Romania's Fake News Fuels Euroscepticism." Last accessed on April 9, 2019 at https://www.euractiv.com/section/justice-home-affairs/news/romanias-fake-news-fuels-euroscepticism/.

Freedom House. 2019. "Nations in Transit 2018: Georgia." Last accessed on April 15, 2019 at https://freedomhouse.org/sites/default/files/NiT2018_Georgia_final.pdf.

Gallarotti, G. 2011. "Soft Power: What It Is, It's Importance, and the Conditions for Its Effective Use." Division II, Faculty Publications. Paper 57. Last accessed on March 14, 2019 at http://wesscholar.wesleyan.edu/cgi/viewcontent.cgi?article=1056&context=div2facpubs.

Ganieva, A. 2018. "Russia's Revisionist History." *New York Times.* Last accessed on June 19, 2019 at https://www.nytimes.com/2018/12/03/gopinion/russia-poland-history-laws.html.

Gomichon, M. 2013. "Joseph Nye on Soft Power." *E-International Relations Students.* Last accessed on January 10, 2018 at http://www.e-ir.info: http://www.e-ir.info/2013/03/08/joseph-nye-on-soft-power/.

GRASS FactCheck. 2018. "Russia Uses Quotes from Salome Zurabishvili'ds Book as an Argument Against Georgia in The Hague." Last accessed on April 9, 2019 at https://factcheck.ge/en/story/37596-russia-uses-quotes-from-salome-zurabishvili-s-book-as-an-argument-against-georgia-in-the-hague.

The Guardian Editorial Board. 2015. "The Guardian View on Russian Propaganda: The Truth Is Out There." Last accessed on January 4, 2018 at https://www.theguardian.com/commentisfree/2015/mar/02/guardian-view-russian-propaganda-truth-out-there?CMP=share_btn_fb.

Human Rights Watch. 2019. "World Report 2019: Russia: Events of 2018." Last accessed on June 19, 2019 at https://www.hrw.org/world-report/2019/country-chapters/russia.

Iancu, N., Fortuna, A., and Barna, C. 2016. *Countering Hybrid Threats: Lessons Learned from Ukraine.* IOS Press.

International Court of Justice. 2008. Application of the International Convention on the Elimination of All Forms of Racial Discrimination (Georgia v. Russian Federation); overview of the case; available at: https://www.icj-cij.org/en/case/140.

Jamnews Tbilisi. 2018. "Nine Steps Georgian Government Took to Improve Relations with Russia in Its Six Years in Power." Last accessed on April 8, 2019 at https://jam-news.net/8-steps-by-georgia-to-settle-relations-with-russia/.

Keohane, Robert O. and Nye, Joseph S. 1977. *Power and Interdependence: World Politics in Transition.* Boston: Little, Brown and Company.

Kintsurashvili, T. 2018. *Anti-Western Propaganda.* Media Development Foundation. Last accessed on April 8, 2019 at http://mdfgeorgia.ge/uploads/library/89/file/eng/AntiWest-2017-ENG.pdf.

Koshkin, P. 2015. "The Paradox of Kremlin Propaganda: How It Tries to Win Hearts and Minds." *Russia Direct.* Last accessed on January 4, 2018 at http://www.russia-direct.org/analysis/paradox-kremlin-propaganda-how-it-tries-win-hearts-and-minds.

Koshkin, P., and Smertina, K. 2016. "Russian Soft Power Still Has Some Hard Edges." *Russia Direct*. Last accessed on April 10, 2019 at https://russia-direct.org/analysis/russian-soft-power-still-has-some-hard-edges.

Krastev, I. 2014. "Russian Revisionism, Putin's Plan for Overturning the European Order." *Foreign Affairs*. Last accessed on March 14, 2016 at https://www.foreignaffairs.com/articles/russia-fsu/2014-03-03/russian-revisionism.

Laruelle, M. 2015. *The "Russian World", Russia's Soft Power and Geopolitical Impact*. Washington, DC: The Center on Global Interests. Last accessed on March 14, 2016 at http://globalinterests.org/wp-content/uploads/2015/05/FINAL-CGI_Russian-World_Marlene-Laruelle.pdf.

Liberali. 2016. "Research: In an Attempt to Discredit West, Russian Foundations Have Become Active in Georgia." (კვლევა: დასავლეთის დისკრედიტაციის მიზნით, საქართველოში რუსული ფონდები გააქტიურდნენ). Last accessed on April 15, 2019 at http://liberali.ge/news/view/20408/kvleva-dasavletis-diskreditatsiis-miznit-saqartveloshi-rusuli-fondebi-gaaqtiurdnen.

Lucas, E. 2014. "Russia Is a Revisionist Power; Greater Dangers Lie Ahead." *Kyiv Post*. Last accessed on March 14, 2016 at http://www.kyivpost.com/opinion/op-ed/edward-lucas russia-a-revisionist-power-greater-dangers-lie-ahead-363081.html.

Lucas, E., and Pomeranzev, P. 2016. *Winning the Information War. Techniques and Counter-strategies to Russian Propaganda in Central and Eastern Europe*. A Report by CEPA's Information Warfare Project in Partnership with the Legatum Institute. Last accessed on March 30, 2019 at https://cepa.ecms.pl/files/?id_plik=2706.

Makarychev, A. 2016. "The Limits to Russian Soft Power in Georgia." PONARS Eurasia Policy Memo No. 412. Last accessed on August 2, 2017 at http://www.ponarseurasia.org/sites/default/files/policy-memos-pdf/Pepm412_Makarychev_Jan2016_1.pdf

MDF. 2015. "Youth Attitudes towards European Integration." *Media Development Foundation*. Last accessed on April 9, 2019 at http://mdfgeorgia.ge/uploads/library/27/file/eng/Research-Publication-ENG.pdf.

MDF. 2017a. "Anti-Western Propaganda." *Media Development Foundation*. Last accessed on April 9, 2019 at http://mdfgeorgia.ge/eng/view-library/65/.

MDF. 2017b. "Kremlin Influence Index." *Media Development Foundation*. Last accessed: 17 April, 2019 at http://mdfgeorgia.ge/uploads/library/67/file/eng/dm_iik_engl-compressed.pdf.

Myth Detector. 2017. "Disinformation on Alleged Opening of NATO Military Base in Poti and the Treaty of Kars." Last accessed on April 8, 2019 at http://mythdetector.ge/en/myth/disinformation-alleged-opening-nato-military-base-poti-and-treaty-kars.

Nye, Joseph S. 1990. "Soft Power." *Foreign Policy* 80: 153-171.

Nye, Joseph S. 2005. *Soft Power: The Means to Success in World Politics.* New York: Public Affairs.

Nye, Joseph S. 2009. *Understanding International Conflicts.* 7th eds. New York: Pearson.

Nye, Joseph S. 2011. *The Future of Power.* New York: Public Affairs.

Pomeranstev, P. 2014. "Russia's Ideology: There Is No Truth." *New York Times.* Last accessed on April 10, 2019 at https://www.nytimes.com/2014/12/12/opinion/russias-ideology-there-is-no-truth.html?_r=1.

Romm, T. 2017. "Tech Is Scary Powerful, and Other Things We Learned when Facebook, Google and Twitter testified to Congress about Russia." Last accessed on January 4, 2018 at https://www.recode.net/2017/10/31/16588032/facebook-google-twitter-congress-russia-election-2016-tech-hearings-franken-cruz-graham.

Russell, M. 2018. "Seven Economic Challenges for Russia: Breaking Out of Stagnation?" *EPRS -European Parliamentary Research Service.* PE 625.138. Last accessed on June 19, 2019 at http://www.europarl.europa.eu/RegData/etudes/IDAN/2018/625138/EPRS_IDA(2018)625138_EN.pdf.

RT. 2017. "Ex-speaker of the Georgian Parliament: Saakashvili Started a Aar in S Ossetia." Last accessed on June 10, 2019 at https://www.rt.com/news/saakashvili-ossetia-war-ivanishvili-163/ https://en.news-front.info/2017/08/08/ex-speaker-of-the-georgian-parliament-saakashvili-started-a-war-in-s-ossetia/.

Shakila, K. 2019. "Russia's New Strategy in Georgia: Creeping Occupation." Last accessed on June 19, 2019 at https://blogs.lse.ac.uk/humanrights/2019/02/05/russias-new-strategy-in-georgia-creeping-occupation/.

Socor, V. 2019. "Russia Launches 'Passportization' in Occupied Ukrainian Donbas (Part One)." Last accessed on June 19, 2019 at https://112.international/opinion/russia-launches-passportization-in-occupied-ukrainian-donbas-part-one-39367.html.

Spectator. 2017. "Slovakia Is Vulnerable to Russian Influence." Last accessed on April 11, 2019 at https://spectator.sme.sk/c/20506478/slovakia-is-vulnerable-to-russian-influence.html.

Kilba. 2017. "Incidents of Poisoning In Tkvarcheli May be Linked to the Laboratory Operating in Georgia (Килба: отравления в Ткуарчале могут быть связаны с лабораторией в Грузии)." Last accessed on April 8, 2019 at https://sputnik-abkhazia.ru/Abkhazia/20170309/102056 8559/kilba-otravleniya-v-tkuarchale-mogut-byt-svyazany-s-laboratoriej-v-gruzii.html.

Stockholm International Peace Research Institute. 2015. "SIPRI Fact Sheet. Trends in World Military Expenditure." Last Accessed on March 14, 2016 at http://books.sipri.org/product_info?c_product_id=496.

Tavadze, G. 2014. "New Russian Imperialist and Georgia": Violent Spatial Practices, Disrupted Places and Destabilized Spaces." *European Scientific Journal* 2: 128. Available at https://eujournal.org/index.php/esj/article/download/4797/4690.

Tugushi, L., Gagua, M., Gvedashvili, G., Lapachi, N., Gaganidze, G., and Dzebisashvili, G. 2016. *Threats of Russian Hard and Soft Power in Georgia*. Tbilisi: European Initiative-Liberal Academy. Available at http://www.ei-lat.ge/images/doc/threats%20of%20russian%20soft%20and%20hard%20power.pdf.

Veebel, V. 2015. "Russian Propaganda, Disinformation, and Estonia's Experience." *Foreign Policy Research Institute*. Last accessed on March 14, 2016 at http://www.fpri.org/article/2015/10/russian-propaganda-disinformation-and-estonias-experience/.

Wagner, J.P. 2014. "The Effectiveness of Soft & Hard Power in Contemporary International Relations." *E-International Relations Students*. Last accessed on March 14, 2016 at http://www.e-ir.info/2014/05/14/the-effectiveness-of-soft-hard-power-in-contemporary-international-relations/.

Watts, C., and Weisburd, A. 2016. "How Russia Wins an Election." *Politico*. Last accessed on January 4, 2018 at https://www.politico.com/magazine/story/2016/12/how-russia-wins-an-election-214524.

4
Analyzing the Potential Causes of Ethno-Political Conflicts in the South Caucasus

Nino Okhanashvili, Ph.D.

This chapter focuses on conflicts occurring in South Caucasus countries in the late 1980s and early 1990s. Two major types of factors can be singled out as the root causes of the conflicts in Abkhazia, the Tskhinvali region, and Nagorno Karabakh: internal and external factors. They often work in concert.

At the external level, artificial escalation of the aforesaid conflicts is linked to Russia's strategic goals. Following the collapse of the Soviet Union, Russia declared the former Soviet territory as the sphere of its vital interest. Russia's interest as a big state is to preserve its superpower status and gain regional hegemony. Russia's aim is to prevent integration of the post-Soviet countries into the European and Euro-Atlantic coalitions controlled by Western powers, and to maintain the status of a hegemonic state in the region (Okhanashvili, 2017, 122). At the external level, the causes of the given conflicts will be determined by verifying the basic theories of international relations. In particular, realism and its progenies are considered: Classical realism; Neoclassical realism; Neorealism; Defensive realism; and Offensive realism. The theory that can best explain developments in the South Caucasus region will be identified based on a qualitative verification of the key assumptions of these theories.

External factors played a lead role in the escalation of conflicts in South Caucasus. However, these factors have received considerable attention in previous research. So, this work will focus more on the internal factors that may have caused these conflicts. Three levels of analysis offered by Kenneth N. Waltz have been used in this study to explain an intra-state conflict. The first level focuses on human nature and mass behavior; the second level addresses the nature of the state and elite behavior, and the third level concentrates on the system's nature. During an ethnic conflict, mass behavior (first level), elite behavior (second level), and the rules of the political system in which the groups interact (third level) must be studied (Kaufman, 1996,149).

There are two ways escalation can start. One case involves mass violence, where ethnic hostility pushes elite actors to take a harsher stance on ethnic issues. Such behavior creates a security dilemma and leads to an ethnic war. Another case involves elite violence, i.e., ethnic war initiated by the ethnic group leaders who are trying to fulfill their political goals. They thus promote ethnic violence so as to create a security dilemma and stoke an ethnic war. In this chapter, the Nagorno-Karabakh conflict is seen as mass-led violence, while the conflicts over Abkhazia and South Ossetia point to elite-led violence. At the initial stage of the Nagorno-Karabakh conflict, the protests and violence were not organized by the elites. In the case of the Abkhaz and South Ossetian conflicts, the elites largely organized and contributed to the escalation of the conflict.

Research Question and Hypotheses

This study investigates the following research question: What are the potential causes of the ethnic conflicts that occurred in Abkhazia, South Ossetia and Nagorno-Karabakh during the period 1988-1994? The following hypotheses are investigated:

1. At the foreign level, the main reason for conflicts is the desire of Russian regional hegemony.
2. At the domestic level, the conflicts are fueled by elite or mass violence, which creates an internal ethnic security dilemma.

Among the many variables that could be studied, the following are regarded as important:

At the external level, the independent variable is Russia's aspiration to achieve regional hegemony and the dependent variable is encouraging and supporting separatism by Russia. At the internal level, the independent variable is mutual perception of the parties' elites/masses, and the dependent variable is conflict escalation.

Established qualitative research methods are applied in this study with the case-study approach selected as the most appropriate for the research questions posed in the chapter. For the purpose of data collection and analysis, secondary sources and literature reviews on the topic were analyzed to create a scholarly basis for the research. Specific techniques such as in-depth interviews with members of expert circles were also used.

The paper offers a comparative analysis of the Nagorno-Karabakh conflict, on one hand, and the conflicts in the Abkhazia and Tskhinvali regions, on the other. Generally speaking, all conflicts are unique, but there are similarities as well as differences between them. Despite a number of differences that will be discussed in this paper, the conflicts in South Ossetia, Abkhazia, and Nagorni Karabakh have certain similar features. All three conflicts occurred after the collapse of the Soviet Union, and in all three cases, there were serious confrontations and high death tolls among civilians.

This issue is particularly important and timely, as the peaceful resolution of the South Caucasus conflicts and the restoration of territorial integrity is a cherished goal of most citizens. The novelty and practical importance of this papers is that it explains the Abkhaz, Tskhinvali region, and Nagorno-Karabakh conflicts through the lens of international relations theories. A theory-based approach is beneficial because it presents a systematic way of understanding events, behaviors, and situations. A theory explains or predicts conflicts by specifying relations among variables.

When studying the causes of a particular conflict, all key related factors need to be considered. The causes of the South Caucasus conflicts can be found at different levels. Internal and external factors are linked and generally complement each other. They are not necessarily mutually exclusive. This chapter aims to show how external factors influence the internal level, and vice versa, including how external factors can exacerbate internal factors, which were then masterfully utilized by Russia. This chapter documents the interaction between these external and internal pressures. This chapter is of practical importance and will provide insights to readers studying the historical root causes of these conflicts. Identifying these causes may provide policymakers with a better understanding of how to prevent such conflicts in the future.

Literature Review

This section provides a detailed review of the relevant literature on international relations theories with regards to conflicts. The review includes the work of some representatives of the realism school, including Thucydides, Niccolo Machiavelli, Thomas Hobbes, Hans Morgenthau, Kenneth Waltz and John Mearsheimer. "The 'international' theory of inter-ethnic war' by Stuart J. Kaufman is also prominent in this section. In his work, Kaufman names mass/elite violence and intra-ethnic security dilemma as the root causes of ethnic war. Other key authors referred to in the historical part of the paper are: Thomas de Waal—"Black Garden"; Ronald Asmus—"A Little War That Shook the World"; Svetlana Chervonnaya—"Abkhazia-1992, a Post-Communist Vendée"; Ghia Nodia—"Causes and Visions of Conflict in Abkhazia"; Shota Malashkhia—"The Anatomy of Conflicts". The aforesaid works present a historical framework of the events that developed over the years and that eventually led to conflicts in the South Caucasus countries. However, this section is less focused on the description of historical facts, as there is plenty of literature on this topic, both in Georgian and other languages. Rather, this section aims to provide a theoretical discussion of the root causes of conflicts.

Dominant International Relations Theories. A theory's descriptive capacity is very important for determining the causes of a particular event. Theory can tell us much about the history of international politics and provide a window into the future. The primary task of international relations theory is, moreover, that it should explain ongoing global developments (Mearsheimer, 2001, 3). Political developments are very complex, so it is hardly possible to make an accurate political forecast without theoretical analysis.

Realism is one of the dominant theories of international relations, with roots that trace back to Thucydides. Modern realists often refer to the classical realists—Thucydides, Machiavelli, and Hobbes—as the 'Founding Fathers'. Realists believe the rudiments of human nature are fear and self-interest; hence, both individuals and states are aggressive and prone to conflict. International politics produces an environment where the main goal of the states is to achieve military security and struggle for power (Wendt, 1992, 395).

Neoclassical realism in the Twentieth Century formed as a result of accumulated historical experience. Hans Morgenthau's work published in 1948 "Politics Among Nations: The Struggle for Power and Peace," has been viewed as a major work in international relations. Power, national interests and politics as a struggle for power are the main themes in his work. The theory mainly focuses on the nature of the politics rather than the actors. Unlike political realism, for which the starting point is the inherent flaws in human nature, neorealism focuses on the international system and considers the peculiarities of the system as a major determinant of international politics.

In his work "Man, the State and War' (1959) Kenneth Waltz described three levels of analysis (also referred to as 'images') in international relations: 1. Individuals; 2. States; and 3. The international system. Waltz thus answers the question of what causes wars. At the individual level, conflicts are often caused by an individual, whose decisions may result in conflict. At the states level, the main cause of war in the state's political system itself. If a state's political system is either authoritarian or totalitarian, the state is more prone to conflicts. At the international level, the international system is oriented towards ongoing processes. According this view, the anarchic structure of the international system is the root cause of wars. The most important thing is how power is distributed in the international system.

Structural realism (neorealism) is divided into two sub-branches: defensive and offensive realism. According to defensive realism (and its main representative Kenneth Waltz), it is more important to maintain power rather than to increase it. Waltz's world consists of states that are satisfied with their power. Under the defensive realism approach, the main goal of a state is to be stronger than its potential rival, since this is seen as the only way to survive. None of Waltz's works suggest that war is the best way to achieve the goal. He actually believes that offensive war is 'a bad idea'.

John Mearsheimer can be regarded as the founder of offensive realism. Mearsheimer's newly formulated theory is different from structural realism, and which explains international aggression. In contrast to Waltz, Mearsheimer argues that the state's search for power is insatiable and has no limits. He disagrees with Waltz on the question of 'how much power states want'. Mearsheimer believes that the international system creates powerful incentives for states to look for opportunities to gain more power and to take advantage of those situations when the benefits outweigh the costs. Mearsheimer's offensive realism predicts many more conflicts and wars than does Waltz's defensive realism. "States are never satisfied; they keep reaching for more power and these power urges seem to collide" (Snyder, 2001, 153). Thus, in Waltz's world, there are 'satisfied' states, while in Mearsheimer's world, there are restless 'maximalists'.

Root causes of conflicts – external level analysis. In the geopolitical layer of South Caucasus, the key actor is post-Soviet Russia, which wants to maintain its influence through these conflicts, and to have an instrument for pressure and control in the post-Soviet area in general. Any attempt to analyze these conflicts without realizing the geopolitical layer will be incomplete. This systemic level has been one of the most important factors leading up to now (author's interview with Giorgi Gvalia — see the list of interviews in the appendix section).

As far as the Caucasus region is concerned, Russia has always been interested in strengthening and maintaining geopolitical, geo-economic and military influence because of the region's proximity to Russia. Abkhazia has always been an integral part of Georgia. However, Russia has its own plan for Georgia's future territorial arrangement. As far back as Tsarist Russia and later, after Russia invaded Georgia, Russia has constantly interfered in the relations between Georgians and Abkhazians, trying to separate them. From the perspective of realism, the main objective of Russia's actions in

Georgia was to establish a dominant position in the region and to create a sphere of influence.

Political realism can best explain Russia's interests and, therefore, can offer rather convincing and comprehensive arguments for explaining and analyzing Russia's actions in Georgia. Russia pursued the same goal in Georgia as in Armenia and Azerbaijan. In terms of realism, Russian motives could be explained as a desire to gain and maintain power, which Russia tried to achieve by carrying out violent policies. Russia aimed to 'restore' the Soviet empire, to stop the democratic processes and suppress the desire for independence.

Abkhazia was declared a socialist republic at a meeting in Batumi on March 28-29, 1921. After that, the Russian Soviet Empire leadership, which instigated the Abkhaz separatists, tried to split away Abkhazia from Georgia. The rise of the national-liberation movement in Georgia fueled tension in Abkhazia, and Russia sought to provoke ethnic conflicts to suppress the republic's aspiration for independence. In November 1990, Mikhail Gorbachev warned Akaki Asatiani, the Deputy Chairman of the Supreme Council of Georgia that if Georgia attempted to withdraw from the Soviet Union, the country, as well as its autonomous entities and the regions populated by ethnic minorities, would face serious consequences.

It was not that difficult to estimate this danger, especially given the numerous examples of Russia fighting against 'disobedient' states in the historical past. Under Bolshevik rule, Russia triggered two Abkhazian and three Ossetian uprisings against democratic Georgia within three years. Mikhail Gorbachev made no secret of Russia's plans either. In a phone conversation with Zviad Gamsakhurdia in 1991, he threatened that 'if Georgia declared independence, it would have to withdraw from the USSR without the Tskhinvali region and Abkhazia' (Gamakharia, 2004, 3).

In her book "Abkhazia-1992, a Post-Communist Vendée", Svetlana Chervonnaya provides a review of the history of Abkhazians, sharing the view that Abkhazia is a part of Georgia. She believes that the war in Abkhazia was the fulfillment of Russia's long-cherished dream; that Georgia was to be stripped of Abkhazia and other ethnic regions as a punishment for leaving the Soviet Union (Chervonnaya, 1993, 9).

Under the offensive realism approach, states are oriented towards regional hegemony. States strive for hegemony and they achieve it through various means. In terms of offensive realism, Russia seeks not only to maintain hegemony in the Caucasus region, but also to expand and pursue the policies that are tailored to Russia's goals. Russia views Georgia as a major strategic state. If Russia fails to establish control over Georgia, it will not be able to become a regional hegemonic power. Expansion of power over Georgia will allow Russia to exercise unlimited control over the North Caucasus. In the case of the region that Russia calls South Ossetia, it was using the same methods as in Abkhazia. Through these conflicts, Russia wants Georgia to be politically and economically dependent on her (author's interview with Nika Chitadze). Kenneth Waltz believes that one possible cause of conflict is when State A possesses something that State B wants. The desire of State B becomes the cause of war and the risk of conflict is further increased by the fact that there is a reason to stop State B. The action of Russia as State B falls under this very example.

In terms of realism, by provoking conflicts in Georgia, Russia was taking care of its bigger interest and was confronting the United States. Realism explains the great powers' interests, taking great powers as a study object, because from a realism perspective, great powers determine the international system and small powers are merely pawns. However, Russia attempted to achieve greater goals using a small power and to confront the superpower (interview with Eka Akobia).

Realism describes international relations from the perspective of power. Russia could not cooperate with Georgia nor engage in talks and pursue a diplomatic solution; it was not within the scope of its interests because Russia's primary concern was its own power. Russia's main goal was to restore the Soviet Union, and Georgia was the first country where Russia tried to revise the internationally recognized borders established after the Cold War. According to realism, states prioritize power and strength, and it was that very attitude that led Russia and Georgia to a conflict. For

Russia, the latter was quite natural, and war was regarded as the only means of survival. Russia aimed to prevent Georgia from becoming a member of the Euro-Atlantic space.

Russian warned on a number of occasions that western aspirations would be detrimental for Georgia. In response to the Bucharest Summit, Russia strengthened its ties with the breakaway regions and started developing a 'creeping annexation' strategy. It was illegally deploying troops and bringing in weapons, which was a precursor for a Russian attack (Asmus, 2011, 15). In 2008, Russian troops openly invaded Georgia. However, Russia failed to overthrow the Georgian government though it did provoke an ethnic confrontation. After the 2008 Russia-Georgia war, it became clear that the Ossetians and Abkhazians were used by Russia as a means of pursuing its national interests.

What had happened in Georgia since the 1990s and again in 2008 is consistent with the international relations theory of realism. Since the South Caucasus countries have been experiencing territorial disintegration but have many similarities in their historical backgrounds, this study aims to find the key factors that caused the tensions. By studying internal dynamics, we will find that the conflicts over the Nagorni Karabakh, Abkhazia and Tskhinvali regions significantly differed from each other. However, Russia's political interests are clearly evident in all three cases.

The Nagorno-Karabakh conflict differs from the South Ossetian and Abkhazian conflicts in that there was a confrontation between the two states. This event has been classified as an inter-state war between Azerbaijan and Armenia, but the ethnic factor is important. While the territory of Karabakh was a part of Azerbaijan, it was predominantly populated by ethnic Armenians.

Russia further aggravated this conflict and its motivation was the same as when it exacerbated the conflicts in South Ossetia and Abkhazia. Those conflicts have been viewed by Russia as an instrument against the West. Russia needs conflicts that are easily manageable and will pose a problem to the West. Instability has always been regarded as a factor hampering the region's integration into the West. The Caucasus region is unique in that it is a highly explosive zone and the 2008 war clearly showed that stability in this region is very fragile and illusory. The reason is that there are at least three hotbeds of conflict in the area (The Nagorno-Karabakh, South Ossetia and Abkhazia conflicts). However, this regional instability ultimately benefits Russia.

Artificial aggravation of the South Caucasus conflicts is linked to Russia's big strategic goals. From the perspective of realism, Russia, as a great power, seeks to restore the global bipolar system and gain regional hegemony. Russia's goal is to prevent integration of the post-Soviet states into the European and Euro Atlantic coalitions, so as to achieve full-fledged representation in the region and maintain its hegemonic status.

When looking for the causes of the Nagorno-Karabakh conflict, recall the collapse of the Soviet Union, when Moscow's policy was to ensure as much controversy and as many 'mines' planted between ethnic groups as possible, and one such mine was planted between the two Soviet republics, Armenia and Azerbaijan. Like the conflicts in Georgia, in Nagorno Karabakh, the violence between ethnic Armenians and ethnic Azerbaijanis also started against the background of these global processes. Being the third party, Russia was covertly involved in this ethnic confrontation and tried to take advantage of it.

Armenians and Azerbaijanis had been sharing the same territory for centuries. The relationship between these two nations of different religions (Christians and Shiite Muslims) has never been easy. The dominant empires (Persia, the Ottomans, or Russia) sometimes took advantage of the tensions between them to advance their own interests, and sometimes promoted their peaceful coexistence for similar reasons. After the collapse of the Soviet Union, the problems between the Armenians and Azerbaijanis were further exacerbated, leading to a territorial conflict (Radvanyi and Beruchashvili, 2011, 70).

The Kremlin pulled all necessary levers to trigger civil confrontations and 'ethnic wars' between the post-Soviet republics. Russia thus made the best use of ethnic and religious diversity and the complex historical past of the South Caucasus, which provided fertile ground for provoking 'ethnic conflicts'. After the early 1990s, the Kremlin fanned the flames of 'ethnic conflicts' and 'civil wars' in all three South Caucasus republics (Malashkhia, 2011, 199). The Kremlin tried to show the international community that after the collapse of the Soviet Union, the people of the Caucasus were still killing each other and only Russia was able to regulate the situation in the region and serve as a mediator. The Kremlin was altering and adjusting the borders in these republics, tailoring them to its own interests. Reflecting those interests, the 'South Ossetian' autonomous district was formed from the territory of Georgia, and the issue of transfer of Nagorno Karabakh either to Armenia or Azerbaijan also served that same interest. Any attempts of to 'disobey' were violently suppressed by the Kremlin, as in the case of April 9 in Tbilisi and 'Black January' in Baku.

The geopolitical layer has a serious impact on the exacerbation of conflicts, and this was the case in the Nagorno-Karabakh conflict. Russia is not interested in conflict resolution because this would cause Russia to lose leverage. Russia uses propaganda instruments to exert pressure on the region and it uses these instruments to further its ambitions. The situation in the region is unlikely to change as long as Russia maintains this attitude, and as long as there is no counter-balancing power in the region to force Russia to revise its policy. The geopolitical context existing in the region is crucial when looking for the causes of conflicts. Russia's motives and behavior are *realpolitik*, and studies must take this into account.

Underlying causes of conflicts-internal level analysis. There have been numerous attempts to explain the causes of ethnic wars. One approach focuses on the role of mass passions; another one suggests that inter-ethnic security dilemmas may be the key cause of ethnic war; the third approach blames ethnic wars on manipulation by belligerent leaders. The research shows that all three factors–hostile masses, belligerent leaders and intra-ethnic security dilemmas–are necessary if ethnic war is to result. These factors cause ethnic war by reinforcing each other in a spiral of increasing conflict; belligerent leaders stoke mass hostility; hostile masses support belligerent leaders; and together they threaten other groups and create a security dilemma, which in turn encourages hostile policy (Kaufman, 1996, 108). When states are swept into wars on the wave of enthusiasm, government leaders often work to create such enthusiasm within the society. Many theorists point out the importance of mass hostility as one of the factors contributing to international war.

A. Mass-led violence. The population's preferences are extreme due to long-held chauvinist and militaristic beliefs, exacerbated by economic hardship. Under these conditions, ethnic conflict is the result of mass pressure: once a particular leader fails to adopt extreme positions on ethnic issues, he/she is replaced by another leader who does. Thus, the elite will either meet the demands of the masses, or the masses will replace them (Welzel, 2003, 341). Consequently, intra-ethnic politics becomes a competition in extremism and this can ultimately result in ethnic war.

The preconditions for mass hostility are the negative ethnic stereotypes and disputes over emotional symbols. A security dilemma arises when there is a fear of ethnic extinction on both sides. Belligerent elites contribute to ethnic conflicts through a process of 'outbidding', which requires either the preconditions or presence of mass hostility, so the masses will be receptive to extremist appeals.

B. Elite-led violence. Ethnic war may be caused by elite violence. It begins with belligerent leaders who come to power when mass hostility is low. The leaders use the power of government and their influence over the media to encourage the growth of mass hostility and provoke a security dilemma, eventually leading to war (Kaufman, 1996, 109). Belligerent elites use monopoly over crucial information, purpose fully disseminating distorted information so as to convince others of their rightness. They try to spread their visions and, whenever possible, influence the mass media.

Elite-led violence occurs when the preconditions for mass hostility already exist. The necessary preconditions for ethnic war are: negative stereotypes, histories of ethnic domination, emotion-laden ethnic symbols, reciprocal fears of group extinction, and military means to act. Horowitz argues that all of these preconditions are present in every case of severe ethnic violence, and that all factors appeared in recent cases of ethnic war, including in the case of Georgia and Azerbaijan. Although all of these preconditions are necessary for the outbreak of war, they are not sufficient. These factors lead to ethnic war only if there is some degree of mass hostility. If preconditions for hostility are merely dormant categories, then war can be averted if elites cooperate to create new institutions that end anarchy. If mass hostility is present, however, the result is mass-led violence; if there is no mass hostility, but elites incite mass violence, the result will be elite-led violence (Kaufman, 1996, 115).

C. Intra-ethnic security dilemma. Under the international relations theory of neorealism, the dominant fact is that the international system is anarchic. There is no central power to determine the rules of conduct for each state. This anarchic environment often creates security dilemmas. In fact, a state's effort to increase its security threatens a neighboring state. The other state, in turn, tries to increase its power and sometimes the result is preemptive action and war (Waltz, 2003).

The security dilemma in ethnic groups differs from that in international relations theory. The neorealist concept of a security dilemma cannot be mechanically applied to ethnic conflict: anarchy and a possible security threat are not enough to create a security dilemma between communities that have been at peace for decades. An ethnic security dilemma requires reciprocal fears of group extinction, and such fears do not arise unless hostile masses define their security in extreme ways; or unless outbidding elites emerge to make the pursuit of such goals public policy (Kaufman, 1996, 112).

An ethnic security dilemma can arise only in a situation of de facto anarchy in which the state is either unwilling or unable to protect major groups. Both groups can think of themselves as potential minorities in danger of extinction. Both sides are then likely to see extreme measures as necessary for their own survival (Kaufman, 1996, 114).

Theoretical Expectations and Empirical Results

Mass-led violence in Nagorno Karabakh. Generally speaking, it is hard to believe that there is no leader behind the masses. Studies show and the definition of mass-led violence explains that a leader will appear at some point, because a leader's existence is essential for achieving an ultimate goal. A leader coordinates the process, though the process splits at an early stage into mass-led and elite-led violence. It is difficult to draw a clear dividing line between mass-led and elite-let violence because they often overlap. It is hard to assert unequivocally that a particular conflict was caused by either mass-led or elite-led violence because the masses always produce a leader who will voice slogans the mass want to hear. And conversely, the elite starts shaping the mass thinking. In fact, the mass acts like a zombie-like element, because it does what the elite wants (author's interview with Nino Pavlenishvili).

To determine the causes of conflict, it is necessary to identify the force that led to violence at the initial stage. As far as the Nagorno-Karabakh conflict is concerned, most scholars share the opinion that masses have had a greater role than local elites. The mood prevailing among Karabakh Armenians that Karabakh is their land and not the land of Azerbaijan, was deeply embedded and this process was driven more by the masses than the elites.

The mass-led pattern of ethnic war can only occur when mass hostility and all of its preconditions are present from the start, to the degree that at least one side feels a fear of ethnic extinction. In these conditions, only the coercive force of the state keeps ethnic conflict under control. When this force is removed, creating the political space for ethnic groups to mobilize, the conflict begins to escalate as people start articulating their hostility and grievances. Mass ethno-nationalistic movements can spring up almost overnight in such conditions. These policies of ethnic domination are of course threating to other groups, which will take defensive positions. The result is a spiral of ethnic extremism leading to war (Kaufman, 1996, 115).

If the initiator of mass-led violence is a subordinate group, the process is one of mass insurgency. In such cases, the security dilemma and the fear of ethnic extinction driving it are particularly severe. The Nagorno-Karabakh conflict illustrates this point: the Armenians of Karabakh remembered the 1915 genocide against them and feared extinction. As soon as Gorbachev's global policy (glasnost, publicity) opened up the necessary political space in 1987, they started agitating for annexation of their region by Armenia. The Azerbaijanians resisted the Armenians. The result was an explosion of mass-led violence and insurgency, propelling nationalists to power on both sides.

The Nagorno-Karabakh conflict is the most acute ethnic crisis that emerged after the collapse of the Soviet Union. Azerbaijanians dispute with the Armenians over Karabakh is a case of a mass-led security dilemma spiral. All the key preconditions for ethnic conflict were in place in Nagorno-Karabakh. There was an ethnic affinity problem. The Azerbaijanians believed that 'Nagorno Karabakh was the same Azerbaijan, but the Armenians haven't realized that yet' (Lynch, 2012, 848). The Armenians in Karabakh had been under Azerbaijani domination throughout the Soviet period. Very quickly, Karabakh became a symbolic issue entwined with each group's stereotype of the other: the Armenian side laid claims to this area, portraying Azerbaijanis as 'bloody-minded' people (Kaufman, 1996, 163). The movement by Armenians in Karabakh to join their region to Armenia was clearly mass-led. There were not any distinguished leaders to guise these processes, like 'Adamon Nykhas' in Tskhinval and 'Aydgilara' in Abkhazia. The Azerbaijanis were perceived by the Armenians as kindred to Turks and the Turkish identity of the Azeris was exposed and exploited at that time.

Initially, neither the rallies nor the violence was organized by top leaders of either republic, or even by opposition leaders. Official media opposed both rallies and violence, and republic leaders were deeply concerned by these actions. Indeed, the top leaders of both republics were replaced as a result of the February events. As for informal groups, the Armenians' Karabakh Committee did not establish its organization in Armenia until the summer of 1988, and the Azerbaijani Popular Front didn't convene its founding congress until the summer of 1989. The conflict further escalated in the next few years. The waves of violence in Armenia and Azerbaijan grew into a conflict in the fall of 1988, causing about 100 deaths and turning 200,000 Armenians and Azerbaijanis into refugees.

Thus, in the case of Nagorno Karabakh, the signs of elite-led violence were less obvious. The hostile attitude and security dilemma had emerged long before the media's tone became hostile, rather than as a result of the media's hostile tone. The security dilemma had risen before the nationalist organizations acquired institutional power to initiate the conflict; consequently, the violence was spontaneous and the escalation of the ethnic conflict took place after the security dilemma had risen.

Elite-led violence in Abkhazia. Unlike the Nagorno-Karabakh conflict in which the underlying cause was a different historical tradition between the two nations and their historic enmity, there was no different historical tradition between the Georgians and Abkhazians, nor any serious confrontation on ethnic grounds between them (Malashkhia, 2011, 207). At the end of the 1980s, against the background of the national-liberation movement in Georgia, anti-Georgian forces intensified their activity in Abkhazia. The Abkhazian Popular Forum 'Aydgilara' (Unity), distinguished by its extreme anti-Georgian sentiments, was set up in Abkhazia in November 1988. Theso-called 'Lykhani Appeal', which was initiated by the 'Aydiglara' and which demanded separation of Abkhazia from Georgia, was adopted on March 18, 1989.

Vladislav Ardzinba, an individual leader of the 'Soyuz' (Union) bloc, who was known for his anti-Georgian position, was elected Chairman of the Supreme Council of Abkhazia in December 1990. The Supreme Council of Abkhazia, through its separatist-minded members of Parliament (MPs), passed a number of anti-constitutional resolutions, including formation of the so-called Abkhaz 'Guard' which contradicted the Georgian Constitution. The Georgian National Council recognized this resolution as illegal.

Ardzinba called on his supporters to resort to violence. He was interested in conflict to strengthen his own power. Long before the armed conflict, Ardzinba was issuing threats, saying: 'We, the Abkhazians, will, at any cost, force Georgians to shoot at us' (Bluashvili, 2016, 330). The key to its success could have been the establishment of a national chauvinist coalition using the organizational resources that would support them. For example, Ardzinba managed to establish control through effective political maneuvers that allowed leaders to manipulate and provide select incentives to supporters. This, in turn, was one of the factors triggering an ethnic war of elites.

POTENTIAL CAUSES OF ETHNO-POLITICAL CONFLICTS   81

In cases of elite-led violence, extremist elites come to power when ethnic tensions are low, turning the preconditions for mass hostility into active hostility. For example, using the propaganda resources of modern political organizations and mass media, leaders can amplify weakly held stereotypes (Kaufman, 1996, 117).

Since 1988, the Abkhazian and Georgian elites, both political and cultural, have been openly voicing their opinions with regard to the independence of Abkhazia. The two conflicting visions of independence provided the basis for escalating the conflict. Both sides had a different answer to the question as to what Abkhazia is. For Georgians, Abkhazia is a Georgian region, like Kartli, Kakheti, etc.; whereas for the Abkhazians, Abkhazia is Abkhazia, a sovereign entity. That is how Stanislav Lakoba, the deputy speaker of the separatist faction of the Abkhazian Parliament, titled an article he published in the West.

In her book "Abkhazia-1992, a Post-Communist Vendée", Svetlana Chervonnaya refers to her private conversation with Yuri Voronov, a historian and chairman of the Human Rights Committee of the Supreme Council of Abkhazia. According to Chervonnaya, Voronov made no secret of his plans with regard to Abkhazia. "My scientific credo and life goal is to free Abkhazia from Georgia's grasp. I'm not going to deviate from that goal, especially now as we are so close to this goal" (Chervonnaya, 1993, 9).

Tracing 'group interests' in the Georgian-Abkhaz conflict can only lead to the Abkhazian ruling elite (Nodia, 1999, 76). According to the 1989 data, ethnic Abkhazians made just 17% of the population of the autonomous republic, while Georgians made up 45%. Despite that, Georgians were less represented in Abkhazian governmental bodies (Malashkhia, 2011, 94). Naturally, they were afraid that the independent Georgian government would stop pursuing such a "kind action" based on general democratic norms. Against such a background, the Abkhazian elite obviously has had the grounds for concern, and it couldn't be said that the Georgian side was trying to prove the opposite either.

It did not help that Zviad Gamsakhurdia had a rigid attitude toward ethnic minorities, which was shared by the Georgian elite. Some radical anti-Abkhazian calls concerning complete abolition of the Abkhaz autonomy were voiced on a number of occasions, although they were not officially adopted. It seems that certain political figures, including Gamsakhurdia, were playing this 'ethnic trump card' and the Georgian elite proved unable to figure out Abkhazian and Russian proprietary interests in advance (Nodia, 1999).

Speaking at the Popular Front assembly in 1989, Zviad Gamsakhurdia stated: "Georgia is a country of Georgians... The Kremlin keeps pursuing the policy of granting privileges to the Ossetians and Abkhazians in Georgia, for some reason the Abkhazians and Ossetians are singled out and the People's Front is struggling for protection of the rights of Abkhazians and Ossetians. They have a pretty good defender in the form of the Kremlin, and you'd better defend Georgia's interests." (Video is available at https://www.youtube.com/watch?v=Kd3FGKfJTtc. Last accessed on July 1, 2018).

Thus, the Abkhazian and Georgian local elites greatly contributed to the escalation of the conflict. Certain groups needed war and then an illusion of independence to ensure that the interests of their regime were met. The elite managed to influence the Abkhazians and Georgians, who had been long sharing their country's history and identity, as well as to manipulate the mass mood through nationalist identity.

Elite-led violence in South Ossetia. The term 'South Ossetia' was first introduced in Tsarist Russia. A newspaper published in 1830 referred to the area of the present-day Java region as 'South Ossetia', a name given by Tsarist Russia to a part of Georgian territory. It was apparently a far-reaching action, for Russia sought to create a sphere of influence in the Georgians' historical territory.

Media propaganda that the Abkhazia and Tskhinvali regions were not historical parts of Georgia was an anti-Georgian campaign that flared up after the beginning of the national-liberation movement in Georgia in the 1980s. The latter was opposed by Russia's triggered separatist movements in the Abkhazia and Tskhinvali regions. Without Russia's explicit support, the separatism would not have been very active in either region. The problems at the intrastate level, namely the mistakes made by the Georgian side that were largely derived from the low level of development of the political class, greatly contributed to the conflict's escalation. The lack of acknowledgement about the need for political crisis management exacerbated the ethnic and ethnopolitical conflicts (Albarova, 2016, 7).

The confrontation between Georgians and Ossetians first started in the 1920s with the support and encouragement of Bolshevik Russia. It was then that Russia first attempted to use Ossetians against Georgia. On March 23, 1920, the Caucasus Regional Committee of the Communist Party, headed by its individual leaders, including Sergo Orjonikidze, convened an emergency session in Vladikavkaz. The only issue on the agenda was: the Bolshevik uprising was supposed to begin on the territory of the present-day South Ossetia to overthrow the government of the independent republic of Georgia. The Ossetian Communists termed the government's struggle to prevent anarchy in Tskhinvali and Samachablo as an anti-national action against the Ossetian population. Having been encouraged by the Bolshevik center, they started separating the Shida Kartli areas, populated by Ossetians, from Georgia, simultaneously proposing to integrate this territory into Soviet Russia (Surguladze, 1992, 210). Finally, in 1921, the Republic of Georgia collapsed. 'South Ossetia' was granted autonomy and Tskhinvali was named its capital.

There had not been any clashes between Georgians and Ossetians up until the 1980s. Ethnic Ossetians and ethnic Georgians peacefully cohabitated in the Soviet era, and there were no conflicts between them. The highest rate of mixed marriages among Georgian ethnic groups was between Georgians and Ossetians. The conflict was started by the Tskhinvali separatist and de-facto government elites with military assistance from Russia. Also, several wrong steps were taken by the Georgian side. Zviad Gamsakhurdia's statements that Ossetians and Abkhazians are "guests" and "Georgia is for Georgians" are such examples (interview with author Tornike Turmanidze). Those were the separatist de-facto government elites that contributed to conflict escalation while receiving military support from Russia.

After electoral legislation passed by the Georgian Supreme Council in the summer of 1990, the regional parties were banned from participating in elections. This move was perceived by the separatists as an act against "Adamon Nykhas". South Ossetia was declared the Soviet democratic republic in September of the same year. This resolution was declared void by the Georgian Supreme Council the next day. The Ossetian side boycotted the October 1990 elections and held the so-called South Ossetian Soviet Republic's Supreme Council elections, despite the Georgian government's numerous warnings to prevent it. By holding the elections, the Ossetian side actually endangered Georgia's territorial integrity. In response, the Supreme Council of the Republic of Georgia abolished the 'Autonomous District of South Ossetia'. Under the Constitution of the Republic of Georgia and the USSR, the Republic of Georgia, as a sovereign state, would enjoy territorial supremacy on its own territory. Despite the legitimacy of this decision, the Ossetian side reacted negatively.

According to Diana Alborova, an Ossetian researcher, back in the 1980-1990s, when the Ossetian people were facing a risk of extinction, self-organizing groups of people were formed to defend their 'homeland'. Those groups later transformed into militia groups that have had great influence on the masses (Albarova, 2016, 9).

Overall, the Georgian nationalistic discourse, in turn, was met by the Ossetian and Abkhazian ones. The Abkhazian and Ossetian leaders' statements were abundant in expressions like: "the enemy confronting us', 'Georgian imperialism', 'Georgian fascism', 'survival of our nation', or 'independence as a guarantee of survival of ethnicity'. The South Ossetia conflict is regarded as elite-led violence, as the elites managed to mobilize the masses by echoing the message that the masses shared. Like the Abkhazian conflict, the South Ossetian conflict was driven by its elites. However, in Abkhazia, there was a more negative attitude towards Georgia than in Tskhinvali region, where the proportion of mixed families was greater (Okhanashvili, 2018).

Structural and Cultural Aspects of Intra-ethnic Security Dilemmas

This section will specify and illustrate how a security dilemma can be used to explain the causes of tensions between ethnic groups and the process by which tensions can escalate into violence.

Like rival states, ethnic groups often find it difficult to determine the relevant balance of power, military force or boundaries between the groups. This uncertainty raises the specter of a security dilemma. The threat of such a dilemma is prevalent in the post-Soviet region where ethnic groups, located in recently liberated states with their underdeveloped institutional structures for minority protection, must provide for their own security and simultaneously may threaten other groups.

There are two approaches related to the use of a security dilemma: the first emphasizes structural conditions. The structural conditions for developing an inter-ethnic security dilemma include: de facto anarchy, demographic fears of extinction, illegitimate borders, and the availability of the means to fight; the second considers both structural and cultural variables, such as language, history and identity.

Intra-ethnic security dilemma in Georgia. The Abkhazians first campaigned to become part of the Russian Federation in 1978. However, the Russian authorities rejected this request. The cultural security dilemma between Georgians and Abkhazians emerged in 1988, when the Abkhazians once again asked to join the Russian Federation. 58 members of the Abkhazian Communist Party sent a letter to officials in Tbilisi and Moscow claiming that the economic and cultural programs had failed to meet Abkhazia's cultural goals. They blamed Georgian hostility for this failure. The Georgians, in turn, charged the Abkhazians with placing restrictions on the use of the Georgian language. The same year, large-scale rallies were launched in Tbilisi protesting discrimination against Georgians by various ethnic minorities, as well as destruction of historical monuments and distortion of the country's history.

A larger confrontation between Georgians and Abkhazians occurred following the Georgian side's decision to separate the

Georgian sector of the Abkhaz State University in Sukhumi and turn that part into a branch of Tbilisi State University. Despite the refusal of the Soviet leadership and Abkhazians, the Georgian side decided to go ahead as planned. Fighting broke out between the two groups in Sukhumi, leading for two weeks of intermittent violence, leaving at least 15 dead and 500 wounded.

When the Abkhazians once again demanded to secede from Georgia and be granted full Soviet Union republic status, the demonstrations in Tbilisi grew in size to over 200,000 people (Cotter, 1999). The security dilemma arose when the Abkhazians' efforts to make themselves more secure, actually made Georgians less secure. Tensions further escalated as the Abkhazians, seeking to maintain their own safety, responded with measures that could undermine Georgians' security. At such times, a dangerous 'ethnic competition' built upon fear and mistrust can develop, pushing both sides closer to violent conflict.

In that period, rumors circulated of Ossetian sympathy for the Abkhazians. The media reported that Ossetians were headed to the area to aid in the fighting against Georgians. The leader of the South Ossetian popular front wrote a letter that appeared in an Abkhaz newspaper, saying that Ossetians sympathized with Abkhazian efforts for autonomy and hoped that their success would set a precedent for other breakaway regions also wishing to join the Russian Federation (Cotter, 1999). At the end of the 1980s, the South Ossetian leaders once again officially voiced their intention to join with North Ossetia. The Ossetian national movement 'Adamon Nykhas' was set up in 1988. On November 10, 1989, the Supreme Council of Georgia rejected the South Ossetian Regional Council's petition to replace the status of the Autonomous District of South Ossetia with the status of the Autonomous Republic within Georgia.

Clashes erupted in Tskhinvali following the August 1989 endorsement by the Georgian Council of Ministers of a draft 'State Program for the Development of the Georgian Language'. The plan called for the increased use of Georgian in all aspects of public life, especially research and education, a move Adamon Nykhas called 'anti-democratic and discriminatory' because the majority of Ossetians did not know the Georgian language. South Ossetia elaborated its own language development program, which declared three official languages – Ossetian, Russian and Georgian. Nationalist strikes and rallies led by 'AdamonNykhas' intensified. It was a classic example of a cultural security dilemma. Mere physical survival is not the only concern of ethnic groups. They also want to preserve historical monuments, native language, national religion, and other important elements of their culture. Ethnic groups seek to preserve their individuality as a group in order to defend their culture, which they believe is under attack. Demands for cultural preservation led to competition between the ethnic groups when the demands put forward by the Ossetians were rejected by the Georgians, who in turn expressed concern about their own cultural security.

The sound defeat of the Communists meant that the last remnants of institutional representation and protection for minority interests were gone, thus solidifying the de facto anarchy in minority regions that had been emerging since 1989. The intra-ethnic security dilemma is a relevant concept for explaining conflicts between ethnic groups in Georgia. The Soviet empire did not satisfy the needs of any of the groups, and ultimately enhanced their fear of cultural decline. Regions set aside for ethnic minorities were granted autonomy. However, against the background of Georgia's institutional and cultural hegemony, they could not halt their cultural decline, and especially the Abkhazian fears of demographic extinction.

Georgians viewed these regions as illegitimate manifestations of Soviet politics, aiming at splitting and 'Russifying" Georgia with sympathetic minorities. The insecure Georgian hegemony allowed Georgian nationalism to persist and eventually came to the surface in increasingly extreme forms. None of the parties to the conflict knew that their actions would be perceived as threatening to others. Under such circumstances, any defensive action that a group resorts to will confirm the fears of other groups that their security is threatened. For example, the Georgians blamed the Ossetians, as the latter aimed to unify North Ossetia within the Russian Federation, forgetting that the Georgian language program was threatening to the Ossetians who had not mastered Georgian.

The Ossetian side believed that the Georgian radical nationalism, which was harming ethnic minorities, was gaining a foothold in Georgia. There were messages about the priority of the Georgian nation (Alborova, 2016, 8). In November 1988, the 'Kommunist' (Communist) newspaper published a draft 'State Program for the Development of Georgian Language' under which Russian language would be purged and all public institutions would start using the Georgian language, which implied that Ossetians would become illiterate. For example, the Ossetians who could not speak the Georgian language would be unable to achieve career advancement and to hold top positions.

Cultural competition occurs in a security dilemma, where the actions of one group protecting their culture and heritage diminishes the cultural security of other groups. In the case of Abkhazians, the demands to revive Abkhazian culture were absolutely necessary from their own perspective, but were threatening to Georgians residing in this area. In addition, Georgians were convinced that the revival of non-Georgian cultures in Abkhazia was inappropriate and ultimately threatened the Georgians who also fought for historical heritage and the restoration of their national identity. The intra-ethnic cultural security dilemma is less common in the Georgian-Abkhazian conflict than in the Georgian-Ossetian one because the cultural competition between these two ethnic groups has been more intensive and prolonged.

In both cases, as Georgia moved closer to independence in the late 1980s and early 1990s, cultural competition became integral to security. The extremist rhetoric of the Georgian nationalist leaders, especially Gamsakhurdia, who would become Georgia's first post-Soviet era president, revealed to Ossetians and Abkhazians that their cultural security was threatened by Georgian independence from the Soviet Union, hence they voted to maintain the USSR and made numerous attempts to join the Russian Federation. Ironically, these demands by the minorities to maintain their autonomy were perceived as a threat to Georgian territorial integrity.

In general, the intra-ethnic security dilemma that addresses both structural and cultural threats and insecurities provides a better explanation of ethnic conflicts than the structural approach alone. Further, the intra-ethnic security dilemma proves that ethnic minorities fear destruction from military weapons as much as they fear a somewhat slower demise from cultural decline and extinction. Consequently, the structural features of the security dilemma only provide a partial explanation for the escalation of tensions.

Intra-ethnic security dilemma in Nagorno Karabakh. In the Caucasus, with its complex geography where small ethnic groups who are living side by side are driven by constant fear of survival, their identity and security predicaments are almost synonymous. The Karabakh conflict erupted in 1988, though its roots can be traced to the early 20th century. The Nagorno-Karabakh Autonomous Region of Soviet Azerbaijan was created in 1923. At that time the Armenian population made up 94% of the region, while in 1989 — it had declined to 75% (Thomas de Waal, 2016). In 1988, against the background of the liberal policy pursued by the USSR leader Mikhail Gorbachev, the Armenian population of Karabakh started campaigning for separation from Azerbaijan and unification with Armenia. Each party engaged in violence out of fear: for the Karabakh Armenians, the threat was that Azerbaijan could absorb it; whereas for Azerbaijanis, Karabakh's unification with Armenia was perceived as a threat to the republic's integrity.

According to Barry R. Posen, the starting point of the security dilemma is the absence of 'a sovereign state'. In 1987, when the conflict escalated, the Soviet Union was a central state, though very weak. It is therefore possible to argue that the Nagorno-Karabakh conflict started at the state level as a result of anarchy. Some scholars consider the Nagorno-Karabakh conflict as an outcome of a security dilemma. This is a situation where the measures taken by one party to enhance its security are perceived by the other party as a threat. The result is escalating tensions, which undermine the security of both parties. The security dilemma arose when Azerbaijan's attempts to preserve its status quo and regain the occupied territories using military force intensified the Armenians' territorial and security interests.

Conclusion

The purpose of this study was to investigate the causes of the conflicts in Abkhazia, the Tskhinvali region, and Nagorno Karabakh by verifying assumptions of the dominant theories of international relations and the 'international' theory of ethnic war. As a result of this research, the hypotheses presented in this paper have been confirmed. In other words, the theories hold in the case of recent ethnic conflicts in the South Caucasus region. At the external level, the main cause of the conflict was Russia's desire to maintain influence in the South Caucasus region.

Mearsheimer's offensive realism best explains Russia's actions in the South Caucasus. Under this theory, the major goal of the state is to increase power and gain regional hegemony. Moscow's policy sought to ensure that there was as much controversy and as many 'landmines' planted between ethnic groups as possible. Russia took advantage of the differences between the peoples of the Caucasus to escalate tensions. The Kremlin exerted political, economic and military pressure. Russia's involvement in the Caucasus region was conditioned by its strategic interest–to increase its power and influence in the region (Freni, 2013, 6).

The underlying cause of the conflicts at the external or systemic level was Russia's intention to use those conflicts to advance its own geopolitical interests, but the conflicts were also conditioned by the factor of ethnic confrontation. The Soviet Union helped to foment hostility between ethnic groups, which was part of the imperialist 'divide and rule' policy. In terms of the 'international' theory of ethnic war, in order to explain the causes of ethnic violence, we must analyze the factors acting at all three levels of analysis. Theoretically, the root cause of ethnic conflict is: ethnicity problem, emotion-driven and negative ethnic stereotypes, and differences over symbolic issues. These conditions lead to ethnic hatred and fear of ethnic extinction. The latter often leads to violence.

In the case of Nagorno Karabakh, the signs of elite-led violence were less obvious at the initial stage. The security dilemma had risen before the nationalist organizations acquired institutional power to initiate the conflict. Consequently, the violence was spontaneous. In the case of the Abkhaz and South Ossetian conflicts, the elite-led violence was enhanced by hostile chauvinist moods, inventing strategic myths and disseminating them through the mass media to justify this aggression. Leaders were spreading myths about certain threats facing a particular ethnic group; some aggressive messages were voiced.

Organizational resources can play an important role. The elites managed to mobilize the masses by voicing the slogans that the mass shared. Emotions contribute to a sporadic pandemic of violence and intensification of the security dilemma, further strengthening fear and animosity. This was exactly the case in Nagorno-Karabakh. As far as the Abkhaz and South Ossetian conflicts are concerned, ruling elites that gained power in one ethnic community threatened the security of other ethnic groups.

The methodological benefit of this approach is that it allows the researcher to examine events and verify or reject the hypothesis. If ethnic violence is waged by masses, the ethnic community can be easily asked about their preferences. If masses opt for confrontation, then violence is initiated by them. If masses prefer to compromise, then violence is driven by elites.

When looking for the causes of conflict at the internal level, we can take the example of the Georgian side, especially in the period of nationalistic sentiments in the Georgian government, which was not aware of the risks of these actions and did not properly evaluate the geopolitical and strategic environment.

Generally speaking, it failed to realize the devastating effect that nationalism and ethnic nationalism can actually bring if chosen as a principle of state strategy in the modern world. Everything that took place in Gamsakhurdia's times, including the official rhetoric, demonstrations, and nationalistic/patriotic discourse, contributed to consolidating the factor of mistrust. In Abkhazia, Georgia was perceived as an enemy that is relatively larger in number and has greater opportunities. Therefore, the ethnic minorities started looking for allies elsewhere to balance the threat and serve as a counterweight. Russia willfully assumed the role of such an ally.

The security and mistrust problem facing Abkhazians and Ossetians was further aggravated partially due to the Georgian leadership's reckless and inappropriate rhetoric and policies. Against the background of this aggravated relationship, Russia took advantage of the situation. If there had not been a local context and confrontation between the elites, if there had not been ethnic hostility and a well-formed mistrust, it would have been more difficult for Russia to achieve its goal. On the other hand, if there had not been Russian factor, the conflict might have been resolved in a different way. Without Russia's interference, no one knows how this confrontation would have developed; perhaps it would have turned to cooperation or war. In fact, the conflict might have occurred without the Russian factor, because if survival is a group's primary concern, the group does everything possible to survive.

Under such circumstances, there were two alternatives or scenarios. In the first scenario, if Russia had been their ally, they would have clung to it so as to balance the threat coming from Georgia. In the second scenario, if Russia had not been their ally and they had no received guarantees that someone would protect them, then more likely than not, they would have clung to Georgia.

If there are no options and you feel that confrontation with a bigger power will lead to defeat, confrontation is not rational. Therefore, it is more likely that the Abkhazians would have started communicating with Georgia from the weaker position and a military confrontation could have been avoided. But the Russian factor was not removed, and that is what shaped the direction of the conflict that occurred. There is therefore an interaction between these factors. If it had not been for the internal factor, Russia would have found it more difficult to escalate the conflict. However, if it had not been for the external factor, the result could have been different. The fact is that these two layers, the internal and external factors, were interacting with each other in Georgia.

References

Asmus, R. 2011. *A Little War That Shook the World*. Tbilisi: Ilia State University.

Alborova, D. 2016. *Institutional Cost of the South Ossetian Conflict: Transformation of Political Institutions in South Ossetia*. George Mason University, USA. ATC-Alliance for Conflict Transformation.

Cotter, J. 1999. "Cultural Security Dilemmas and Ethnic Conflict in Georgia." *Journal of Conflict Studies* 19(1): 43-81

Chervonnaya, S. 1993.*"Abkhazia - 1992: Post-Communist Vendée"*. Moscow.

Freni, S. 2013. *Causes of Violent Conflict in the Caucasus Since the Collapse of Communism*. Inquires Journal/student Pulse.

Gamakharia, J. 2004. *Zviad Gamsakhurdia's Policy in Abkhazia (1990-1993)*. Lika Publishing House.

Kaufmann, J. 1996. *Spiraling to Ethnic War. Elites, Masses, and Moscow in Moldova's Civil War*. Cambridge, MA: MIT Press.

Kuntzsch, F. 2009. "Drawing Boundaries: The Politics of EthnicViolence and the Case of Nagorno-Karabakh." Working paper. Available at https://www.cpsa-acsp.ca/papers-2009/Kuntzsch.pdf.

Lynch, D. 2012. "Separatist States and Post-Soviet Conflicts." *International Affairs* 78(4): 831-848.

Malashkhia, S. 2011. *Anatomy of Conflicts*. Tbilisi: Forma Publishing.

Mearshaimer, J. 2001. *The Tragedy of Great Power Politics*. New York, NY: Norton.

Nodia, G. 1999. *Conflict in Abkhazia- Reasons and Understanding*. Tbilisi, Georgia: CIPDD.

Okhanashvili N. 2017. *Causes of the August War in the Perspective of the Defensive and Offensive realism*. Tbilisi: The Intellectual.

Okhanashvili, N. 2018. "Causes of the Nagorno-Karabakh Conflict in the Perspective of Constructivism." *International Journal of Science and Research* 7(4): 1262-1264.

Onuf, N. 1989. *World of Our Making: Rules and Rule in Social Theory and International Relations*. Columbia, SC: University of South Carolina Press.

Snyder, G. 2001. *Mearsheimer's World – Offensive Realism and the Struggle for Security*. New York, NY: Norton.

Surguladze, A., and Surguladze, P. 1992. *History of Georgia*. Tbilisi: Merani.

Waal, T. 2003. *Black Garden*. New York, NY: New York University Press.

Waal, T. 2016. *Prisoners of the Caucasus: Resolving the Karabakh Security Dilemma*. Carnegie Europe.

Welzel, C. 2003. "The Theory of Human Development: A Cross-cultural Analysis." *European Journal of Political Research* 42(3): 341-379.

Wendt, A. 1992. "Anarchy Is What States Make of It: The Social Construction of Power Politics." *International Organization* 46(2): 391-425.

Appendix

List of interviews with experts:

Nika Chitadze. Expert and Professor — International Black Sea University. Tbilisi. 22/06/2017.

TornikeTurmanidze. Professor — Ivane Javakhishvili Tbilisi State University. Tbilisi. 05/12/2017.

Nino Favlenishvili. Professor — Ilia State University. Tbilisi. 16/12/2017.

David Matsaberidze. Assistant Professor — Ivane Javakhishvili Tbilisi State University. Tbilisi. 22/02/2018.

Giorgi Khelashvili. Policymaker and Professor — Ivane Javakhishvili Tbilisi State University. Tbilisi. 06/04/2018.

Eka Akobia. Professor — Ivane Javakhishvili Tbilisi State University. Tbilisi. 12/04/2018.

Gia Siamashvili. Scientist of Political Institute. Tbilisi. 16/04/2018.

Avtandil Tukvadze. Professor — Ivane Javakhishvili Tbilisi State University. Tbilisi. 19/06/2018.

Giorgi Gvalia. Professor — Ilia State University. Tbilisi. 07/05/2018.

Oliver Reisner. Professor — Ilia State University. Tbilisi. 22/05/2018.

5
Voter Turnout of Ethnic Azerbaijani Women in Georgia

Aytan Hajieva

Active engagement by all citizens, irrespective of gender, religion, and ethnicity, in the social and political life of a country is vital for a healthy democracy and sustainable governance. People's participation in the selection of leaders and the determination of public policy through voting in competitive elections is an essential component of democracy.

> "Participation in conventional ways, such as voting, enhances people's sense of having a stake in the system, encourages them to become more knowledgeable about politics, and enables individuals to channel their demands to the political system in legal and peaceful ways. Hopefully this will lead to political legitimacy, stable political institutions, effective public policy, and ultimately the betterment of society. These issues may be particularly important with respect to ethnic minorities who are more likely to feel discriminated against, become alienated from electoral politics, and become more motivated to engage in political violence" (Just, 2017).

The above-mentioned factors are of great importance for Georgia—a country with a rich ethnic palette. The country is stepping forward and seeking to build a democratic state and has successfully implemented major policies aimed at forming appropriate administrative and political institutions. From the view of understanding how a broad voter turnout can be achieved, it is important to examine the extent of electoral participation by Azeri citizens, especially Azerbaijani women, who are the largest ethnic minority in Georgia.[1] Data on elections in Georgia show that voter turnout of women living in the regions mostly populated by ethnic Azerbaijanis is weak. This chapter addresses the question of: *What factors are associated with lower turnout among ethnic Azerbaijani women in Georgia?*

---

1   Source: National Statistics Office of Georgia, http://www.geostat.ge.

Background on Voter Participation for Minority Women

Since its independence, Georgia has been struggling with the challenges and difficulties of transitioning to and building a democratic state and improving the situation of women and ethnic minorities. The country has made a number of commitments under key international documents to move towards eliminating discrimination against women, and particularly relating to access for women in political life. Among the steps taken by the Georgian government to address women's issues was the establishment of the first state institution for the advancement of women in 1998. Moreover, Georgia joined the Convention on the Elimination of All Forms of Discrimination Against Women (CEDAW) in 1994, which showed its readiness to fight discrimination against women and support the establishment of gender equality.

Parallel to this, the Georgian government has taken serious and consistent steps towards the formation of a state strategy and the creation of institutions dedicated to integrating national minorities. The first such step was made after 2006, when the Council of Europe Convention for the Protection of National Minorities went into force. From 2008, the Office of the State Minister for Reintegration (currently called the State Minister for Reconciliation and Civil Equality) was created and charged with implementing policies to integrate national minorities.

Furthermore, the adoption of the National Concept on Tolerance and Civil Integration and Action Plan in May 2009 was another important step towards integrating national minorities. Simultaneously to all of this, the role of the Public Defender of Georgia must be mentioned as well. In December 2005, its official mission and mandate was expanded when the Council of National Minorities was established. This council unifies most organizations of national minorities operating in the country and seeks to provide consultations and promote collaboration between these national minorities and the government. The adoption of the National Concept on Tolerance and Civil Integration further expanded the role of the Council of National Minorities (Sordia, 2014, 3).

In spite of all these efforts, there has been little substantive change in the status and rights of women in Georgia (Chkheidze, 2011). The situation looks even worse when it comes to political participation of ethnic minorities, especially Azerbaijani women in Georgia. These Azerbaijani women are often regarded as the most vulnerable members of society due to the double burden of belonging to the historically discriminated gender, and also because of traditional and religious factors. While religion factors into the different roles attributed to men and women throughout the Caucasus, the strict division of gender roles typical for Muslim societies may place Azeri women in a particularly difficult position (Peinhopf, 2014).

In the Kvemo Kartli region, mostly populated by Azerbaijani people, the rate of political participation is very low among women, and there are almost no Azerbaijani women representatives at the regional level. According to expert remarks and studies conducted in Kvemo Kartli, the region has always had a particularly wide gap in political participation between the genders. It is also known that the general lack of interest in politics is even more widespread among women than men (Kachkachishvili et al., 2012, 20).

Table 5.1 Electoral Activity of Women in 2017 Municipal Elections in Ethnic Azerbaijani-Populated Areas in Georgia

Municipal elections 2017		
	Female %	Male %
Voter turnout in Georgia	50.28	49.72
Voter turnout according to regions - Kvemo Kartli	47.02	52.98
Voter turnout according to election districts mainly populated with ethnic Azerbaijanis		
Gardabani	45.5	54.5
Marneuli	40.46	59.4
Bolnisi	44.57	55.43
Dmanisi	46.59	53.41

Source: CEC Municipal elections 2017, Voter Turnout. Retrieved on August 23, 2018 from http://cesko.ge/res/docs/Aqtivoba20.002017ENGGENDER.pdf.

Table 5.1 contains data from the Central Election Commission of Georgia for the 2017 municipal elections, while Table 5.2 provides a population breakdown by gender as reported in the 2014 census. As Table 5.1 shows, female voters comprised 50.28% of those voting in municipal elections throughout Georgia in 2017, while male voters comprised the remaining 49.72%. However, in the Kvemo Kartli region, female voting activity is lower than for any other region in Georgia, with women making up only 47.02% of the voters in this region. When examining the four election districts that are mainly populated with ethnic Azerbaijanis—Gardabani, Marneuli, Bolnisi, and Dmanisi—we can see that women formed an even smaller percentage of voters in these districts compared with the Kvemo Kartli region as a whole.

Table 5.2 Population of Georgia and the Kvemo Kartli Region by Gender

Area	Women	Men	Total
Georgia	52.26%	47.74%	100.00%
	(1,940,940)	(1,772,864)	(3,713,804)
Kvemo Kartli	50.82%	49.18%	100.00%
	(215,454)	(208,532)	(423,986)

Source: Geostat, Population by Gender, 2014 General Population Census.

To get a sense of how large the turnout gap is in Kvemo Kartli, we can contrast the share of voters who are women in Table 5.1 with the share of the population who are women in Table 5.2. In the country of Georgia, women make up 52.26% of the population, but only 50.28% of the voters in the 2017 municipal elections. This 1.98 percentage point drop-off indicates that women are less likely to vote than men across the nation. In the Kvemo Kartli region, the gap is even greater. The population is a bit more gender-balanced in Kvemo Kartli, with 50.82% of residents being women. However, women only comprised 47.02% of voters in the region. Hence, in Kvemo Kartli there is a 3.8 percentage point drop-off from the percentage of the population that is female to the percentage of voters that is female. Overall, then, the gender gap in turnout is much higher in Kvemo Kartli than it is nationwide. The analysis of the data provided in Tables 5.1 and 5.2 demonstrates the low level of political participation of ethnic Azerbaijani women, even though voting is a simple form of political activity. This chapter specifically seeks to explain this lower level of turnout among ethnic Azerbaijani women.

Literature Review

Over the years, researchers have studied the voting habits and behaviors of women and ethnic minorities. These studies have mainly focused on Western democracies and especially the United States. There are relatively weak statistics and data on female and minority participation in the politics of developing countries. In the case of Georgia, there are few studies on political participation of women and minorities and almost no studies on voter turnout of Azerbaijani women in the country.

This lack of basic information is partly due to Georgia's status as a Soviet republic during much of the Twentieth Century. The Soviet Union's elections consisted of centralized rules applying to all elections in a one party authoritarian system, including those in Georgia. Suffrage was universal and voting was considered secret, but in practice, voters could submit a blank ballot to vote for Communist Party candidates but they had to enter a polling booth to vote for other candidates. This practice likely suppressed voter turnout and distorted election results. Hence, Georgia's historical voting data is not comparable with data compiled since Georgia declared independence from the Soviet Union in the early 1990s and began holding democratic elections (Shapiro 19,77; Nohlen and Stover, 2010).

The literature cites many factors that can affect voter behavior. These factors can appear in unique and complex combinations in various countries, and can depend on certain circumstances. These factors can be grouped together as: a) socio-economic factors, which include population size, population stability, and economic development; b) political factors, which include closeness of elections, perception of the political issues at stake, campaign expenditures, and political fragmentation; c) institutional factors, which include electoral system, compulsory voting, concurrent elections, registration requirements, and voting arrangements; and d) individual factors such as age, education, political interest, and civic duty (Solijonov, 2016). There are also some factors that affect only certain groups of the population such as women, minorities, or youth.

For an investigation of voter turnout of ethnic Azerbaijani women in Georgia, several important factors should be taken into consideration: First, the issue should be viewed from the gender perspective, as women are the more vulnerable gender group in society. Second, Azerbaijani women in Georgia belong to the largest minority group in the country. Third, unlike other minorities living in Georgia, Azerbaijanis are mainly Muslim. Thus, these women also belong to a religious minority group within the country.

Starting with gender, despite the removal of legal barriers to women's political participation in many countries, governments remain largely male-dominated (Shvedova, 2005). She asserts that the political arena is organized according to male norms, values and lifestyles. This is otherwise known as the masculine model of politics (Shvedova, 2005). In an investigation of barriers to women's political participation in case of Georgia, Blomgren (2010) divides hindrances for women's political participation in Georgia into two groups of obstacles: First, psychological, cultural, and socio-economic obstacles, which are related to public opinion, the Soviet past, and resources; and second, political obstacles, which are connected with political culture and the electoral system.

Turning to ethnicity, Hansen (2009) investigates what factors motivate members of minority groups to vote based on an ethnic attachment. She argues that

> "ethnic voting is more likely to emerge when individual socialization experiences and dissatisfaction increase the salience of ethnic identity, contextual factors serve to politicize this salient identity, and the mobilization potential of the ethnic group is high, making it more likely that an ethnic-based appeal will be successful" (Hansen, 2009, 1).

Given that Georgia is a country with a rich ethnic makeup and is geographically located in a region where geopolitical interests intersect, Hansen's findings suggest that ethnicity could be particularly important in the country.

In Georgia, some research has been done regarding gender and ethnicity issues. Particularly relevant to this study are the works of Sabedashvili (2007), who has done valuable studies about gender and the democratization process in Georgia. Sabedashvili (2011) has also studied gender equality and women rights in Georgia (2011), where she does comprehensive research and provides broad information regarding the topic during the post-Soviet period. She stresses that:

> "without engaging women or representatives of other excluded and marginalized groups of the population, democratization processes–as understood in a broader sense rather than as structural or system reform–are doomed to fail" (Sabedashvili, 2007, 44).

Stefanczak (2015) examines the political representation of women in independent Georgia in the context of political and electoral systems and the broader socio-economic environment of the state. The author argues that the transition from a Soviet republic to an independent state had a negative impact on women's public involvement and influence. She concludes that this transition

> "...brought an end to the formal structures that had supported women's political engagement while at the same time the reassertion of 'traditional values' with the social perception of gender roles and the growing influence of the Orthodox Church mitigated ideas of gender equality that would have supported calls for women's political participation" (Stefanczak, 2015, 5).

The work done by Sordia (2014) on minority governance and political participation in Georgia is of particular interest. In that work, the author discusses state policies towards national minorities in Georgia. The article explores the institutional framework of minority governance and identifies the main challenges the state is facing in the process of civil integration and participation of minorities (Sordia, 2014).

Scholars have identified sociological factors, such as income, occupation, education, gender, age, religion, ethnic background, geography, and family, which affect voter behavior in elections. Regarding income, researchers have found a strong relation between income and voting rates. It was found that wealthier people vote at higher rates, and when the national economy declines, turnout from the most affected citizens is likely to decrease (Harder and Krosnick, 2008). There are also theories predicting that occupational involvement generates wider political participation, and that a high-status job substantially increases an individual's likelihood to vote (Sobel, 1993).

Age is another factor that may affect voter turnout. Most people seem to vote more frequently as they grow older, although participation in voting tends to decrease in their retirement years (Strate et al., 1989). Scholars mention a number of reasons that can cause differences between age groups in turnout rates, such as the 'generational effect'. This term suggests that historical events occurring when a particular generation of people is at a particular age can shape their political views for the rest of their lives (Harder and Krosnick, 2008). For instance, in regards to partisanship, for people who grew up before the fall of the Soviet Union, the socialization hypothesis would suggest a greater attachment to the communist successor parties among older respondents (Hansen, 2009).

Regarding gender, feminist political scientists and scholars have used a supply and demand model to explain women's political participation (Norris and Lovenduski, 1995). Supply factors are those that motivate individuals to participate in public life and politics, such as political knowledge, material and financial resources, skills, support networks, time, and so on. Demand factors, in contrast, are the factors that hinder women's access to venues of power and play a key role in their exclusion. Demand factors would include the

> "…male-dominated nature of social, economic, cultural and political institutions and political and legal-historical cultures which see women as inferior citizens and therefore not admissible to spheres of influence and power" (Joly and Wadia, 2017, 24).

The role of gender in voter turnout has greatly changed over time. In the United States, from the early years of women's suffrage until the 1980s, women's turnout rate was very low in comparison to men: This was explained by the fact that women often felt less efficacious, were less well informed and politically interested than men, and often had less power and responsibility in the workplace. However, starting from the mid-1980s, women's turnout rate started increasing and would eventually equal or even exceed the rate of men in some cases (Harder and Krosnick, 2008).

In another vein, scholars have developed a civic education theory to explain the link between education and political participation. According to this theory, "education provides both the skills necessary to become politically engaged and the knowledge to understand and accept democratic principles" (Hillygus, 2005, 27). There is general agreement in the literature that education is positively related to voter turnout (Putnam, 2000). Scholars believe that education is likely to broaden people's outlooks, help them to understand the need for norms of tolerance, and increase their capacity to make rational electoral choices (Chevalier and Doyle, 2012). Studies have also found out that college graduates who took more social science classes have an increased feeling of civic duty, and they also vote more often than other graduates (Hillygus, 2005).

Theoretical Framework

An investigation of lower voter turnout among ethnic Azerbaijani women in Georgia should include the above-mentioned factors, such as education, residency, and fluency in the official state language. The lower level of voter turnout among ethnic Azerbaijani women can be partially explained by factors that are known to affect turnout such as language, education, religion, and living in a rural area. Once these factors are accounted for, the turnout rate for ethnic Azerbaijani women may be similar to other Georgians. Yet the turnout rate of Azerbaijani women may be lower because on average they are less fluent in the Georgian language, have less formal education, are more likely to be Muslim and have higher levels of religiosity, and participate in customs that subordinate women's roles in society.

Why can language, education, and religion explain these differences in Georgia? Consider education: Huseyn Yusupov, who is the Head of the Congress of Ethnic Azerbaijani people in Georgia and former Kvemo Kartli region deputy governor, argues that an increased level of political education and an informed electorate will lead to a solution of the problem. He states that:

> "A big part of the population did not have information about other political parties in Georgia. Only the ruling party had an office in Kvemo Kartli. People vote for the political party, which they know. Personal contacts are very important. Ethnic Azerbaijani people mostly vote for the parties where their relatives and acquaintances are members. It may be strange, but in the regions inhabited by ethnic Azerbaijani people, those political parties win who have no visions about ethnic minorities in their election agendas. It is caused by political illiteracy" (Mammad, 2016).

It has been well established in the literature that education is important for political participation. Here, Huseyn Yusupov confirms that political knowledge is lower in the Kvemo Kartli region and that this can affect Azerbaijani turnout due to a lack of political learning among the uneducated. We can therefore expect that education continues to have an effect on turnout in Georgia and that this is one of the main reasons for lower turnout among Azerbaijani women.

Turning to language, interviews conducted by Azeri researchers (on September 1, 2015) regarding the political participation of ethnic Azerbaijanis in Georgia can offer insight. Regarding these interviews, one scholar said:

> ...today ethnic Azerbaijanis are a non-integrated community in Georgia. They speak Turkish. They preserve their traditions and customs. But they are not involved in politics in the administrative sense. They do not speak Georgian. They are culturally and socially isolated. They cannot nominate a candidate in elections because they cannot fulfill the criteria for the application — the knowledge of Georgian, to be in official correspondence, to speak Georgian (Yılmaz and Öğütcü, 2016).

Lack of state language proficiency can serve as a barrier to voter activity of ethnic Azerbaijani women. According to a survey done by the National Integration and Tolerance in Georgia Program (NITG) in 2006, in Kvemo Kartli, only 16.9% of inhabitants who belong to national minorities say they speak Georgian (Wheatley, 2009). Thus, this factor hinders their integration into the sociopolitical life of the country. This lack of language ability is likely to dampen political participation as well. In Georgia, most national news and political information is in the Georgian language, meaning those who are not fluent in Georgian are less able to learn about politics. With less learning, citizens are less likely to engage with political issues and the candidates seeking office. Therefore, any citizen who is not fluent in the Georgian language will be less likely to participate in politics. This means that that lower language fluency may be a major cause of lower voter turnout among ethnic Azerbaijani women.

Regarding religion, Georgian Azerbaijanis are predominantly Muslim. As a result of the lack of proper interpretation of the Islamic religion, like women of other Muslim nations, the socio-political activity of Azerbaijani women in Georgia has been limited in a certain sense. Although 70 years of Soviet atheist rule exacerbates this issue, the misinterpreted religious factor persists in the form of traditions in the lifestyle of Georgian Azerbaijanis. The way Islam is practiced in Georgia is likely to discourage women from engaging in public life. Hence, Muslim Georgians are less likely to vote, and this is a major reason why predominantly-Muslim Azerbaijani women are less likely to vote themselves.

A final important factor is whether a respondent lives in an urban or rural area. The majority of the ethnic Azerbaijani population lives in the rural areas of Kvemo Kartli. The absence or weak functioning of political parties and related organizations in rural areas, unlike in urban areas, leads to weak political competition among the rural population, and, ultimately, a lack of interest in political processes. Hence, the rural settlement patterns of most ethnic Azerbaijanis likely contribute to lower voter turnout rates. Based on the foregoing discussion, this study formulates the following hypotheses:

Hypothesis 1. Low fluency in the official state language negatively affects voter turnout in Georgia.

Hypothesis 2. Lack of education has a negative influence on voter activity in Georgia.

Hypothesis 3. Identifying with Islam as a religion is negatively related to voter turnout.

Hypothesis 4. Living in a rural area has a negative influence on voter turnout.

Hypothesis 5. Once language ability, education, religion, and ruralism are accounted for, there will not be an additional effect of being an ethnic Azerbaijani woman on voter turnout compared with other Georgian women. That is to say, the low turnout for this group can be explained by its differences from other Georgians on these four factors.

Data and Methods

This research is based on data from Caucasus Barometer, a regular survey about socio-economic issues and political attitudes conducted by the Caucasus Research Resource Centers (CRRC) that covers Georgia for the year 2017.[2] The sample size is 2,379 respondents (with 2,356 complete cases for our analysis), and the sample population consists of adults (18 years old and over), excluding people living in territories affected by military conflict (South Ossetia and Abkhazia). The response rate is 58%. The sample design is multi-stage cluster sampling with preliminary stratification, and the survey mode is face-to-face paper-and-pencil interview (PAPI).

The hypotheses are tested with a logistic regression model in which voter turnout is the dependent variable. The model is specified as follows:

$$P(\text{voter turnout}) = B0 + B1\text{woman} + B2\text{azeri} \\ + B3\text{woman*azeri} + B4\text{educ} \\ + B5\text{muslim} + B6\text{rural} + B7\text{language} + \text{error term}$$

In this model *P(voter turnout)* refers to the probability that a survey respondent turns out to vote. The *woman* variable is a dummy variable for a woman respondent, *azeri* is a dummy variable for an Azeri respondent, *educ* is an eight-category ordinal measure of education of respondents, *muslim* is a dummy variable for a respondent who adheres to the Muslim religion, *rural* is a dummy variable for a respondent who lives in a rural area, and *language* is a dummy variable for whether the respondent took the interview in a language other than Georgian (specifically, in Armenian or Azeri).

Analysis and Results

Two logistic regression models of voter turnout are estimated to see how much of the participation gap can be explained by measurable factors. In Table 5.3, a simple logistic regression model of voting was used. The model has three predictors: a dummy variable for woman, an Azerbaijani dummy variable, and the interaction of the two. This model produces a significant negative coefficient for being a woman, which shows that women in Georgia in general are less likely to vote than men, on average. This model also shows a

---

2 Data source: https://caucasusbarometer.org/en/cb2017/downloads/.

significant negative relationship to the interaction effect between Azerbaijani and woman. This means that ethnic Azerbaijani women are even less likely to vote that non-Azerbaijani women.

Table 5.3   Partial Model of Voter Turnout with Gender and Ethnicity as Predictors

Variable	Coefficient	Std. Error	z value	p value
Intercept	1.2823	0.0875	14.661	0.0000
Woman	-0.2331	0.1068	-2.183	0.0291
Azeri	0.0218	0.2731	0.080	0.9364
Woman*Azeri	-0.5694	0.3401	-1.674	0.0941

Notes: N = 2,356; AIC = 2640.7.

In the second model, which is shown in Table 5.4, a logistic regression model of voting again includes the three predictors of woman dummy variable, Azerbaijani dummy variable, and the interaction of the two. However, this model also includes four control variables: an ordinal variable for education (ranging from 1-8), a dummy variable for Muslim, a dummy variable for rural, and a dummy variable for a non-Georgian language interview.

When controlling for these additional predictors, the significant interaction effect between Azerbaijani and woman from the first model goes away. According to this model, education is a significant variable. This is important because ethnic Azerbaijani women tend to have lower levels of education and limited education opportunities. Since education has an important positive relationship with voting, Azerbaijani women's lower levels of education is a simple explanation for the lower turnout.

Additionally, those who completed the survey in a language other than Georgian were also less likely to vote. This, too, is an important reason why Azerbaijani women might be less likely to vote—they are less likely to be fluent in the state language. It should be noted that there is still a gender gap between men and women in general in Georgia, even when controlling for these other predictors. However, the gap does not seem to be larger for Azerbaijani women compared to non-Azerbaijani women.

Table 5.4 Full Model of Voter Turnout with Gender and Ethnicity as Predictors, and Controls

Variable	Coefficient	Std. Error	z value	p value
Intercept	0.5129	0.2128	2.411	0.0159
Woman	-0.2027	0.1086	-1.867	0.0620
Azeri	0.3531	0.4392	0.804	0.4214
Woman*Azeri	-0.5424	0.3427	-1.583	0.1135
Education	0.1075	0.0352	3.055	0.0023
Muslim	0.5235	0.2892	1.810	0.0702
Rural	0.5136	0.1053	4.878	0.0000
Non-Georgian Language	-1.0261	0.2342	-4.381	0.0000

Notes: N = 2,356; AIC = 2596.6.

Conclusion

The paper is dedicated to understanding why voter turnout of ethnic Azerbaijani women is particularly low in Georgia. The paper analyses the impact of variables like religion, language, education, and ruralism on voter turnout. The study uses data from Caucasus Barometer related to a specific region of Georgia in 2017. A logistic regression model was used to estimate the relationship between the dependent and independent variables. The findings show that state language fluency and education have significant impacts on voter turnout in Georgia, which supports the first and second hypotheses. The paper did not find a significant impact of religion or ruralism on voter turnout. However, the most important result is that the significant negative effect of being an Azerbaijani woman diminished once education and language were controlled for in the model, offering a likely explanation for why voter turnout is lower for this group. There is still a general gap in participation between men and women, but the additionally lower turnout for Azeri women can be explained to a large degree.

There are two avenues for future research. One is to consider more deeply how education or language training might remedy unequal participation rates. The two factors often fit together, in that higher education access can be limited for those who cannot speak Georgian. Conversely, those with less education probably have more language difficulties. If the language barrier could be removed, it would open the way for the Azerbaijani community to gain greater access to the Georgian higher education system. Therefore, language skills could directly increase participation in the political process, especially in the election process, and it also could have an indirect effect on education levels among the Azerbaijani people. A particularly important program to study further is the 1+4 program that is in place to help students from minority groups learn Georgian and earn a higher education degree.

Another avenue for research is to consider that there might be deeper cultural factors affecting turnout that are difficult to quantify. Qualitatively, it might be useful to undertake case studies of Azeri families. In this way, we could compare families based on their degree of conservatism or national traditions. Whether these differences have an effect on women's political involvement and behavior could be discerned from these qualitative contrasts. Both types of studies could inform future research on this topic. Perhaps such studies can help lead to new public policies that help close the voter turnout gap for Azeri women and make Georgian democracy more vibrant.

References

Blomgren, Emelie. 2010. "Women and Political Participation. A Minor Field Study of Hindrances for Women's Political Participation in Georgia." Thesis. Linnaeus University.

Chevalier, Arnaud, and Doyle, Orla. 2012. "Schooling and Voter Turnout: Is there an American Exception?" IZA Discussion Paper No. 6539. Available at http://ftp.iza.org/dp6539.pdf.

Chkheidze, Ketevan. 2011. "Gender Politics in Georgia." Heinrich Böll Stiftung: Gunda Werner Institute for Feminism and Gender Democracy. Available at https://www.gwi-boell.de/en/2011/02/07/gender-politics-georgia.

Hansen, Holley E. 2009. "Ethnic Voting and Representation: Minority Russians in post-Soviet States." Thesis. University of Iowa.

Harder, Joshua, and Krosnick, Jon A. 2008. "Why Do People Vote? A Psychological Analysis of the Causes of Voter Turnout." *Journal of Social Issues* 64(3): 525-549.

Hillygus, D. Sunshine. 2005. "The Missing Link: Exploring the Relationship Between Higher Education and Political Engagement." *Political Behavior* 27(1): 25-47.

Joly, Danièle, and Wadia, Khursheed. 2017. *Muslim Women and Power: Political and Civic Engagement in West European Societies.* London: Palgrave Macmillan.

Just, Aida. 2017. "Race, Ethnicity, and Political Behavior." In *Oxford Research Encyclopedia of Politics*. DOI:10.1093/acrefore/9780190228637.013.238

Kachkachishvili, Iago, Korinteli, Nino, Mataradze, Teona, and Nadareishvili, Mamuka. 2012. *Study of Social and Economic Conditions and Attitudes of Kvemo Kartli Population.* Tbilisi: Universal.

Mammad, Nurana. 2016. "Ethnic Azerbaijani People and Elections." *Human Rights in Georgia*. Available at http://www.humanrights.ge/index.php?a=main&pid=18901&lang=eng.

Nohlen, Dieter, and Stöver, Philip. 2010. *Elections in Europe: A Data Handbook*. Baden-Baden, Germany: Nomos.

Norris, Pippa, and Lovenduski, Joni. 1995. *Political Recruitment: Gender, Race, and Class in the British Parliament*. New York, NY: Cambridge University Press.

Peinhopf, Andrea. 2014. "Ethnic Minority Women in Georgia—Facing a Double Burden?" ECMI Working Paper #74. Available at https://www.ecmi.de/publications/working-papers/74-ethnic-minority-women-in-georgia-facing-a-double-burden.

Putnam, Robert. 2000. *Bowling Alone: The Collapse and Revival of American Community*. New York, NY: Simon & Schuster

Sabedashvili, Tamar. 2011. "The Identification and Regulation of Domestic Violence in Georgia (1991-2006)." Thesis. Central European University.

Sabedshvili, Tamar. 2007. *Gender and Democratization: The Case of Georgia 1991-2006*. Tbilisi: Heinrich Böll Foundation.

Shapiro, Leonard Bertram. 1977. *The Government and Politics of the Soviet Union.* Abingdon-on-Thames, the UK: Taylor & Francis.

Shvedova, Nadezhda. 2005. "Obstacles to Women's Participation in Parliament." In Ballington, Julie, and Kara, Azza eds., *Women in Parliament: Beyond Numbers.* Stockholm: International IDEA.

Sobel, Richard. 1993. "From Occupational Involvement to Political Participation: An Exploratory Analysis." *Political Behavior* 15(4): 339–353.

Solijonov, Abdurashid. 2016. *Voter Turnout Trends Around the World.* Stockholm: International IDEA.

Sordia, Giorgi. 2014. "Challenges of Minority Governance and Political Participation in Georgia." *Caucasus Analytical Digest* 64(July 9): 2-5.

Stefanczak, Karolina Ó Beacháin. 2015. "Georgian Politics: Gender Imbalance and Women's (Under)Representation." *Caucasus Analytical Digest* 71(March 30): 2-5.

Strate, John M., Parrish, Charles J., Elder, Charles D., and Ford, Coit. 1989. "Life Span Civic Development and Voting Participation." *American Political Science Review* 83(2): 443-464.

Wheatley, Jonathan. 2009. "Managing Ethnic Diversity in Georgia: One Step Forward, Two Steps Back." *Central Asian Survey* 28(2): 119-134.

Yılmaz, Aytaç, and Öğütcü, Özge Nur. 2016. "Borçalı Türkleri: Sosyo-Ekonomik Durum, Siyasi Katılım ve Entegrasyon." In Aydingün, A., Asker, A., and Yavuz Şir, A. eds., *Gürcistan'daki Müslüman Topluluklar: Azınkık Hakları, Kimlik, Siyaset.* Ankara: Avrasya İncelemeleri Merkezi.

Part II

Public Policy and Administration in Georgia

6
Low Performance Issues in Public Elementary Schools in Georgia: Implications for Policy-Makers

Ana Laitadze

How would the reduction of class size affect elementary school students' learning outcomes in Georgia? Based on empirical studies from other countries, policy makers in Georgia have argued that class size reduction would be an effective method for improving academic achievement among students in Georgian public elementary schools. For instance, in the latter part of the twentieth century, the policy gained wide popularity in the United States, as it was believed that learners benefited from increases in individual attention from teachers made possible in smaller classes (Bressoux et al., 2009; Bonesronning, 2003). Additionally, the thinking has been that teachers are less stressed and expend less effort on classroom management and discipline when class size is smaller.

Literature about possible impacts of class size reduction on student achievement has produced contradictory results, however. On one hand, many scholars who study class size reduction agree that smaller classes create beneficial circumstances for teachers to raise student achievement if they adapt and modify their instructional strategies in ways that are not possible in larger classes (Ehrenberg et al. 2001). Since the most significant outcome of the system of education is students' learning, often measured by test scores, we should expect to see a negative correlation between class size and student performance. That is, as class size declines, student performance should increase.

Nevertheless, the research on reduction of class size has produced disagreement as to the efficacy of the public educational policy of introducing reduced classes, known as CSR (class size reduction) for improving student performance in public schools (Graue et al., 2007, 672). Additionally, research on the topic suggests that the pattern of the relationship between reduced class size and educational outcomes differs across countries and even between school districts and communities within the same country. Thus, it is not always possible to state that the relationship is universally negative between CSR and student performance. These varied findings beg for further research to examine this effect in new settings and from new perspectives. What is more, it is important to identify and to explain the mechanisms underlying any relationship discovered in order to understand fully the conditions when class size reductions may actually be beneficial.

In general, improvements in student performance outcomes are a result of complex, multi-faceted teaching and learning processes. In addition, the factors that generate desirable outcomes are all interdependent in numerous ways, where class size reduction maybe just one of the main variables. Measuring the effect of class size reduction on achievement is then an attempt to single out a component from a complex system and to identify its share of impact on student achievement. Student performance has been shown to depend on various factors apart from class size, including factors such as teacher characteristics (such as verbal skills, education, qualifications, and competence), characteristics of a student's family, the quality of the school and community environment, and individual student characteristics.

One common argument discussed in the articles on CSR is that reductions in class size are thought to be particularly important in elementary education and should be seen as a foundational segment of any system of education (Jepsen and Rivkin, 2009). For this reason, the research in this chapter focuses on an analysis of data obtained from Georgian public elementary schools. I examine the final scores of students in their fifth grade or year in school. The fifth grade is the first graded year and exemplifies what the learners have been introduced to throughout the entire elementary education level and the assessment of how well individual students and schools perform is critical for policy makers. In the remainder of this chapter, I first proceed to review prior research on the question of how class size affects students' achievement. Next, I describe the original dataset of 1,058 students and their performance, spread across 50 schools throughout Georgia. Third, I describe the results from my analysis of these data. Finally, I explain some of the practical and policy implications of this study.

Literature Review

Prior evaluations of the impact of class size typically have concluded that smaller classes are better for students. However, these studies vary in terms of their conclusions about *how* effective class size reduction is, which other factors are central to students' learning, and whether CSR is the best choice out of a menu of options for improving education. Some studies evaluate the effect of class size in the context of attributes of *teachers*. Others make this determination in the context of *students'* characteristics. Finally, a few others consider the *resources* that are dedicated to the classroom. In this section, I review past findings on class size in the context of what we know about teachers, students, and resources, respectively.

Class size and teacher related variables. One of the most comprehensive studies of the impact of class size reduction on student performance is by Ehrenberg et al. (2001). They review over 100 experiments and research projects and find a positive effect of class size reduction on student performance, especially in early elementary grades and in groups of 20 and few students (Ehrenberg et al., 2001, 19). The effects of reduction, however, are less noticeable for test scores in large class sizes (Ehrenberg et al., 2001, 4). One program they analyzed was a class size reduction project in the Tennessee STAR Project, a state level program in the United States. They found several benefits of reduced class size, including better teaching conditions, better schooling outcomes, better learner behavior in the long run after the experiment, and fewer disruptions in the learning process (Ehrenberg et al., 2001, p.16). The analysis of the STAR Project supports arguments for smaller class sizes and find that benefits introduced during early elementary grades are maintained throughout the upper elementary grades.

On the other hand, the results of the Wisconsin's SAGE program (Student Achievement Guarantee in Education), another state level program in the United States, found that there was little improvement in the test scores of elementary students in classes of 12 to 15 as compared to others in groups of 21-25. In addition, an evaluation of a CSR program implemented in the state of California in 1996 identified little statistically significant improvement in mathematics, reading, and writing skills in response to the class size (Ehrenberg et al., 2001, 20). This article concludes that class size reduction is effective given that teachers *modify methods of instruction* accordingly. Teachers in smaller groups need to change their behaviors to take full benefit of the new teaching environment. Improvement in achievement is a result of improved teaching strategies, and a reduced class is a supportive factor (Ehrenberg et al., 2001, 20). When learners get individual attention and consistently engage in activities such as small group work, problem solving, discussion, and extensive writing, they benefit from a reduced class size (Ehrenberg et al., 2001, 21). Unfortunately, as Hargreaves, Galton, and Pell (1998) show, teachers' methods were often not modified as the class size was reduced. This outcome was linked to issues where teaching was an institutionalized routine with little room for autonomy, and where the standardization of teaching practices was further preconditioned by national curriculum goals and requirements, such as coverage of mandatory material, testing, and assessment. Thus, CSR alone is an insufficient policy to help student performance without the changes on the teacher related variables.

Teacher training emerges as an influential factor in the improvement of student achievement in small classes, especially teacher education including verbal activity, subject knowledge, and academic degrees. These are related to improved achievement levels among learners in smaller classes (Ehrenberg et al., 2001, 25). In a study of third grade student achievement in France, Bressoux, Cramer, and Prost (2009) consider the cost-effectiveness of class size reduction over other performance improvement policies such as teacher training factors. Among factors influencing positive test score dynamics, class size reduction works when paired with teacher qualifications, with teacher training being on average as effective as reducing class size by 10 students. Angrist and Lavy (2001) estimate teacher training's impact on student achievement in

Israel and find a positive correlation between these two variables, both in turn significant for student performance. In terms of cost-effectiveness, Angrist and Layy (2001) agree with Bressoux, Cramer, and Prost (2009) that raising teacher competence may be more cost-effective class size reduction, all else equal.

Another possible drawback to CSR is that it requires many more teachers to fill classrooms. Jepsen and Rivkin (2009) also evaluated California's 1996 CSR program. Their investigation did find positive effects, such as a rise in achievement in math and reading. However, reducing the student-to-teacher ratio required the opening of 25,000 new teacher positions in the state. Filling these positions was difficult as an inflow of less experienced and less qualified teachers became a real issue and resulted in negative effects on schooling outcomes (Jespen and Rivkin, 2009, 223).

Organizational behavior literature also shows that another important factor behind student success is how *motivated* the teacher is. Michaelowa and Wittmann (2007, 57) also find evidence in support of a positive effect of CSR on student achievement. Their primary research focus was identification and measurement of the determinants of teachers' motivation, however. Their model shows that there is a positive influence of teachers' job satisfaction and good attendance at work on student achievement, as well as a curvilinear impact of class size (with very big classes showing a drop-off in students' success, despite teacher motivation levels). Clearly, then, teacher training, adaptability, and motivation are important factors for students' success that also can condition the impact of class size on student performance.

Class size and student related variables. The backgrounds of students themselves can be important not only as a direct predictor of their grades but also as a conditioning factor for the impact of a variable like class size. For example, Bonesronning (2003, 952) studied student achievement in Norwegian low secondary schools and found that smaller classes were helpful in schools with a majority of students originating from intact families. He also found that reduced class size generates opportunities for students to attain more by taking advantage of a higher proportion of teacher attention. In general, it is learners who are highly motivated who benefit from the opportunity of CSR and may significantly improve their achievement (Bonesronning, 2003, 954). As a third finding, grading practices seem to affect student behavior in reduced-size classes. In the presence of strict grading practices, motivated male students and students from small families use the opportunities created by reduced-size classes more productively than female learners and students from relatively bigger families (Bonesronning, 2003, 963). Bonesronning concludes by recognizing that teachers' and learners' efforts are the ultimate determinants of schooling outcomes, with CSR producing conditional effects across the cases in which it is exercised.

The body of literature also shows that race, past student performance, and economic background are important control variables when modeling students' performance. Using longitudinal data across all grades of elementary education in a study of 649 schools in the US state of Connecticut, Hoxby (2000) found that class size reduction was independent from student achievement when other student characteristics such as low-income and minority backgrounds were accounted for in the models. Hoxby cautions, however, that estimates in her research would likely apply only to elementary schools in the American states, where class sizes may range significantly between 10 and 30 students per classroom. She notes that class size is typically much higher in developing countries (Hoxby, 2000, 1280). Meanwhile, Graue et al. (2007, 675) in their study of Wisconsin's SAGE program observe that African American students as well as underachieving students show a lot of benefit from class size reduction. Relatedly, Bressoux et al. (2009, 560) find, in contrast to some of the aforementioned results, that low-performing students actually show more improvement with smaller classes than from the education and training variables of their teachers. They also observe that there can be contrasts between students in rural areas versus urban areas. It is worth noting that Bressoux et al.'s (2009, 551) study of France is completed in a context where the system of secondary education is highly centralized, and where the practice of mixed grade classes and small size classes occurring often in rural schools.

Class size, school context, and resource allocation. Schooling outcomes are associated with other factors apart from teacher related variables, student related variables, and class size. The fact that not only teachers but also the learning environment in which students are educated affects student achievement is studied in Carrasco and Torrecilla (2012) in Latin American countries. On the point of technology in the classroom, the mere presence of computers is not a means of enhancing high performance, but it is the frequency (2 or 3 times a week) of usage during the teaching and learning process that is associated with improved test performance in mathematics by 23 points and reading by 25 points (Carrasco and Torrecilla, 2012, 1125). Thus, access to technology resources and their regular usage is an important factor for student performance.

Many studies more generally find that resource availability is a factor on influencing student achievement. For example, Graue et al. (2007, p.681) admit that, although reduced class size is helpful, the best ways to improve student achievement are a comfortable setting for a teacher to lead a change in the learning process in the classroom, an increase in resources such as space, and special training in classroom management skills for teachers (Graue et al., 2007, 692). Organizational changes promoted by CSR include expanding the number of teaching staff, extra space, more teaching and learning materials, introducing and implementing cooperation in co-teaching, and dealing with children with special needs. For effective use of resources, Graue et al. (2007, 677) suggest sharing best practices within and between countries.

In their evaluation of the Tennessee STAR social experiment, Jepsen and Rivkin (2009, 224-225) find that class size reduction is an effective tool for achieving improved learner performance at early years of elementary education, with long-lasting influence on the educational attainment experience during later years at school. However, they show that resources and wealth matter as well. Low-poverty schools take more advantage of CSR than high-poverty schools, where the share of new teachers is higher and adoption of the program takes longer in the initial years of policy implementation (Jepsen and Rivkin, 2009, 246). Jepsen and Rivkin (2009, 228) further add that changes in school policy, variation in size of the cohort entering the school (which entails a chain of changes, such as mobility of students among grades), increases in teacher experience, and the reallocation of teachers across grades are additional factors that help to improve student performance.

When policymakers change the resources dedicated to schools, how effective are various reforms? Results can be mixed and context dependent. School reforms including student testing, changes in curriculum, and systems of accountability for teachers, learners, and schools often fail to produce long-lasting or large-scale changes in educational attainment level (Ehrenberg et al., 2001, 2). Meanwhile, when Wisconsin's SAGE program was implemented in the presence of a space deficiency, a 30-student class would be taught by two teachers (Graue et al., 2007, 691). Effective patterns of cooperation included tag-team teaching, where one teacher was leading a teaching process and another was assisting in organizational and instructional areas. Drawbacks, however, included the fragility of partnerships between teachers, as some proved to be able to communicate constructively more than others due to prior experience in teams, friendship, or other human capital factors associated with co-teachers. Altogether, though, it is clear that local resources and school policies are important in the context of evaluating student performance.

Based on the literature review of the covariates of student performance and the key covariate of interest, my primary *hypothesis* is that the distribution of students' grades will be lower in larger classes than in smaller classes. Ehrenberg et al. (2001, 11) differentiate between pupil per teacher ratio and class size as two differing measures used by scholars. The former is an administrative dimension and identifies economic parameters of the relationship, referring to all administrative and teaching staff involved. The latter is a direct measure of how teaching resources influence learner development, and class size is connected with the way learners are engaged in the learning process as well as how they interact with the teacher. Class size varies day by day according to attendance rates, which leads to a variance in the pupil per teacher ratio for each student in the same class at different stages of an academic year (Ehrenberg et al., 2001, 1-2). Accurate measurement is essential to the success of a study, so as I will explain, I focus on measures of class size of students selected into the dataset that come directly from school rolls. Again, all of this is to test the hypothesis that students' grades are lower in larger classes. To that end, I now describe the data that I collected in order to test this hypothesis.

Data and Univariate Statistics

The unit of analysis in the study is a student, studying at a fifth-grade level in a Georgian public school. The fifth grade was selected due to the fact that it represents the first year that students receive formal assessment, as students are not formally graded from the first to the fourth grades. Quantitative data on the performance of fifth year students at elementary schools are public information and are obtained directly from the schools. A total of 50 schools were randomly selected using a stratified selection method, and then random students' information was chosen from each selected school. The initial number of students selected in this two-stage process was 1,075, but that number decreased to 1,058 due to missing information on grades for 17 students in the target sample. Reasons for this problem vary and include mobility, absenteeism, or a shift to a non-public form of education.

The distribution of sample schools across the regions of Georgia is described in Table 6.1.[1] Each numeric row represents one of Georgia's 12 regions, with a row of totals at the end. The first numeric column presents the total number of schools that are open in each region. The second column presents the percentage of all schools that this comprises. The third and final column shows how many schools were randomly chosen from that region for inclusion in the sample. Knowing that I wanted a sample of 50, I determined how many schools to draw from each region based on the percentage of all the nation's schools falling in the region. For example, Ajara has approximately 11% of all of Georgia's schools. By

---

[1] A list of all schools and contact information is publicly available on a web page of the electronic catalog of educational institutions functioning in Georgia (http://ecatalog.emis.ge).

randomly choosing 5 schools from Ajara, this region makes 10% of my sample, giving it appropriate weight in the results.

Table 6.1 The distribution of schools by regions of Georgia

Region	Number of schools in region	Percentage of schools in region	Number of schools in the sample
Ajara	229	10.99%	5
Guria	97	4.65%	2
Tbilisi	176	8.45%	4
Imereti	370	17.77%	9
Kakheti	185	8.88%	4
Mtskheta-Mtianeti	84	4.03%	2
Racha-Lechkhumi	67	3.21%	2
Samegrelo-Zemo Svaneti	241	11.57%	6
Samtskhe-Javakheti	204	9.79%	5
QvemoQartli	253	12.15%	6
Shidaqartli	163	7.82%	4
Aphkhazeti	13	0.62%	1
Total	2082	99.93%	50

Turning to the descriptive statistics from the sample of 1,058 students across 50 schools, the distribution of students by class sizes across the sample is illustrated in Figure 6.1. This variable serves as my explanatory variable. In this histogram, the horizontal axis designates the size of the class that students are in. The vertical axis presents how common each class size is. For clarity, each bar is also labeled with the exact number of students in the sample who were in a classroom of that size. As the figure shows, larger classes are generally a more common experience for students. The mode is a classroom with 26-30 students, with class sizes of 31-35 and 21-25 being the next two most common categories.

Figure 6.1 Distribution of class sizes across schools in the sample

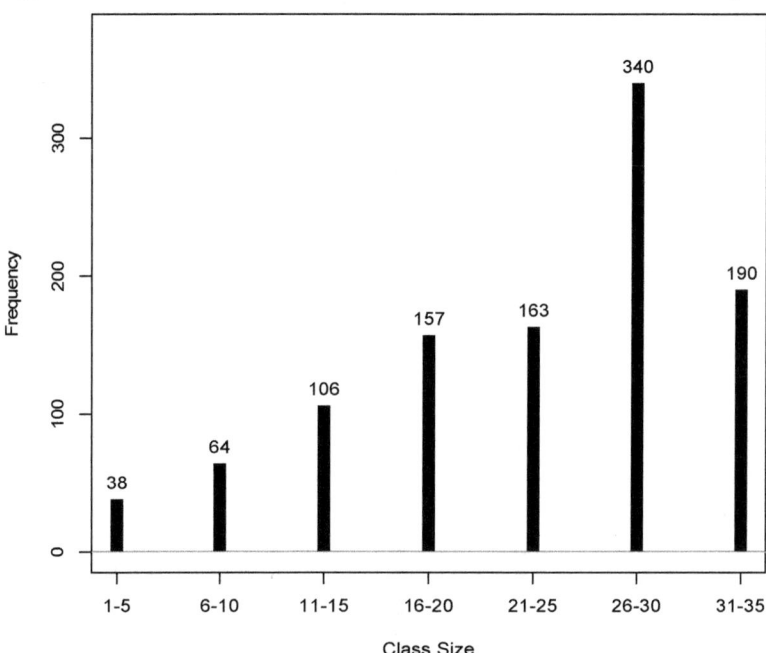

Turning to the dependent variable, I use students' annual grades as indicators of performance. These observations were collected through e-mail correspondence. Grades range on a scale from a low of 1 to a high of 10. Figure 6.2 illustrates the distribution of student grades from lowest to the highest for the sample of schools. The grades shown in this graph are the average marks across nine subjects.[2] The horizontal axis shows the grade a student received. Note that all grades from 1-5 were aggregated together, as they were infrequent. Each score from 6 to 10 is presented separately. The vertical axis presents the number of students in the sample receiving each mark, and this exact number of students is also written at the top of each bar. As is clear, the highest grades are the most common. The mode is a grade of 10, with each subsequently lower grade being the next most frequent score that students

---

2   These subjects are Georgian language, English, Russian, mathematics, science, IT, history of Georgia, arts, and music.

receive. With a univariate review of both the explanatory and dependent variables, I now turn to an analysis of how they relate to one another.

Figure 6.2 Distribution of awarded grades

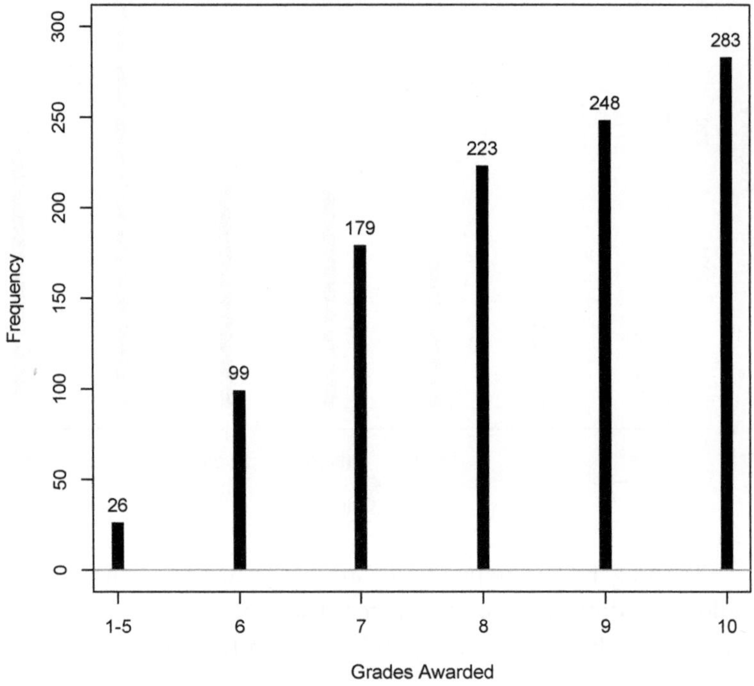

Bivariate Analysis

Table 6.2 is a crosstabulation in which the relative frequency of grades is considered contingent on the size of the classroom. The rows offer the distribution of the dependent variable of averaged grades across nine subjects. For a clearer view of the distribution of all student grades across classes of different sizes, I examined three grade categories: the number of high performers (students with annual grades of 9 and 10) which totaled 531, the number of mid-level performers (students with annual grades of 7 and 8) which totaled 402, and the number of low performers (students with annual grades from 1 to 6) which totaled 125. The columns divide the data based on six categories of class size, with 1-10 students as the group of the smallest classes and 31-35 as the group of the largest classes.

Table 6.2 The distribution of students by grade awarded and class size

Grade A-warded	Class Size					
	1-10	11-15	16-20	21-25	26-30	31-35
High: 9-10	53%	60%	43%	52%	47%	52%
	(54)	(64)	(68)	(85)	(161)	(99)
Medium: 7-8	37%	35%	41%	35%	37%	43%
	(38)	(37)	(64)	(57)	(125)	(81)
Low: 1-6	10%	5%	16%	13%	16%	5%
	(10)	(5)	(25)	(21)	(54)	(10)
Total	100%	100%	100%	100%	100%	100%
	(102)	(106)	(157)	(163)	(340)	(190)

Notes: Cell entries are percentages within columns.
Numbers in parentheses are raw frequencies.

Examining Table 6.2, there does not appear to be evidence of a class size effect—at least not without control variables. Looking at the percentages of students earning the highest grades (9 and 10), the absence of a meaningful pattern is clear when contrasting the smallest and largest class sizes: 53% earned top marks in the classrooms of 1-10 students, and 52% of students in classes of 31-35 earned top scores. These percentages are effectively the same. Meanwhile, the very lowest percentage of top performers (43%) comes in medium-sized classes of 16-20. From the other end, percentage of low performing students (scoring 1-6) is highest in midsized classes with anything from 16-30 students, with smaller percentages of low performers in classes sized 1-15 or 31-35. Thus, this bivariate table does not provide evidence that class size affects student's performance.

To consider this relationship in greater depth, Figure 6.3 analyzes separate grades for six of the nine subjects that data are recorded for. The horizontal axis presents the groups of class size. The vertical axis shows the average grade for a given subject among students in that class size. The six lines, drawn with different patterns represent the subjects of Georgian language, English, arts, IT, history of Georgia, and science, respectively. (The subjects of Russian, mathematics, and music are omitted for graphical clarity, but exhibit similar patterns to those displayed.)

Figure 6.3 The Illustration of Dynamics of Annual Grades across Six Subjects

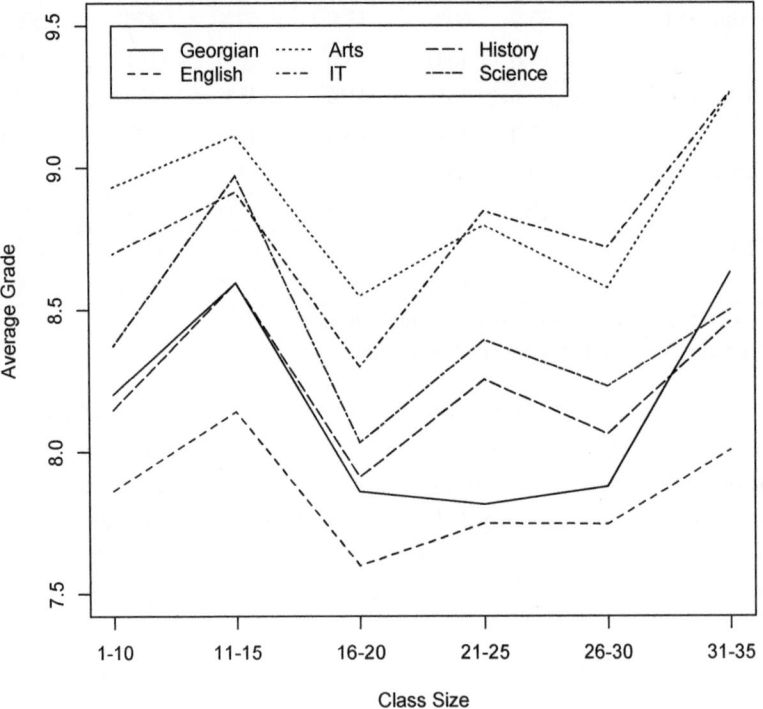

As Figure 6.3 shows, the lowest average score for all classes is for history. The highest average score for smaller classes is arts, but for larger classes is IT. Examining these means provides us with a similar conclusion as the percentages reported in the crosstabulation. There is no clear evidence that class size affects student performance. For each respective subject, the average grades move up and down across categories without a clear trend. My hypothesis would have implied clear downward trends in these lines, with the highest averages on the left in small classes and the lowest averages on the right in the large classes. However, we do not see this. It certainly is possible that with control variables the expected pattern would emerge. Therefore, I now turn to some of the limitations of these data and the need for additional research.

As was discussed in the literature review, there are a few factors that are known to affect students' performance besides (arguably) student class size. In particular, the socioeconomic status of the student's family and the training of the teacher have both been repeatedly shown to affect students' performance. Unfortunately, the measures of these two variables are unavailable. This inability to control for other factors could be suppressing a real relationship if, for example, wealthier areas with better-trained teachers on average have smaller classes. It is possible that if we were able to compare students with similar backgrounds and teachers, but different classroom sizes, then we might see that classroom size has the expected effect when other factors are held constant.

Anecdotally, it does appear that control variables would help this analysis. When searching for outliers in the sample, I found two schools, each with class sizes ranging from 29-35. One outlier was located in the region of Imereti and represented the highest of all high-performer student rates. The other outlier was located in the capital of Tbilisi, and it had the lowest rate of low performer students. Tbilisi and Imereti are the first and second most populous of Georgia's 12 regions, together comprising about half of the nation's population. This is meaningful because highly populated areas in Georgia, as in many parts of the world, face a different socioeconomic situation compared to lower-populated areas. In 2017, the percentage of the Georgian population under the poverty line was 21.9% overall. In urban areas it was 18.6%, but in rural areas it was eight points higher at 26.6%. Because of this large gap in the economic situation, I consider an analysis that only examines the other 10 regions of Georgia, excluding Tbilisi and Imereti. By excluding the two most populous regions, where there is more likely to be a wide variance in the other factors that shape student performance, I can consider whether class size may have an effect when holding population factors constant.

Table 6.3 Crosstabulation of grades by class size for regions of Georgia (excluding Tbilisi and Imereti)

Grade Awarded	Class Size					
	1-10	11-15	16-20	21-25	26-30	31-35
High: 9-10	54%	61%	42%	52%	35%	34%
	(45)	(35)	(59)	(85)	(48)	(11)
Medium: 7-8	34%	33%	43%	35%	38%	47%
	(28)	(19)	(60)	(57)	(53)	(15)
Low: 1-6	12%	5%	16%	13%	27%	19%
	(10)	(3)	(22)	(21)	(38)	(6)
Total	100%	100%	100%	100%	100%	100%
	(83)	(57)	(141)	(163)	(139)	(32)

Notes: Cell entries are percentages within columns.
Numbers in parentheses are raw frequencies.

Table 6.3 presents the results of this bivariate analysis. It is formatted just as Table 6.2 was above, with class size defining the columns and grades awarded defining the rows. Only 10 regions are included in the analysis, with two most populous ones omitted. Importantly, Table 6.3 shows a clearer pattern that is in line with the hypothesis, once the two largest regions of Tbilisi and Imereti are removed. Looking at the percentage of top-scoring students (with grades of 9 and 10), the lowest percentages are in the largest classes, sized from 26-35. The highest percentages are in the smallest classes, sized 1-15. To illustrate the pattern, going from the smallest class size of 1-10 to the largest class size of 31-35, we see a 20-percentage point drop in the rate of high scores (54% to 34%). Meanwhile, the percentage of low-scoring students (with grades of 1-6) is highest for the large class sizes from 26-35, and the percentage is lowest for the small class sizes from 1-15. This is the result we expected to find, based on our formal hypothesis.

Conclusion

In univariate and bivariate analyses of an original dataset, I do not find evidence that class size affects students' outcomes when reviewing all regions in Georgia. However, when two regions with extreme outlier populations in the data were excluded from the analysis, the expected negative correlation between class size and student performance did emerge. This suggests that deeper investigation into the factors affecting elementary school students' learning outcomes can be worthwhile. With control variables or an experimental research design, a clearer policy recommendation will be possible.

As past studies have shown, school policies and resources affect student achievement. Are there incentives for teachers to use newly adapted strategies oriented at increasing material delivery, input quality, and student achievement? Further, the socioeconomic background of students and the competence of the teachers are also important factors. In this study, while I did not have measures of these factors, a model that eliminated the two most populous regions, Tbilisi and Imereti, may indicate that there are still omitted key factors that need further evaluation. Future work should seek to gather quantitative measures of teacher training, funding per student, district poverty rate, and others. With control variables like these, it will be possible to get a clearer sense of just how much class size does or does not influence students' performance.

It should be noted, however, that a simple policy of class size reduction is unlikely to be or should be the only alternative. In comparison to class size reduction, which can be costly due to infrastructural expenses, a more cost-effective tag-teaching model could be reviewed as a less costly alternative that may improve educational outcomes (Graue et al., 2007). The primary expense of tag-teaching basically concerns recruitment of teaching assistants. Tag teaching would be expected to influence learner performance through teacher-student ratio reduction and appears to be a feasible and viable alternative for public schools in Georgia at all educational levels from elementary to secondary levels. A potential long-run benefit of this plan is that teaching assistants would become new professionals in the educational sector who gain substantial practice for future work as lead teachers. This would institutionalize continual development of human capital in a sustainable way.

To policymakers seeking to improve primary education in Georgia, one possible next step would be to conduct a trial policy intervention. By choosing some classrooms to receive a teaching assistant, others to be divided into smaller classes, and yet others to remain in place and serve as a baseline, the effectiveness of these policies can be evaluated more clearly. With a limited trial, if none of these interventions are effective, then perhaps an emphasis elsewhere (such as teacher training) might be a better goal. If the cost-effective teaching assistant approach clearly helps, then it may be worth a larger-scale investment. If the higher cost of shrinking class sizes has a clear effect over others, then slowly phasing in and further evaluating such a policy may be worthwhile. The menu of potential education policies is long; it is a matter of finding the best set of choices for Georgia's children.

References

Angrist, J.D., and Lavy, V. 2001. "Does Teacher Training Affect Pupil Learning? Evidence from Matched Comparisons in Jerusalem Public Schools." *Journal of Labor Economics* 19(2): 343-369.

Bonesronning, H. 2003. "Class Size Effects on Student Achievement in Norway: Patterns and Explanations." *Southern Economic Journal* 69(4): 952-965.

Bressoux, P., Cramer, F., and Prost, C. 2009. "Teachers' Training, Class Size and Srudents' Outcomes: Learning from Administrative Forecasting Mistakes." *The Economic Journal* 119(536): 540-561.

Carrasco, M.R., and Torrecilla, F.J. 2012. "Learning environments with technological resources: a look at their contribution to student performance in Latin American elementary schools." *Educational Technology Research and Development* 60(6): 1107-1128.

Ehrenberg, R.G., Brewer, D.J., Gamoran, A., and Willms, J.D. 2001. "Class Size and Student Achievement." *Psychological Science in the Public Interest* 2(1): 1-30.

Graue, E., Hatch, K., Rao, K., and Oen, D. 2007. "The Wisdom of Class-Size Reduction." *American Educational Research Journal* 44(3): 670-700.

Hargraves, Linda, Maurice Galton, and Anthony Pell. 1998. "The Effects of Changes in Class Size on Teacher-Pupil Interaction." *International Journal of Educational Research* 29(8): 779-795.

Hoxby, C.M. 2000. "The Effects of Class Size on Student Achievement: New Evidence from Population Variation." *The Quarterly Journal of Economics* 115(4): 1239-1285.

Jepsen, C., and Rivkin, S. 2009. "Class Size Reduction and Student Achievement: The Potential Tradeoff between Teacher Quality and Class Size." *The Journal of Human Resources* 44(1): 223-250.

Michaelowa, K., and Wittmann, E. 2007. "The Cost, Satisfaction, and Achievement of Primary Education — Evidence from Francophone Sub-Saharan Africa." *The Journal of Developing Areas* 41(1): 51-78.

7
Georgian Higher Education Policy and Ethnic Minority Performance

Giorgi Tchumburidze

The Twenty First Century is an age of globalization. This is a time when the majority of countries are multiethnic and multicultural. According to the 2014 general population census, 13% of Georgia's population are ethnic minorities. Among these minorities the largest groups are ethnic Azerbaijanis (6.3%) and ethnic Armenians (4.5%). There is no information about ethnic Abkhazians and ethnic South Ossetians, as those parts of Georgia are occupied by Russia and a census could not be held reliably there. Those four groups are compactly settled in different parts of Georgia. 48% of the ethnic Armenian population of Georgia lives in the Samtskhe-Javakheti region, while 75% of the ethnic Azerbaijani population lives in the Kvemo Kartli region.

One can argue that Georgia is an emerging democratic country, which is also a multi-ethnic country. So, in accordance with democratic values, Georgia faces the challenge to integrate those minorities and create a tolerant living environment where representatives of the dominant culture as well as ethnic minorities will have common civil values and opportunities. This is important, as an essential condition of democracy is the peaceful coexistence of citizens, which in a multicultural environment means a tolerant approach to minorities as well as their full and unhindered civic engagement. Therefore, equal opportunity for higher education is important to democracy. Gupta (2006) points out that in the 21st century higher education has transitioned from elitist to mass oriented. Universities and colleges should do more to make access better while also keeping high quality standards and excellence of academic performance. Many countries face these dual goals, and Georgia is not an exception.

Higher education is necessary for better integration of minority groups. But if we look at the Caucasus Barometer survey from 2008, we can easily see that out of participants who had higher education diplomas, 97% were ethnic Georgians, while only 2% were from ethnic Azerbaijani, Armenian, Abkhazian or Ossetian groups combined. This number compared to the total percentage of ethnic minority groups in Georgia's population clearly describes the seriousness of integration problems that Georgia faces. This can be one of the major reasons why the Georgian government decided to implement a kind of affirmative action plan called "1+4." The aim of this study is to ask: How does this 1+4 policy influence the levels of higher education attainment among ethnic minority citizens in Georgia and educational performance of ethnic minority students?

Policy Context in Georgia

Since 2005 Georgia has implemented a set of new university entrance examinations, which are called national entrance examinations. These standardized and centralized exams are held by the National Assessment and Examination Center (part of the Ministry of Education), and everyone who wants to carry on studying at a university level must pass them, instead of passing examinations that each individual university held on their own before 2005. The new exams consist of three general subjects, which are the Georgian language, a foreign language (participants can choose from English, Russian, French, or German), and a general aptitude test (conducted in the Georgian or Russian language). Starting in 2020, instead of the general aptitude test, students will be given a choice to either take a subject-focused test on history or a subject-focused test on mathematics. (Some universities, however, may continue to require students to take the general aptitude test as a fourth exam.) Additionally, students who apply to study medicine in 2020 will have to take an additional exam in biology.

Of course, either exam structure since 2005 creates some problems for ethnic minorities as their primary language is not Georgian. Moreover, because minority citizens often live in compact settlements and are isolated from Georgian speakers, their knowledge of the Georgian language frequently is not strong. Certainly, the government has known about this issue and has tried a few things to make the situation better. For example in 2008 general aptitude tests were administered in the Armenian and Azerbaijani languages in addition to Georgian and Russian. In 2009 the Abkhazian and Ossetian languages were introduced too.

In late 2009, the Georgian government began to implement a new university program called "1+4." They decided that institutions of higher education had to admit students only on the scores they got on the general aptitude tests held in the Armenian, Azerbaijani, Abkhazian, or Ossetian languages. Those members of ethnic minority groups no longer needed to pass the other subjects. Additionally special quotas were created. Universities had to create an additional 5% of places for ethnic Azerbaijani students, 5% for Armenian students, 1% for ethnic Abkhazian students, and 1% for Ossetian people.

After passing this general aptitude test and getting accepted into universities, these students must spend one year in a special Georgian language-learning program. This program helps ethnic minorities to develop necessary skills (reading, listening, speaking, and writing) for enrolling in bachelor's programs or continuing in certification programs, so that they can obtain a bachelor's degree or certification in a number of vocational and professional areas. This one-year training program contains 60 credits (1 credit = 25 hours). After finishing this one-year program and earning all the necessary credits, students receive a certificate, which is necessary to continue their studies at the bachelor's or certified professional level. All the universities that participate in this program have their own Georgian language courses, which are accredited by the Ministry of Education. In addition to being allowed to proceed with a higher education degree program, successful ethnic minority students receive funding from government, so they do not have to pay for their studies.

Review of Affirmative Action Programs around the World and in Georgia

Many countries in the world have some kind of an affirmative action policy for their ethnic minorities. Almost all of those programs offer resources and assistance programs to these minority students, to make their studies possible. Most of these students either lag behind in their educational aptitude to succeed at a university without extra preparation or academic support or they do not have money to cover college tuition and fees.

Orlans (1992) describes affirmative action in the United States. He talks about the importance of such programs and the various ways in which they have been implemented. He says that, at the beginning, those policies were implemented to invite more women and black Americans to academic fields. In the next decades other minority groups like Hispanics and Asian Americans were invited to carry on their studies in higher education institutions though affirmative action programs. Orlans describes that institutions that had a certain amount of income had to enroll a certain amount of women and minority students. Women were the main force for this action, and so they became primary beneficiaries of enrollment goals for higher education institutes.

As for ethnic minority members, some interesting things have happened. Orlans says that affirmative action was instituted for black Americans, but in advanced degrees and faculty appointments, Asian Americans were the ones who have prospered. He thinks that the reason for this is earlier education, where Asian Americans typically are educated in better schools than African Americans.

Arcidiacono (2005) talks about the connection that financial aid for minorities has on their future earnings. He claims that race-based benefits had little influence on black Americans' future earnings. However, if those assistance programs are removed, it affects other outcomes for black Americans. In particular, removing advantages in admissions greatly decreases the number of black students at top-tier schools, while removing financial aid decreases the attendance number of those black students. Hence, both financial aid and racial quotas play a positive role for minority students. The same can be said about minority student programs in Great Britain. Leslie and Drinkwater (1998) argue that financial aid greatly influences chances of college completion for ethnic minorities. Almost all minorities in Great Britain are using some kind of aid systems. Authors say that while using those financial aid programs, minorities excel in their studies.

Of course in some cases affirmative action policies are not viewed positively, and there are many cases in the United States where people questioned the justice of such programs. Lehmuller and Gregory (2004) reviewed such cases in their paper. They bring up examples of white Americans who were left out of college because there was a quota system that designated places for minority group members, who scored lower in their exams, than those white Americans. Of course, those that were negatively affected by affirmative action rules argue that this is a form of injustice and even discrimination. However, in the case of Georgia, we will not see the same kinds of problems. Places for ethnic minority students are created additionally to existing levels of student matriculation, and they are, in principle, not taking any places from other students. Universities have to decide how many students they are going to accept in each program, and then they have to create an additional 12% of places, which are fully funded by the government.

Poor knowledge of the state language is another serious problem, which many ethnic minority students face when they decide to carry on their studies in higher education institutes. Maher (1997) discusses Japanese minorities and the education policies that are implemented by the Japanese government. One of the major minority groups in Japan are citizens of Chinese descent. Those people use the Chinese language for their communications most of the time. There are schools where every subject is taught in Chinese. The Japanese government is doing a number of things to improve this minority group's involvement in Japanese society. They have a Japanese as a second language program to improve minority students' integration.

Georgia has a similar program, which is taught at the primary school level. However, according to the data of the National

Assessment and Examination Center of Georgia, this program has not been enough as only a small number of ethnic minority students has continued their studies at higher level. Hence, "1+4" has been implemented to close the gap in Georgian language skills of ethnic minority students in Georgia.

Another study by Clothey (2005) discusses the Chinese case. The author describes that there are more than 100 million minority people in China. Most of them use a different mother tongue than Chinese. Of course, the Chinese government is trying to integrate these people into Chinese culture, often forcibly against their will. Several groups within China complained that their languages, cultures, and religions have been under deliberate attack under forced assimilation policies. There are, nevertheless, many policies implemented, which help minority students to learn the nation's language and continue studies at institutions of higher education. When asked, those minority students answered that language policies were great, as they helped them to get a higher level of education, which increased their chances of getting jobs and earning higher salaries.

If we look at the "1+4" program in Georgia, we can see that it has the key components mentioned above (with the exception of forced assimilation, which is not only undemocratic but also morally and legally objectionable in any normal society). First of all, in this program you can find a quota system for ethnic minorities. As Arcidiacono (2005) mentions, having a certain level of quota system for ethnic minorities is really important, and it significantly increases chances that members of those groups will start studying at the university level. Another important feature is that the "1+4" program offers financial aid for ethnic minority students. As Leslie and Stephen (1998) mentioned, financial aid increases chances of college completion, as students do not have to worry about earning money for their studies and can instead focus on studying university subjects. As Georgian ethnic minorities are language minorities as well, it is important for them to learn the Georgian language better, because studies in Georgian universities are conducted predominantly in Georgian. Of course, successful participants who complete this program may become examples for other ethnic minority members, who might become more interested to take part in this program. So if we look at those reasons, it is quite logical to expect that the "1+4" program is of interest to both the citizens and policy makers.

Theoretical Framework

There are several reasons why "1+4" should work in the Georgian case. First of all, when we look at Georgian minorities, we can see that most members of a minority group live in the same geographic proximity. So, even if only a few of those minority group members start using this program, it will become more visible for other members through observation that there is something that will help them in their university studies. For example, if a minority group member sees his or her neighbor who is from the same group using this "1+4" program, he or she might become interested in the program and start thinking about using it in the future. This is especially important for school children, who will see that after finishing school they can continue their studies in Georgian universities instead of going to neighboring countries that offer instruction in other languages that the minority students might be more comfortable with.

Another important reason why this program should work is the fact that there is a quota system and no payment for studies. The quota system makes it easier for Georgian minorities to apply to the universities and gain degrees in the field that they are interested in. This is possible because they are not competing with ethnic Georgian students, and most of the tests for National Exams are written in Georgian, which minority students do not have to take. For ethnic minority students, passing exams successfully thus might have been harder just because their knowledge of the Georgian language was not on par with that of any ethnic Georgian student. With quota spaces, minority students face a more balanced pool of competition from a language standpoint. As for the financial scholarship for their studies, this makes it easier for those students to focus on their studies instead of thinking about earning money to pay their university fees.

One more reason why this program should work is the initial 1-year portion, where ethnic minority students are learning the Georgian language. During this year participants interact with other students, learn more about student life, and of course learn the Georgian language. After the first year passes, these students should be almost as adapted for university life as any ethnic Georgians.

If we look at all of those reasons above, as well as to the cases of the other countries, we can expect that the "1+4" program should produce positive results in Georgia. As a result, this paper's *hypothesis* is that, starting in 2015, the education gap between ethnic Georgians and ethnic minorities should begin to narrow. 2015 marks the first year that the program could credibly have an effect on education levels, hence my desire to see how education levels change before and after that time.

In-depth Interviews

As a first examination of how effective this policy is, I turn to qualitative evidence from student interviews. To find out what ethnic minorities thought about "1+4" program, five in-depth interviews were held with current or former university students from ethnic minority groups. Four of them were enrolled Tbilisi State University students in 2019. Two of them were ethnic Armenian and two of them were ethnic Azeri. All four of these students were taking part in the "1+4" program. As for the fifth student, he was an alumnus of Tbilisi State University who graduated in 2012, before the "1+4" program was available. All five of the respondents said that they believed that the "1+4" program is useful. They all believed that this program should be kept.

When talking about his experience with higher education, the 2012 TSU alumnus said that it would have been much easier for him if there had been a program like "1+4" when he started studying. He said: "I had to hire a tutor who taught me Georgian. Of course, I had studied the Georgian language as a second language, but national exams showed that I did not know much. It got harder after entering the university. Lecturers gave us too many books to read and all of them contained different subjects. So, I had to pay university tuition and fees, as I had not received funding from the government because of my scores, and I had to pay to my Georgian language tutor. Fortunately after lots of practice my reading skills became better and I didn't have to keep paying for tuition as I received a scholarship in later years."

When asked if any of his friends or family members wanted to carry on studying at the higher education level, he said that two of his classmates took the national exams, but were not able to pass. He thinks that the program helps minorities to get higher education:

> "You see, when you don't have to pay for your studies, your family support increases. Go try it they will say. But when they have to pay for your studies, accommodation, and Georgian language tutoring in my case — well in many cases — this support decreases. Of course I was lucky, as my family kept supporting me until the end. But in many cases, it's simple: They say, 'just go do something else, there is no need for you to get a university degree.'"

As for the current students, all four of them said that they would not be studying at a university level if not for this program. "Even right now it's hard for me to speak in the Georgian language. It would have been just impossible for me to pass the entrance exams," said one of the students. When asked to assess their knowledge of the Georgian language on a five-point scale, all four of them placed themselves at 3 points.

When asked if they wanted more time to be spent on learning Georgian, they said no, because two years of learning only the Georgian language and then four years for their bachelor's degree is too much time. Some of them think that some kind of Georgian language courses should be added specifically for them, where they would be able to spend some of their free credits (ECTS) and increase their level of Georgian. "There are some courses in Georgian at the university, but it's very hard for us," said one of the respondents.

They also mention that the program helped them to gain new friends of different ethnicities. For their future plans, two of the respondents said that they were going to carry on their studies at the graduate level, and the other two said that they were going to return to their hometowns and work there. These students say that they would absolutely suggest to everyone they know to take part in this program because it really helps. One respondent said, "It was not easy for me, to be away from my family, in a different city, where my mother tongue was not major, but with the help of this program I started to overcome those hardships. It's not easy, but it's doable. I would suggest to anyone who wants to stay in Georgia and work here, to take part in this "1+4" program."

From these interviews it is evident, that ethnic minority members believe that the "1+4" program is useful. Participants in the program can explain how the program has helped them succeed. An ethnic minority alumnus who did not have the benefit of the program also described how similar pressures to those facing today's students made it difficult to complete his degree. Hence, the importance of this program's linguistic and financial opportunities are clear both for those who received the program as well as for an alumnus who could not benefit from it. For these reasons the "1+4" program provides a chance for these ethnic minority members to get a higher education, which otherwise would be nearly impossible.

Data Description

The qualitative evidence implies that the "1+4" program is effective in helping minority students attain higher education. Has the program shown the hypothesized effect of raising degree completion among minority residents of Georgia? To test my hypothesis, I gathered data from six waves of the Caucasus Barometer, from 2009-2017. The Caucasus Barometer contains data from three countries, Azerbaijan, Armenia and Georgia. As my interest was only in Georgia, which implemented the "1+4" program, I have excluded Azerbaijan and Armenia from the sample. Also the respondents whose age was lower than 22 were excluded, as the minimal age for having a bachelor's degree in Georgia is typically 22.

This analysis requires a comparison by ethnicity. For this reason, I recoded survey information about ethnic groups. Ethnic

Georgians were included in one group (the control group), and minorities for whom "1+4" program was created were in another (the case group, consisting of Azeris, Armenians, Abkhazians and South Ossetians). All other minority groups were excluded from the analysis. The dependent variable is respondent's education, which was also recoded into a new variable containing two levels — those with a college degree versus no college degree.

The test of the "1+4" policy treatment comes by evaluating how much education levels differ by ethnic groups before and after the policy came into effect. Hence, after the recoding was done, I computed crosstabulations for each wave of the survey, with education as the dependent variable and ethnicity as the predictor. After calculating each year's percentage point differences in educational attainment between ethnic Georgians and ethnic minorities, I looked at a figure of the percentages throughout the years in order to see how the education gap between those two groups has changed. For reference, the separate crosstabulation tables for each year can be seen in the appendix.

Analysis

Figure 7.1 presents an analysis of education level for ethnic Georgians and ethnic minority citizens over time. The horizontal axis represents the year in which the survey was conducted. The vertical axis represents the percentage of an ethnic group that has a college degree. The continuous line represents the percentages with a degree for ethnic Georgians. The dash-dotted line represents the percentages with a degree for ethnic minorities. The vertical dashed line represents the start of 2015, the year when the program would begin taking effect.

Figure 7.1 Percentage of Ethnic Georgians and Ethnic Minorities with a College Degree, 2009-2017

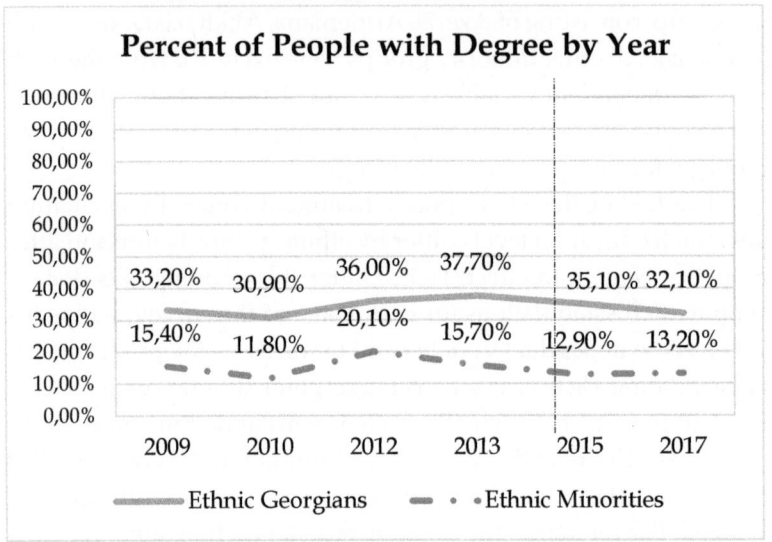

Source: Caucasus Barometer Surveys, various years.

As the figure shows, ethnic Georgians consistently are more likely to have a college degree. In 2009, Georgians were 17.8 percentage points more likely to have a degree than ethnic minority respondents. In 2010, they were 19.1 percentage points more likely to do so. The gap actually dropped in 2012 to 15.9 percentage points. However, the gap reopened to wider levels with a 22-percentage point gap in 2013, a 22.2 percentage point gap in 2015, and an 18.9-percentage point gap in 2017. If we look at the last two years, 2016-2017, when the program would still be in its initial years, we can see that the gap between ethnic Georgians and ethnic minorities continues to hold. It would be interesting to see what the gap looks like in 2020 and 2021 when the first cohorts of graduates with "1+4" program would begin to graduate. More data will help to better evaluate this program in future years.

Conclusion

Although this study uses broad nationwide survey data, this analysis tentatively suggests that the "1+4" program has not produced results yet. It is understandable because the first cohort of graduates will be leaving universities in 2020-2021. Studies of these later periods will be necessary for empirical assessments of the impact that "1+4" program had in Georgia. Furthermore, some features of this program, like providing examples to younger children of ethnic minorities of what is available, will take a longer time to have an effect that only future years can reveal. Also, with a closer look at micro-level data it is possible that we would find more of an effect. Nevertheless, the available quantitative data do not yet offer evidence in support of the program.

While there is not evidence that the nationwide policy goal of closing the education gap has begun yet, the qualitative evidence suggests that allowing the program to run longer could possibly produce effects in the future. As it seems from the in-depth interviews, ethnic minority students think that "1+4" program is useful for them and gives them chance to get higher education. The experiences both of an alumnus who did not have access to this program as well as students who do participate in the program all point to linguistic and monetary difficulties they have had to face, and how a program like "1+4" can help overcome these obstacles to higher education. If the factors that faced these interviewees fairly describe the experience of most prospective students from ethnic minority populations, then it seems likely that the degree gap between ethnic Georgians and ethnic minorities may narrow in the future.

In the future there are more questions about the "1+4" program that can be answered with both further qualitative and quantitative research. On the qualitative side, it might be interesting to study more about minority students who use this program. What do they think about it? Are they receiving the kind of education they were expecting? How satisfied are they with the program? Maybe something happens during those years that prevent the degree gap between Georgians and minorities from closing, such as an issue that hinders minority graduation rates. On the quantitative side, it will be interesting to see what will happen when the next wave of the Caucasus Barometer is held. It might show that gap between ethnic Georgians and ethnic minorities is getting closer, which might indicate that the program is doing its job.

References

Arcidiacono, P. 2005. "Affirmative Action in Higher Education: How Do Admission and Financial Aid Rules Affect Future Earnings?" *Econometrica* 73(5): 1477-1524.

CRRC. 2017. *Caucasus Barometer*. The Caucasus Research Resource Centers. Retrieved on October 16, 2018 at http://www.caucasusbarometer.org/.

Clothey, R. 2005. "China's Policies for Minority Nationalities in Higher Education: Negotiating National Values and Ethnic Identities." *Comparative Education Review* 49(3): 389-409.

Gupta, A. 2006. *Affirmative Action in Higher Education in India and the US: A Study in Contrast*. Center for Studies in Higher Education.

Lehmuller, P., and Gregory, D. E. 2005. "Affirmative Action: From Before Bakke to After Grutter." *NASPA Journal* 42(4): 430-459.

Leslie, D., and Drinkwater, S. 1999. "Staying on in Full-time Education: Reasons for Higher Participation Rates Among Ethnic Minority Males and Females." *Economica* 66(261): 63-77.

Maher, J. 1997. "Linguistic Minorities and Education in Japan." *Educational Review* 49(2): 115-127.

Orlans, H. 1992. "Affirmative Action in Higher Education." *The Annals of the American Academy of Political and Social Science* 523(1): 144-158.

Appendix

Crosstabulations of Each Year's Caucasus Barometer

Year 2009			Ethnicity		Total
			Georgian	Minority	
Education	No University Degree	Count	1033	236	1269
		% within ethnicity	66.8%	84.6%	69.5%
	University Degree	Count	513	43	556
		% within ethnicity	33.2%	15.4%	30.5%
Total		Count	1546	279	1825
		% within ethnicity	100.0%	100.0%	100.0%

Year 2010			Ethnicity		Total
			Georgian	Minority	
Education	No University Degree	Count	1158	254	1412
		% within ethnicity	69.1%	88.2%	71.9%
	University Degree	Count	518	34	552
		% within ethnicity	30.9%	11.8%	28.1%
Total		Count	1676	288	1964
		% within ethnicity	100.0%	100.0%	100.0%

Year 2012			Ethnicity		Total
			Georgian	Minority	
Education	No University Degree	Count	1318	230	1548
		% within ethnicity	64.0%	79.9%	66.0%
	University Degree	Count	741	58	799
		% within ethnicity	36.0%	20.1%	34.0%
Total		Count	2059	288	2347
		% within ethnicity	100.0%	100.0%	100.0%

Year 2013			Ethnicity		Total
			Georgian	Minority	
Education	No University Degree	Count	1067	264	1331
		% within ethnicity	62.3%	84.3%	65.7%
	University Degree	Count	646	49	695
		% within ethnicity	37.7%	15.7%	34.3%
Total		Count	1713	313	2026
		% within ethnicity	100.0%	100.0%	100.0%

Year 2015			Ethnicity		Total
			Georgian	Minority	
Education	No University Degree	Count	1210	217	1427
		% within ethnicity	64.9%	87.1%	67.5%
	University Degree	Count	655	32	687
		% within ethnicity	35.1%	12.9%	32.5%
Total		Count	1865	249	2114
		% within ethnicity	100.0%	100.0%	100.0%

Year 2017			Ethnicity		Total
			Georgian	Minority	
Education	No University Degree	Count	1308	308	1616
		% within ethnicity	67.9%	86.8%	70.9%
	University Degree	Count	617	47	664
		% within ethnicity	32.1%	13.2%	29.1%
Total		Count	1925	355	2280
		% within ethnicity	100.0%	100.0%	100.0%

8
Roadmap to Employability: The Relationship between Generic Skills and Employment

Elene Jimsheleishvili

Current Unemployment Rate (UR) in Georgia is approximately 12%, which is 1.5 times higher than respective global unemployment figures indicated by the ILO in its *World Employment and Social Outlook*. Also, there is a significant misclassification or underemployment for approximately 24% of potential labor force participants in the country (or about 65% of persons outside the labor force part- or full-time). These are persons that continually remain outside the labor force due to limited skills capacity or specific individual reservations to engage in work for pay or profit. As suggested by Dr. Hans Gutbrod, it is likely that "the real unemployment number is above 30%" (Gutbrod, 2013). Thus, increasing the levels of individual prospects for employability and facilitating greater levels of labor productivity in the country are one of the immediate government priorities.

The concept of employability (i.e. the state of being employable) relates to the likelihood of getting and retaining a job. It became the subject of active considerations from the 1980-90's. By then, along with vocational consultations and trainings of citizens, governments of several Western countries turned their attention to a wholesome concept of employability as an important component of the labor market. It was considered necessary not only to offer vocational services to obtain certain skills, but the vocational programs had to be tied to the surrounding realities of those stuck outside the labor market. In other words, the labor supply side programs had to be aware of both the individual characteristics of the citizens, the typical channels or professions that these citizens would engage in, and steer them toward professions that were perceived to be generally unavailable to them by matching the training skills to the broader features of the demand side in the labor market. Not only the citizens would be actively encouraged to seek employment in spite of their cultural or social surroundings, but those who would seek vocational training could be matched to a particular set of jobs in demand by employers. Development of individual employability, therefore, became a key contributor in the process of improvement of employment accessibility. Employability is now considered as an essential part of governmental strategies addressing unemployment and social inclusion.

In the same period, together with actualization of the concept of *Employability*, concepts of *Career* and *Career Management* and *Work* itself have also been in the process of transformation. The latter includes salaried jobs as well as volunteering, which enables one's personal self-actualization. So, work is defined broadly as a human activity that is initiated

> "for individual success and satisfaction, to express achievement and strivings, to earn a living… to further ambitions and self-assertions… and to link individuals to a larger social good" (Richardson 1993, 428, cited in Patton and McMahon 2014, 156).

The emphasis has been shifted from the organization to individuals developing own careers in the 21st century, which is adjustable and boundary-less in nature. The protean career displaces the notion of a linear and vertical career and acknowledges opportunities for a flexible and idiosyncratic career construction or career building; it includes all aspects of an individual's life as relevant to one's career, and places the individual at the center of a career in organizational and occupational contexts (Patton and McMahon, 2014, p.402). The term *Career* under this new understanding means a lifelong experience of work and self-actualization. For lifelong careers, the skills and competencies, which ensure successful management of this experience, are becoming ever more important for individuals, especially for managing careers through different stages of life in the context of continuous changes.

The ability to manage one's career successfully is an integral component of becoming and being employable. Employability and career management are interrelated concepts and respective competencies are identified and successfully institutionalized since the 1980's in developed countries, led by Australia, Canada, New Zealand, and the United Kingdom. Institutionalization applies to two core change components — dynamics developments in education to match the shifts in the labor market. The focus competencies then serve as a common ground for parents, teachers, employment service providers, and other parties related to assisting citizens in their life and career changes to better support target beneficiaries in managing achieving self-actualization. Currently, several countries are also elaborating their own Employability/Career Management Competencies: Italy, Spain, Turkey, Greece, Romania, and Norway (Sultana, 2012, p.225).

Georgian government is actively addressing issues related to employment markets and employability. According to an analysis conducted in cooperation with the Millennium Challenge Georgia Fund (MCF-G, 2015, cited in Resolution of the Government of Georgia №167 2016, 2), local workforce lacks skills required by the labor market. In addition, according to a report of the International Competition Index, another main obstacle for doing business in Georgia is low-qualification of its workforce. It is notable that unlike the EU countries, where unemployment is concentrated mainly among low-educated individuals, 50% of unemployed or underemployed in Georgia have high-school education, while 40% of unemployed or underemployed have higher education. There is a dearth of empirical research then that would explain what is missing between the levels of education and the skills that are inadequately matched with the composition of the labor markets in Georgia.

Figure 8.1 Georgian labor market structure, 2019, population estimates are in thousands.

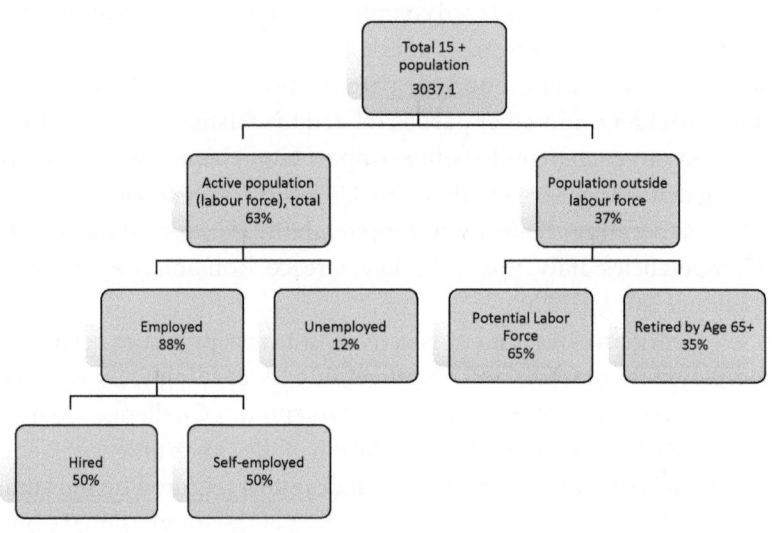

Source: National Statistics Office of Georgia.

The general structure of the Georgian labor is presented in Figure 8.1. Of the 3 million or so individuals aged 15 and older, official statistics show a labor force participation rate of 63%, split equally between for hire and self-employed jobs. Among the 37% not participating in the labor force, the size of the potential labor force that could be tapped into is over 1.1 million individuals. To address the concerns of unemployment and underemployment, since 2015 Georgia's Government has been implementing the Concept of Development of "Lifelong Professional Consultancy and Career Planning Accessible Public Services" as part of its State Strategy for Labor Market Development. At the moment, the project is mainly focused on raising citizens' awareness regarding existing employment opportunities (job-openings) and vocational orientation (e.g.,

Worknet—online database of jobseekers and current vacancies coordinated by the Social Service Agency of the Ministry of Internally Displaced Persons from the Occupied Territories, Labour, Health and Social Affairs of Georgia).

Georgian Context

Employability is a multifaceted concept. It is essential for individuals as a tool toward, self-realization, psychological wellbeing, and social inclusion, required by employers as guarantee for highly qualified workforce and entrepreneurial success, and is essential for governments as a foundation for labor productivity and wealth in the country. However, "full, or even approximately full, employment is of rare and short-lived occurrence . . . an intermediate situation which is neither desperate nor satisfactory is our normal lot" (Keynes 1964, 249). Here, we will review the existing literature from the three points of view, starting from the state and narrowing to an individual level, with a focus on the likelihood of being employable and the specifics of the context in Georgia.

Georgia is a former Soviet country. It became independent in the early 1990's and sought to align itself with Europe and away from the resurgent and increasingly belligerent Russian efforts to dominate the South Caucasus. This re-orientation caused the worsening of its relationships with Russia, and Georgia had to face a series of drastic challenges like the civil war to settle competing political visions for the country's future, two separatist secessionist rebellions backed by Russia in what are now the self-proclaimed Republics of South Ossetia and Abkhazia. These challenges culminated in 2008 in the so-called 'August War' and the Russian incursion deep into the heart of the country, a confrontation that uprooted and displaced tens of thousands in the country and continues to simmer to this day. Due to these events that Georgia faced in the early 1990's up o the war in 2008, the economy suffered several serious blows to its gross domestic product (GDP). While in 1992 the decline in the rate of GDP was -44.9%, the country slowly began its recovery process (EBRD 2001, 59). The growth path was remarkably stable until 2008, however the August War has wiped out almost a decade of growth (Saha and Giucci 2017). Nevertheless, Georgia continues to diversify its economic orientations by leveraging its potential as a transit route for oil and gas exports from the Caspian region, gaining substantial U.S. and EU economic trade concessions, and actively engaging Turkey as a trading partner, (Bremmer 2006).

Georgia's key positives lie in its economic and trade diversification, the success of implemented reforms, its economic resilience, low public debt level and a well-regulated, stable and strong banking sector. Between 2010 and 2019, Georgia's GDP per capita grew at an average annual rate of 4.8%. The World Bank's Doing Business (DB) 2020 report shows that Georgia remains one of the most business friendly countries globally, ranked 7 out of 190 countries. It is also attractive for investments, specifically in labor intensive sectors, due to a competitive wage level. Country's general image is positive, related to beautiful nature, unique cultural heritage hospitality and good governance (Saha and Giucci 2017).

Georgia has also become an important and reliable energy transit country through significant foreign and domestic investments into new power plants and power lines. The construction of a new deep-water port in Anaklia and projects related to the Chinese "New Silk Road" initiative lead to the improvement of transport connections within and out of Georgia, reducing transport costs for imports and Georgian exports. Solving the productivity problem will further unlock potential for growth in agriculture and downstream food processing industries. Finally, domestic and international tourism is becoming an important factor in the Georgian economy. The Travel & Tourism Competitiveness Report in 2019 ranked Georgia 68th among 140 nations, a steady improvement from previous years. From 2015 to late 2019, the average number of visits made by inbound visitors increased by 47%. The largest increases came from Iran, Israel, and the EU member countries.

By the end of 2019, dynamic changes in the country's GDP mean that construction and real estate sector is 20% of the economy; followed by wholesale, retail trade, and hospitality; and education, social, health, culture and other professional activities at 18% each.

Energy and manufacturing as well as high-tech (i.e. Information and communication and Financial and insurance activities) comprise 10% of GDP each. The economy, however, remains dependent on 71% of import activity and 18% exports, excluding re-export and 11% re-export/transit. It is notable that trade was focused mostly on neighboring partners. In terms of export these are (and the picture with imports is similar):

- CIS countries (53%) where Russian language would still be the lingua franca as main trade partners here are Russia and Azerbaijan (13% each), Armenia (11%) and Ukraine (7%), followed by Kazakhstan, Kyrgyzstan, Turkmenistan and Uzbekistan (approx. 2% each)
- EU countries (22%) are headed by Bulgaria (8%) and Romania (5%), and followed by Germany to a far lesser extent (1%). It is noteworthy that the largest EU trading partners for Georgia are the former Communist bloc countries in Eastern Europe.
- Other countries (25%) are headed by China (6%) and Turkey (5%), and followed by the US (3%), Iran, Switzerland, and United Arab Emirates (approx. 2% each).

Literature Review

Employment structure in Georgia, however, does not generally follow the country's current economic profile. Agriculture, forestry and fishing are the leading employment sector comprising 38% of the employed, though comprising just 7% of the economy. In recent years, nevertheless, the Education, health, culture and other professional activities sector as well as the Wholesale, retail trade, and hospitality sector provide 18% and 15% of jobs, respectively. Based on the data for Georgia's context, it's heavy dependence on imports, the destination markets for the country's exports, and the labor activity profile in the country, the potential skills that are relevant for employability appear to be largely geared toward the former-Soviet and post-Communist partners.

Education is generally perceived to be a highly valued achievement in Georgia. Currently its key role lies in providing higher chances of finding a job rather than in raising individual incomes. These results could be due to the relatively slow process of job creation in Georgia. To the extent that the improvements in the quality of education result in the increased productivity of the workforce, as well as the expansion of applications of individual skills in the labor market, the relationship between education and incomes should improve in the future. Existing analysis of the Gergian labor market reveals, however, that post-Soviet education yields a lower income impact compared to the education acquired during Soviet times. Note that the probability of employment itself has not increased. At the same time, comparisons between post-Soviet university education and post-Soviet lower levels of educational attainment show the unconditional marginal effect: university education pais off substantially as the earnings of workers increase by 131.75% (relative to incomplete secondary education). This number is 14.26% for completed secondary education, 63.15% for completed technical education—both versus incomplete secondary education levels (Khitarishvili 2010). Thus, the size of the impact from university education is twice the size of completed technical or vocational education, and almost ten times the impact of completed secondary education.

According to a recent overview of the Higher Education System in Georgia in 2017, obtaining a Master's degree does not guarantee a significant increase in income, but increases the chance of getting a job by at least 70% when compared to an individual with only a bachelor's degree. Therefore, graduate studies are a means of increasing employment chances in Georgia (EACEA, 2017). Meanwhile, according to the 2017-18 edition of the Global Competitiveness Index, the quality of higher education and vocational training in Georgia remains substandard. Georgia is ranked below the 100th (out of 137 countries) place in areas such as the quality of higher education system (107), quality of math and science education (103), quality of management schools (113), local availability of specialized training services (131). These results confirm the findings in the 2012 Employer Survey conducted by the World Bank, which reveal deficiencies such as a lack of knowledge of foreign languages—69%, followed by weak leadership skills—55%, weak creative thinking—40%, and deficient problem-solving skills—30% (Pignatti 2018).

In terms of language skills, though Georgian has been the state language in Georgia, minorities have a right to obtain information in their own language and up to 10% cent of total broadcasting time is allowed in other languages (Dietrich 2005). At the same time, many are fluent in Russian, though the younger generation is certainly shifting away to other languages in addition to Georgian. In the post-Soviet period, English is becoming a popular second language, associated with being successful, having better job opportunities, becoming a part of the global marketplace, learning more about the outside world, or having greater mobility (Pearce and Rice 2014). According to the Caucasus Research Resource Centers (CRRC) surveys in 2009-2010, there was a mildly positive but significant correlation between knowledge of Russian and employment (r-squared of 0.111 in 2009 and 0.13 in 2010) as well as between knowledge of Russian and life satisfaction (r-squared of 0.112 in 2010). Also, knowledge of English seemed to correlate moderately and significantly with knowledge of Russian (r-squared of 0.300 in 2009 and 0.331 in 2010). Although English is replacing Russian as the prestige language, and state policy continues to be directed towards giving English primacy among foreign languages, the case of Georgia illustrates the path dependencies in an increasingly globalized job market, where Russian remains a desirable language skill (Blauvelt 2013).

Furthermore, with regards to gender and ethnicity, there are noticeable inequalities in employability. Female labor force participation in Georgia for 2019 was 49.5%, while the same figure for the male population is at 62.8% (National Statistics Office of Georgia 2019). Survey data in 2014 has shown that being a housewife was considered a fulfilling status among more than half of the population, while 83% of respondents perceived that men are breadwinners for the family. Up to 81.8% of the younger respondents agreed with the statement that the "main duty of a man is to provide financial support for the family" (United Nations Population Fund 2014, 21). It is also notable that ethnic minorities have strongly aligned with this standpoint. Yet, while cultural and social traditions certainly influence individual perceptions and choices with regards to labor force participation, over the last two decades the service sector became to employ the largest portion of the workforce, especially among women (Khitarishvili 2016, 7-8).

In addition, the first experimental evidence regarding ethnic discrimination in the labor market of Georgia was provided in 2017. The field experiment studied attitudes towards job candidates through callback trends. The findings showed that gender had no effect on the probability of callback, but an ethnic Georgian job applicant was twice more likely to be called for a job interview than an equally skilled ethnic non-Georgian (Azeri or Armenian). The study also showed that as unemployment rates increased in Georgia by 1%, the gap in the probability of a callback between Georgians and non-Georgian job applicants increases by about 2% (Asali, Pignatti and Skhirtladze 2017).

Theoretical Framework

There is no one single theory to aid in understanding the multiple facets of employability. Rather, there is an amalgamation of theories on human capital, career management, competence signaling, and labor market demand views of employability. Each of these views or theoretical frameworks help us in drawing a picture of an aggregate nature of employability (Cole and Tibby, 2013). As a foundation for our research, we are following the Bridgestock's model, which argues that in the context of a rapidly changing economy, workers must not only maintain and develop knowledge and skills that are specific to their own discipline or occupation, but must also possess generic human capital skills that are transferable to many occupational situations and areas and enables them to both be immediately and sustainably employed. Our framework, given the Georgian context in the study, is that certain individual skills have value for employers, and therefore, will be preferred during hiring decisions.

Given the lingering orientation of the Georgian economy toward the post-Soviet and post-Communist countries, in addition to educational attainment, generic skills such as knowledge of

Russian, and increasingly English, will be significant for employability. In line with existing empirical evidence, individual characteristics, such as gender or ethnic background, are expected to matter for one's employability. Georgian government has conducted a number of research projects, which mainly focused on skills gap and unemployment (MLHSAG 2015; MLHSAG 2016a and 2016b; MESDG 2017a and 2017b). However, these studies and their respective findings lack an analysis of the generic skills associated with employment. Our research is focused on an analysis of competencies or skills qualifications (education, languages, language skills, or computer literacy), and thus, offers evidence for a 'skills roadmap' toward employment. A theoretical framework tested in the chapter is presented in Figure 8.2.

Figure 8.2 A model for individual skills capital and employability

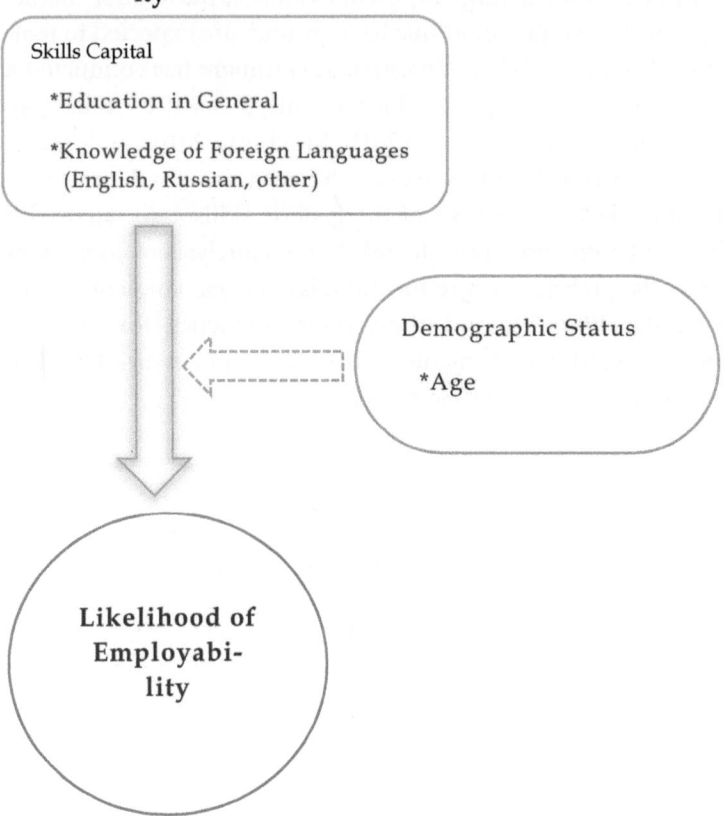

Following the model of employability in Figure 8.2, we develop the following formal hypotheses:

a) Skills capital improves the likelihood of individual employability. Our hypothesis is that easily transferable generic skills in Georgia will positively influence individual employability.

Hypothesis 1 = there is a significant relationship between an individual's skills capital and the likelihood of being employed.

b) Individual characteristics will influence the likelihood of employability. Our hypothesis here is that variables such as age, gender, and ethnicity will moderate the effect of skills capital on the likelihood of being employable.

Hypothesis 2 = there is a significant relationship between an individual's demographic characteristics and the likelihood of being employed.

Data and Descriptive Statistics

The data used for modeling employability (the binary likelihood of employment) is drawn from a representative nationwide public opinion survey of individual respondents in Georgia from the Caucasus Barometer's 2017 wave. Caucasus Barometer fields an annual survey of socio-economic issues and political attitudes, conducted by the Caucasus Research Resource Centers (CRRC) in the three countries of the South Caucasus—Armenia, Azerbaijan, and Georgia. The Caucasus Barometer sample is designed using a multi-stage cluster sampling approach with preliminary stratification, focusing on the population of adults (18 years old and over), excluding the populations living in territories affected by the frozen conflicts (South Ossetia and Abkhazia, which are currently occupied by Russia). The survey was conducted using Computer-assisted personal interviews (CAPI). The survey yielded 2,379 respondents, based on a response rate of 58%.

As discussed in the previous section, the chapter focuses on two areas—skills capital and individual characteristics, including a set of interactions between them, and the likelihood of being employed. For our analysis, we have following variables:

The dependent variable is *Employment*, constructed as a binary outcome measure from item "EMPLSIT #76" in the 2017 wave of the Caucasus Barometer in Georgia. Table 8.1 shows the scales in the original data set and the measurement approach we took for this study. We exclude all categories for respondents outside the labor force—the largest excluded sub-sample is comprised of the retired respondents, which is over 26% of completed responses; this is followed by respondents self identified as house-wives, an additional 15% of completed responses. The likelihood of employment aggregates respondents who are-employed for hire or self-employed to equal 1, and the unemployed are equal to 0. The working sample retained for the analysis after this step decreases to 1,284, where 850 respondents are employed and 434 are unemployed.

Table 8.1 Variables and measurement

Variable	Code	Meaning	#	% of Obs	Re-Coded	Interpretation	% of Obs
Employment	−3	Interviewer Error	11	0.46%	excluded	outside the labor force	46.03%
	−2	Refuse to answer					
	−1	Don't Know	1	0.04%	excluded	outside the labor force	
	1	Retired, not working	625	26.27%	excluded	outside the labor force	
	2	Student, not working	59	2.48%	excluded	outside the labor force	
	3	Housewife not working	360	15.13%	excluded	outside the labor force	
	7	unable to work	33	1.39%	excluded	outside the labor force	
	8	Other	6	0.25%	excluded	outside the labor force	
	4	Unemployed	434	18.24%	0	Unemployed	18.24%
	5	Employed	529	22.24%	1	Employed	35.73%
	6	Self-employed	321	13.49%	1	Employed	

Education	-3	Interviewer error					
	-1	Don't know					
	1	No primary education	18	0.76%	0	No Education	0.76%
	2	Primary education	61	2.56%	1	Below Secondary Education	11.27%
	3	Incomplete secondary education	207	8.70%	1	Below Secondary Education	
	4	Competed secondary education	694	29.17%	2	Secondary or Secondary Technical Education	59.90%
	5	Secondary technical education	669	28.12%	2	Secondary or Secondary Technical Education	
	6	Incomplete higher education	62	2.61%	2	Secondary or Secondary Technical Education	
	7	Completed higher education	662	27.83%	3	Higher Education	28.08%
	8	Post-graduate degree	6	0.25%	3	Higher Education	
Computer skills	-3	Interviewer error	1	0.04%	0	No Computer Literacy	70.49%

	-2	Refuse to answer			0	No Computer Literacy	
	-1	Don't know	68	2.86%	0	No Computer Literacy	
	1	No basic knowledge	1359	57.12%	0	No Computer Literacy	
	2	Beginner	249	10.47%	0	No Computer Literacy	
	3	Intermediate	512	21.52%	1	Computer Literacy	29.51%
	4	Advanced	190	7.99%	1	Computer Literacy	
English skills	-2	Refuse to answer	1	0.04%	0	No Knowledge of English	83.56%
	-1	Don't know	68	2.86%	0	No Knowledge of English	
	1	No basic knowledge	1513	63.60%	0	No Knowledge of English	
	2	Beginner	406	17.07%	0	No Knowledge of English	
	3	Intermediate	300	12.61%	1	Knowledge of English	16.44%

	4	Advanced	91	3.83%	1	Knowledge of English	
Russian skills	-1	Don't know	17	0.71%	0	No Knowledge of Russian	29.55%
	1	No basic knowledge	193	8.11%	0	No Knowledge of Russian	
	2	Beginner	493	20.72%	0	No Knowledge of Russian	
	3	Intermediate	1140	47.92%	1	Knowledge of Russian	70.45%
	4	Advanced	536	22.53%	1	Knowledge of Russian	
Other foreign language skills	-3	Interviewer error	2	0.08%	0	No Knowledge of other foreign languages	87.81%
	-2	Refuse to answer	6	0.25%	0	No Knowledge of other foreign languages	
	-1	Don't know	107	4.50%	0	No Knowledge of other foreign languages	

	1	No basic knowledge	1616	67.93%	0	No Knowledge of other foreign languages	
	2	Beginner	358	15.05%	0	No Knowledge of other foreign languages	
	3	Intermediate	212	8.91%	1	Knowledge of other foreign languages	12.19%
	4	Advanced	78	3.28%	1	Knowledge of other foreign languages	
Ethnicity	-3	Interviewer Error					
	-1	Don't know					
	1	Armenian	124	5.21%	0	Ethnic Minorities	15.76%
	2	Azerbaijani	203	8.53%	0	Ethnic Minorities	
	3	Georgian	2004	84.24%	1	Ethnic Georgian	84.24%
	4	Other Caucasian ethnicity (Abkhazian, Lezgin, Ossetian, etc.)	14	0.59%	0	Ethnic Minorities	
	5	Russian	14	0.59%	0	Ethnic Minorities	
	6	Kurd or Yezid	7	0.29%	0	Ethnic Minorities	

	7	Other ethnicity	13	0.55%	0	Ethnic Minorities	
Gender	1	Male	867	36.44%	0	Male	36.44%
	2	Female	1512	63.56%	1	Female	63.56%
Educated x female	CrossTab		1502	63.14%		Female with Education	63.14%
Georgian x female	CrossTab		1282	53.89%		Female of Georgian Ethnicity	53.89%

Two sets of predictor variables are constructed from the 2017 wave of the Caucasus Barometer survey. Skills capital measures are *Education* (item RESPEDU#185); *Computer Literacy* (item COMPABL #192); English (item KNOWENG#190); Russian (KNOWRUS#189); Other foreign languages (item OTHLANABL #191). Education is an eight choice categorical variable, ranging from no education to postgraduate education. We recoded this into a four choice ordered measure, where 0 equals to no education, 1 equals to less than secondary (high school) education, 2 equals to secondary or technical (high school or vocational training) education, 3 equals to a university/graduate or postgraduate degree. The remaining skills variables are binary measures, where intermediate and advanced skills are coded as 1, else coded as 0.

Table 8.2 Descriptive statistics for dependent and predictor variables

Variable	Obs.	Mean	Std. Dev.	Min	Max
Employment	2379	0.357293	0.479303	0	1
Female	2379	0.635561	0.481374	0	1
Age	2379	51.96637	18.51907	18	102
Ethnic Georgian	2379	0.842371	0.36447	0	1
Education	2379	1.887348	0.853876	0	3
English	2379	0.164355	0.370675	0	1
Russian	2379	0.704498	0.456364	0	1
Other language	2379	0.1219	0.327239	0	1
Computer	2379	0.295082	0.456176	0	1
Educated x female	2379	1.209332	1.138764	0	3
Ethnic Georgian x female	2379	0.538882	0.498591	0	1

Three variables capture individual characteristics — Age (item AGE#7); Ethnicity (item ETHNIC#183); and Gender (item RESPSEX#214). Age is a ratio measure that ranges from 18 to 102. Ethnicity is coded to equal 1 for ethnic Georgians, and to equal 0 for all other minorities. Finally, females are coded 1, else are coded 0. Descriptive statistics for the dependent and predictor variables are presented in Table 8.2.

Analyses and Results

Binary logistic regression was applied to analyze relationships between the dependent and predictor variables. Given multicollinearity between language skills, we present four competing models. The first three models focus on Russian, English, and other foreign language skills, respectively. The last regression is a nested model for all languages, where the absence of any foreign language skills is the omitted comparison category. Binary logistic regression results are presented in Table 8.3.

Overall, in line with existing research (Khitarishvili 2010), more educated individuals are found to be more likely to be employed. Every unit increase in the education measure is associated with an increase of the likelihood of being employed by about 36% to 43% across the four models (logistic coefficients are exponentiated for likelihood interpretations). A difference in the likelihood of employment between less than a secondary degree and a graduate/postgraduate degree is then anywhere between over 70% to almost 90%. Among language skills, Russian is significantly and substantively associated with the likelihood of employment, which confirms earlier findings (Blauvelt 2013). All else equal, Russian language skills appear to have about 60% higher likelihood of employment than non-Russian speakers. Other languages, however, are not found to matter for employability in the general survey of Georgia's population. The results hold through models 1 to 4.

Table 8.3 Regression models for the likelihood of employment

Variables	Model 1	Model 2	Model 3	Model 4
Female	-0.932**	-1.040**	-1.039**	-0.936**
	(-2.76)	(-3.08)	(-3.08)	(-2.76)
Age	-0.02***	-0.02***	-0.02***	-0.02***
	(-5.85)	(-5.58)	(-5.50)	(-5.99)
Ethnic Georgian	1.124***	1.122***	1.108***	1.130***
	(5.27)	(5.24)	(5.16)	(5.24)
Education	0.307***	0.356***	0.351***	0.314***
	(3.51)	(4.1)	(4.05)	(3.58)
Russian skills	0.470***			0.483***
	(4.11)			(4.19)
English skills		-0.148		-0.182
		(-1.07)		(-1.32)
Other language skills			-0.0029	-0.0525
			(-0.02)	(-0.37)
Computer skills	0.183	0.282*	0.249*	0.225
	(1.53)	(2.29)	(2.09)	(1.82)
Educated x female	0.111	0.147	0.141	0.119
	(0.99)	(1.31)	(1.26)	(1.06)
Ethnic Georgian x female	-0.146	-0.164	-0.161	-0.147
	(-0.48)	(-0.53)	(-0.52)	(-0.48)
Constant	-1.160***	-0.902***	-0.935***	-1.112***
	(-4.18)	(-3.29)	(-3.41)	(-3.97)
N	2379	2379	2379	2379
AIC	2789.4	2805.4	2806.6	2791.5
BIC	2841.3	2857.4	2858.5	2855

t statistics in parentheses; * $p < 0.05$, ** $p < 0.01$, *** $p < 0.001$.

Furthermore, in terms of individual characteristics, age appears to have an inverse association with the likelihood of employment. Older respondents are found to be less likely to have employment, all else equal — though the relationship appears to be non-linear (polynomial results for age are omitted). In line with existing research with regards to possible discrimination patterns in

Georgia's labor market (Asali, Pignatti and Skhirtladze 2017), regression results show that, all else constant, ethnic Georgians are more likely to be employed than minority respondents. The magnitude of this difference is large—the odds of being employed for ethnic Georgians vs. minorities are greater by a factor of 3.07, or more than a 200% gap in the likelihood of being employed. Also, in line with existing research (Khitarishvili 2016), women are less likely to be employed, other predictor variables equal. They are less likely to work than men by almost 60%. Interestingly, however, more educated women are not necessarily any more likely to be employed than women with lower levels of education. The coefficient for the interaction effect is not statistically significant. At the same time, minority women are not any more likely to be unemployed than ethnic majority Georgian women as well.

Conclusion

Employability is an individual characteristic that affects and enhances the individual-work interface. Although employability does not assure actual employment, it enhances an individual's likelihood of gaining employment. The analysis in this chapter focuses on person-centered factors—skills capital and demographic characteristics—and their associations with the likelihood of employment. As individuals often do not have control of employers' hiring criteria (e.g. years of experience and job specific skills) or of market factors in rapidly changing times, investment in own skills capital demonstrates an adaptive orientation and a commitment to continuous learning, and boosts employability. However, the development of only individual skills capital is not always a sufficient condition for employment—individual demographic characteristics, unfortunately, tend to have an influence here. Knowing the specifics of this influence, often based on socio-cultural systemic factors, policy makers can better manage employability in the labor markets.

The results of empirical analysis in this chapter lend support for both of the formal hypotheses. Based on these findings, the following are key conclusions with regards to individual employability in Georgia:

Gender moderates the skills capital relation with employability. Women are less likely to work by almost 60% compared to men. Taking into account that, all held equal, educated women are not more likely to be employed compared to relatively less educated women, as well as the outcome that minority women are not more likely to be unemployed than ethnic Georgian women, this underemployment among women may have structural roots. It could be that socio-cultural undercurrents in Georgia dictate that women must make work-family orientated choices more often relative to men, which limits their labor market participation behaviors. Further research is necessary here to develop a more precise explanation for the gap between female and male employment. Such research would reveal the points for improvement to attend to gender disparities in the labor market because access to employment to all is important for prospects toward robust, sustainable, and inclusive growth of the economy. Relevant policies should, therefore, seek to bring more women to the labor force by bridging potential gender disparities in access to jobs or desirability of employment.

As age and ethnicity appear to be significant for employability, policies targeting age or ethnicity-based job access disparities must be adopted. The fact that older people are more likely to report unemployment is problematic for a couple of reasons. The first one has to do with learning capabilities that can fade with age and older individuals would find themselves at a disadvantage compared to younger generations. The second one is critical because many in the older generation in Georgia may have lost their life savings or social security with the collapse of the Soviet Union and the civil war in the 1990's. The finding that ethnicity is significant for the likelihood of employment also needs further research and policy focus. One of the culprits here could simply be the issue of fluency in Georgian. According to the National Statistics Office of Georgia 2003 data, only 15% of ethnic Azeris spoke Georgian fluently, while the same figure for ethnic Armenians stood at 35%.

Furthermore, without proper command of Georgian, ethnic minorities would have little if any chances to get higher education in Georgia. The statistic that, while 39% of ethnic Georgians reported higher than secondary education, the corresponding indicator for Armenians and Azeries stood at 25% and 9%, respectively (PSA 2014). Thus, policies should accommodate fluency in Georgian for non-ethnic Georgians to facilitate their access to university and postgraduate education. This would subsequently improve entry to the labor market via strengthening of Georgian language skills among ethnic minorities in the country.

Education, as a foundation of individual human capital, indeed appears to have a positive relationship with one's employment. More educated individuals are more likely to be employed relative to less educated individuals. This confirms the human capital expectations in the labor market, and education should continue to be a key policy priority in the country. Furthermore, knowledge of Russian as an element of individual skills capital continues to have a positive association with employability. This result signals that post-Soviet and post-Communist markets (including Russia), which generally operate in Russian, are still important to the Georgian economy and Georgians. Even beyond that, at least as far as remittances are concerned, Georgia continues to depend on Russia, more so than on the EU, where Russian is certainly a language of importance (Labadze and Tukhashvili 2013). These trends are likely to change away from Russia as Georgia seeks to break away their dependence on the Russian economy.

In terms of other skills, proficiency in English, or indeed another foreign language, as an element of individual skills capital are not significant in any of the models. Computer literacy skills appear to be only marginally significant. Despite insignificance, however, while there is no definitive empirical evidence is available, a large number of entry- and mid-level leadership employees in the Georgian government, businesses, the NGO community, and the private sector have experience of visiting or education in the EU, the UK and/or the US. Certainly, a recently introduced visa free regime to the Schengen member states will only accelerate this trend. This experience is likely to become a considerable source of cultural and social change, and serve for the coming generation as a reorientation toward other countries. This conjecture is supported by a trend showing that employment and educational reasons to travel to Europe are emerging as a significant rival to former orientation on Russia (Labadze and Tukhashvili 2013).

Research in this chapter is the first step for Georgia toward a roadmap to employability, stressing generic skills and demographic characteristics as key covariates. As noted, future research should venture into deeper details of the relationship between gender and employment; age and employment; and minority communities and their access to employment. Next steps should also account for different measurements or operationalizations of education, such as by degree type, university resources, and university specializations. Further research would also benefit from better measurement of employment related skills—beyond languages and computer proficiency. These next steps would certainly help with constructing a more dynamic and generalizable roadmap toward individual employability in Georgia.

References

Akhvlediani, T., and Havlik, P. 2019. *Georgia's Economic Performance: Bright Spots and Remaining Challenges*. The Vienna Institute for International Economic Studies, No 29, Policy Notes.

ILO. 2010. *A Skilled Workforce for Strong, Sustainable and Balanced Growth: A G20 Training Strategy*. Geneva, CHE: International Labour Office.

Artess, J., Hooley, T., and Mellors-Bourne, R. 2017. *Employability: A Review of the Literature 2012 to 2016*. Higher Education Academy.

Asali, Muhammad, Pignatti, Norberto, and Skhirtladze, Sophiko. 2017. *Employment Discrimination in a Former Soviet Union Republic: Evidence from a Field Experiment*. IZA, DP No. 11056.

Blauvelt, Timothy K. 2013. "Endurance of the Soviet imperial tongue: the Russian language in contemporary Georgia." *Central Asian Survey* http://dx.doi.org/10.1080/02634937.2013.771978.

Bremmer, Ian. 2006. "The Post-Soviet Nations after Independence" in *After Independence, Making and Protecting the Nation in Postcolonial and Postcommunist States* eds., Lowell W. Barrington. Ann Arbor: University of Michigan Press.

Brown, P., Hesketh, A., and Williams, S. 2003. "Employability in a knowledge-driven economy." *Journal of Education and Work* 16(2): 107-126.

Capannelli, Giovanni, and Kanbur, Ravi. 2019. *Good Jobs for Inclusive Growth in Central Asia and the South Caucasus Regional Report*. Asian Development Bank.

Cole, D., and Tibby, M. 2013. *Defining and Developing Your Approach to Employability: A Framework for Higher Education Institutions*. The Higher Education Academy, the UK.

Government of Georgia. 2014. *Concept for Development of Lifelong Vocational Consultancy and Career Planning Accessible Public Services and Its Action Plan*.

Government of Georgia. 2016. *Strategy for Active Labour Market Policy and Action Plan for Its Execution in 2016-2018*. Government of Georgia.

De Grip, A., Van Loo, J., and Sanders, J. 2004. "The Industry Employability Index: Taking account of supply and demand characteristics." *International Labour Review* 14(3): 216.

Dietrich, Ayse. 2005. *Language Policy and the Status of Russian in the Soviet Union and the Successor States outside the Russian Federation*. Working paper.

Bowman, K. 2010. *Background Paper for the AQF Council on Generic Skills*. Available at: http://www.academia.edu/8365066/Generic-skills-background-paper-FINAL.

European Bank for Reconstruction and Development. 2001. Transition Report 59.

Frederiksen, M.D., Thomsen, S.M., and Slot, A.L. 2019. *Labour Market Analysis 2018-19, EU4Youth*. Connectio 2018/2019.

Fugate, M., Kinicki, A. J., and Ashforth, B. E. 2004. "Employability: A Psycho-social Construct, Its Dimensions, and Applications." *Journal of Vocational Behavior* 65: 14–38.

Gutbrod, H. 2013. *Correcting Unemployment Numbers – A Call for Government Action*. Available at: https://iset-pi.ge/index.php/en/iset-economist-blog-2/entry/correcting-unemployment-numbers-a-call-for-government-action.

Japaridze, E., Zhghenti, N., Barkaia, M., and Amashukeli, M. 2013. *Gender Attitudes and Perceptions among Young People in Georgia*. Center for Social Sciences, Georgia.

PMCG. 2019. *Inequality in Education, Economic Outlook and Indicators*. PMCG Research, Issue #109. Available at: https://pmcresearch.org/publications_file/92ed5c8fbc3cd723e.pdf.

Kakulia, M., Kapanadze, N., and Bakhtadze, L. 2019. *Quarterly Review of the Georgian Economy- II Quarter of 2019*. Georgian Foundation for Strategic and International Studies (Rondeli Foundation).

Kariuki, A., Wasike, Sh., and Ambula, R. 2016. "Intellectual Capital and Employability Proposing A Conceptual Framework. *International Journal of Economics, Commerce and Management* 4(4): 1149.

Keynes, J.M. 1939. *The General Theory of Employment, Interest, and Money.*

Khitarishvili, T. 2016. *Gender and employment in the South Caucasus and Western CIS.* UNDP.

Khitarishvili, T. 2016. *Gender Dimensions of Inequality in the Countries of Central Asia, South Caucasus, and Western CIS.* Levy Economics Institute of Bard College.

Khitarishvili, T. 2010. *On Education: Assessing the Returns to Education in Georgia.* Levy Economics Institute of Bard College.

Knight, P., and Yorke, M. 2003. *Learning, Curriculum and Employability in Higher Education.* London, the UK: Routledge.

Labadze, L., and Tukhashvili, M. 2013. *ENPI – Costs and Benefits of Labour Mobility between the EU and the Eastern Partnership Partner Countries.* Country Study: Georgia. EuropeAid/130215/C/SER/Multi.

McQuaid, R.W., and Lindsay, C. 2005. "The Concept of Employability." *Urban Studies.* 42: 197-219.

MLHSAG. 2015. *The Survey Report of Labour Market Demand Component.* Ministry of Labor, Health and Social Affairs of Georgia.

MLHSAG. 2016a. *The Study of Youth Attitudes, Motivation and Employment Strategies.* Ministry of Labor, Health and Social Affairs of Georgia.

MLHSAG. 2016b. *Report on Key Indicators of Labour Market.* Ministry of Labor, Health and Social Affairs of Georgia.

MESDG. 2017a. *The Analysis of Labor Market of Georgia.* Ministry of Economy and Sustainable Development of Georgia.

MESDG. 2017b. *The Study of Skills Demanded by Enterprises.* Ministry of Economy and Sustainable Development of Georgia.

Monogan, James E. 2015. *Political Analysis Using R.* Springer International Publishing.

Noga, A. 2016. *Special Theory of Employment and Co-Productive Goods.* Kozminski University.

EACEA 2017. *Overview of the Higher Education System, Georgia.* European Comission, Education, Audiovisual and Culture Executive Agency (EACEA).

Paadi, K. 2014. "Perceptions on Employability Skills Necessary To Enhance Human Resource Management Graduates Prospects of Securing a Relevant Place in the Labour Market." *European Scientific Journal.*

Patton, W., and McMahon, M. 2014. *Career Development and Systems Theory.* Rotterdam, the Netherlands: Sense Publishers.

Pearce, K. E., and Rice, R. E. 2014. "The Language Divide – The Persistence of English Proficiency as a Gateway to the Internet: The Cases of Armenia, Azerbaijan, and Georgia." *International Journal of Communication* 8: 2834–2859.

Peeters, E., Nelissen, J., De Cuyper, N., Forrier, A., Verbruggen, M., and De Witte, H. 2017. "Employability Capital: A Conceptual Framework Tested Through Expert Analysis." *Journal of Career Development*. 1-15.

Pignatti, Norberto. 2018. *Higher Education Reform in Georgia: Challenges and Opportunities*. ISET.

UNPF. 2014. *Population Situation Analysis of Georgia 2014*. United Nations Population Fund.

Posadas, Josefina, Makovec, Mattia, Jaef, Roberto Fattal, Gruen, Carola and Ajwad, Mohamed Ihsan. 2018. *Georgia at Work: Assessing the Jobs Landscape*. Washington, DC: World Bank.

Riegl, Martin, and Tomáš, Vaško. 2008. *Comparison of Language Policies in the Post-Soviet Union Countries on the European Continent*. Charles University.

CSS. 2017. *Return on Education, Labor Market and Job Satisfaction in Georgia*. Center of Social Sciences, Nekeri Publishing.

Rothwell, A., Herbert, I., and Rothwell, F. 2008. "Self-perceived Employability: Construction and Initial Validation of a Scale for University Students." *Journal of Vocational Behaviour* 73(1): 1-12.

Saha, David, and Giucci, Ricardo. 2017. *Towards Strong and Balanced Growth: Georgia's Economic Policy Priorities in 2017-2020*.

Shaffer, L. S., and Zalewski, J.M. 2011. "Career Advising in a VUCA Environment." *NACADA Journal* 31(1): 64–74.

Sultana, R.G. 2011. "Learning Career Management Skills in Europe: A Critical Review." *Journal of Education and Work* 25(2): 225-248.

Williams, S., Dodd, L., Steele, C., and Randall, R. 2015. "A Systematic Review of Current Understandings of Employability." *Journal of Education and Work* 29(8): 877-901.

9
How Do Mining Activities in Georgia Affect Local Public Health?[1]

Natia Tchigvaria, Ph.D.

How does proximity to a mine affect local public health in Georgia? There are gains achieved from the mining sector to the economy, but there also are significant environmental, health and social costs to the nation of Georgia. The extent to which pollution from mining activities in Georgia affects the ecosystem and human health is a matter of growing concern, especially in cases when the mining industry is not properly managed. This chapter addresses an important potential consequence of this industry, whether ongoing mining activities have an impact on local public health.

I evaluate the impact of mining on local public health outcomes by studying all Georgian municipalities (excluding Tbilisi, the capital city of Georgia, and the occupied territories) in 2016. Each municipality is coded as having a toxic mine in its presence, a semitoxic mine, or no mining activity at all. Whether this aspect of mining in a municipality affects public health, measured by a variety of diseases, is then tested. Specifically, I use Poisson regression models for count outcome variables, to assess whether the rates of certain diseases are elevated for municipalities that have toxic or semitoxic mines in their geographic proximity.

Tbilisi, the capital of Georgia, is left out of the list for several reasons. The city is densely populated with 1.5 million people, and air pollution is very high because of automobile emissions, a potentially important confounding factor. Another reason to exclude Tbilisi is that many of the patients for the conditions studied are often from other regions, but they visit Tbilisi hospitals for their medical

---

1   I would like to express my gratitude towards the University of Georgia (U.S.) faculty for implementing a University Research Program in Georgia and for their support in conducting my research.

needs. This implies that there are different processes driving health statistics generation in Tbilisi versus various other regions in the country.

This chapter proceeds first by reviewing some background on mining in Georgia. Second, it describes past findings about the relationship between mining and public health—both abroad and in Georgia itself. Third, the chapter explains why, theoretically, mining practices in Georgia could affect nearby residents' health. Fourth, I describe the data that are collected about the municipalities and how the count regression model is selected and used. Fifth, the results of these regressions are presented. Finally, this chapter concludes with a discussion of policy implications.

Background on Mining in Georgia

Favorable conditions for development of the mining industry in Georgia were created by the existence of various metal and non-metal natural reserves (such as polymetals, manganese, coal, oil, barite, arsenic, diatomite, and bentonite clay). Mining enterprises generally have developed in the country and drove urban developments outside the capital city, both in the time prior and during the Soviet Union. In the context of this general development of the mining sector, often at a fast pace industrialization rates in a centralized planning system, appropriate attention was not necessarily paid to the negative impacts of mineral extraction and processing on the environment (namely terrain, air quality, water, soil, flora, and fauna). These adverse influences on the environment in turn are expected to affect public health. Degradation of the natural landscapes and creation of anthropogenic pollution from open quarries of metal or non-metal mineral resources are noticed in all regions of Georgia. One of the most obvious examples is the Tchiatura Plateau. Large-scale extraction of manganese and quartz started there in the 1950's, and particles from open quarries can be detected in significant concentrations all around the plateau.

The negative impact of the mining industry's development on the natural and socioeconomic environment in Georgia has not been studied adequately. Only in recent years was attention drawn to the environmental impacts of some of the mining enterprises and deposits. From this standpoint, it is important to define the manner and scale of the impact of mining operations not only on the environment, but also on public health. During the Soviet period the mining industry was a highly developed field. The collapse of the entire system was followed by degradation of all industries in Georgia. There were several attempts since 2014 to enforce reforms in the mining industry, but regulating mining activities properly continues to remain problematic.

Reforms enforced by Georgian governments were largely unsuccessful. Georgia did not have a state policy or long-term strategy in this field. Studies regarding mining activities in Georgia reveal that the mining industry in Georgia is far from practicing responsible mining principles. Environmental experts and local populations living near mines have a lot of concerns (CENN, 2016). Specifically, scientists and doctors emphasize environmental issues caused by mining activities, such as damage of terrain, air, water, and soil, which subsequently have an impact on public health.

It is also important to examine the national legislation framework on mining to understand the institutions around mining regulation. The Constitution of Georgia, article 37.3, states: "Everyone shall have the right to live in a healthy environment and to use the natural and cultural environment." (For additional constitutional text, see the appendix.) The main public law that directly refers to mining industry is the Georgian Law about Mines of 1996, with amendments in 2005 and 2013 (Legislative Herald of Georgia, 2018). This law includes an obligation that companies return the terrain to the same form it had before mining activities have begun. The law aims for a reasonable use of natural resources taking into account the potential impacts on the environment, future generations' interests, and core principles of sustainable development. Extraction of natural resources must be reasonable within the framework of economics and ecology. Other relevant laws include Georgian law on licensing and permissions, which is directly linked to the law about the mining industry and the regulation of firms directly involved in the extraction and processing of natural resources. Also, Georgian environmental protection law serves as a framework for ecology legislation in the country. Altogether, some requirements for the mining industry are included in Georgian laws, but regulation of this field remains weak as legislative instruments and implementation of laws are still developing.

Evidence of Mining's Consequences around the World

Academic articles reveal that, besides the fact that the mining industry is an important economic sector for many countries, it is also dangerous and requires a very cautious and standardized approach from government policy, especially when it comes to public health issues. The impact of mining activities on community health occurs in various ways, namely adverse health effects that result from environmental exposure to contaminated air, water, and soil. Mining also poses health risks through noise pollution and events such as mining disasters. Few research studies have been conducted on the exposure and relative risk for residents living in the area of a mine when compared to the number of studies on occupational exposure. It is worth noting that many adverse effects are only noticed in risk groups such as children and elder people since their health is more likely to be affected due to their relative vulnerability (Coelho, Teixeira, and Gonçlaves, 2011).

However, there are certain significant studies about how varying types of mining, for example coal mining versus gold mining, affect public health. Research conducted in a Chinese province showed that the cadmium concentration in local soil is increased significantly by the mining activities there (Pyatt and Grattan, 2001). This poses risks to local residents of the affected Chinese province, whose intake of cadmium from rice and vegetables grown in soils in the vicinity of the mine has been measured at 596 grams per day.

Another study, based on data from a survey in West Virginia, investigated the relations between health indicators and residential proximity to coal mining sites. Results of hierarchical analysis indicated that high levels of coal production were associated with worse adjusted health status and with higher rates of cardiopulmonary disease, chronic obstructive pulmonary disease, hypertension, lung disease, and kidney disease (Hendryx and Ahern, 2008). Further research conducted by these authors narrowed down their sample to non-smokers and non-miner individuals living near surface coal mining sites in the United States. They measured blood inflammation among these people versus people living farther away in Indiana and West Virginia. None of these people reported current acute illness. Results showed that mean C-reactive protein levels were significantly higher for residents who lived near mining, and that mining residents reported more cardiopulmonary disease conditions and more illness symptoms (Hendryx and Entwhistle, 2015).

A study investigating pollution from tar sand industrial activities in northeastern Alberta, Canada showed high health risks for the nearest settlements (Timoney and Lee, 2009). Chronic exposure to polluted air is associated with cardiovascular disease, increases in respiratory symptoms, and lung cancer. The highest particulate matter (PM2.5) concentrations in Alberta in 2006 were observed at the Suncor Millennium tar sands mine. Both the quantity and the chemical constituents of the particulates pose health concerns. Meanwhile, elevated levels of mercury and arsenic in local fish are a concern there (Shavlishvili et al., 2017). Pregnant women, women of childbearing age, and children should consume no more than one fishmeal per month sourced from local rivers. Arsenic is a known carcinogen that can lead to skin cancer, vascular diseases, and Type II diabetes. Hence, negative health outcomes from mineral resource extraction from tar sands can occur both through air and water pollution.

Evidence of Mining's Effects in Georgia

For the Republic of Georgia, as a developing country, it is vital to take into account the mining industry experiences of developed countries. Although mining activities started in Georgia in the 19th century, the negative impacts of mineral extraction have not been defined clearly for terrain, air quality, water, soil, flora, or fauna. In recent years, Georgian researchers started investigating environmental problems caused by mining. Presently, progressive annual increases of extraction of metal and non-metal mineral resources continue, while entirely or partially ignoring proper uses of necessary public health technologies. This can affect the ecological equilibrium in the natural and human environments. If not properly managed, the mining industry causes undesirable geomorphologic changes at the locations of mines, ore processing facilities, and manufacturing locations. In other words, open quarries often cause complete or partial destruction of the natural terrain at the quarries and their adjacent territories. This also causes pollution of the hydrographic network, of soil with harmful toxic substances, and severe degradation of vegetation and wildlife, resulting in a reduction of the environmental biodiversity.

In this regard, the case of Bolnisi, one of the most significant agricultural regions in Georgia, serves as a good example. It supplies most of the country with vegetables; thus, its ecological condition is of great importance for the entire Georgian population. The region has an effective irrigation system supplied by the waters of the Mashavera River, yet many mining companies have been operating in the region upstream (Avkopashvili et al., 2017). One of the largest mines is JSC Madneuli, which etxracts barite and copper ore. According to Hanauer et al. (2011), this plant pollutes the Kazretula and Mashavera Rivers with copper and cadmium. The region's irrigation system draws heavily from the two rivers' confluence; therefore, the agricultural soil of a large region is potentially contaminated with heavy metals. Eventually this process will dramatically reduce soil fertility, which is undesirable since Bolnisi is one of Georgia's significant producers of vegetables and greens.

Pollution of surface waters with harmful chemicals and biogenic elements continues up to the present in a range of mines. During floods, polluted overruns affect vast areas adjacent to the riverbed (CENN, 2016, 33). As a result of this process, the soil in these areas becomes polluted to different degrees. For example, in the city of Kutaisi, several thousands of cubic meters of clay containing solid residues are left behind as a result of the barite enrichment activities at the former Litofoni Chemical Factory of Paints. This plant was located on the lower floodplain terrace of the river Rioni.

During floods, a large portion of the polluted waste escaped into the river. Strong winds take into the atmosphere barite powder that pollutes the air, which moves afterwards into the populated quarters of Kutaisi. Similar examples include cases when the treatment of arsenic-containing ores contaminated waters in the Ambrolauri and Lentekhi municipalities (CENN, 2016, 8), as well as waste oil disposal in bore-holes of the Iori River's floodplain in Sagarejo municipality (CENN, 2016, 36). Hence, soil contamination can occur from both air and water transmission channels, which bring harmful elements from the mines to populated areas.

In summarizing the overall literature about the effects of mining in Georgia and internationally, scholars do not generally argue with the fact that the mining industry provides jobs, supports infrastructural development in the regions it enters, and offers opportunity for diversification of state revenues. However, there also are costs when pollution from mining activities, if not properly monitored and mitigated, damages the environment and creates public health hazards. In fact, in some cases the human cost of mining can outweigh its economic benefits, as Hendryx (2008) argued was the case for coal mining in the Appalachian region of the United States. To evaluate what these costs are, it therefore is important to determine to what degree mining affects public health in Georgia.

Theoretical Framework

While any type of mining potentially has a serious impact on the environment, features of certain mines can elevate or lower the environmental and public health costs. It has been well established, for example, that the method of mining is important. Namely, open pit mining is particularly damaging, as environmental hazards are present during every step of the open-pit mining process. Hard rock mining exposes rock that has lain unexposed for multiple geological eras. When crushed, these rocks expose radioactive elements, asbestos-like minerals, and metallic dust. Underground mining can release toxic compounds into the air and water. As water takes on harmful concentrations of minerals and heavy metals, it becomes a contaminant (Miranda et al., 1998).

However, the most important problem of mining for public health concerns is whether toxic substances are used in mining activities, and, if so, how they are handled. When safety rules are violated, these toxins are hazardous for the environment and for public health (see https://www.atsdr.cdc.gov/substances/index.asp for more information.) Toxic or semitoxic substances often are used in gold, copper, silver, manganese, and coal mining to dissolve rock around the valuable material. The residual fluid from this process can contaminate nearby soil and water (International Atomic Energy Agency, 2005).

Toxic substances that are used in the mining process and byproducts of different mining activities pollute the environment in different ways: the air is polluted with dust, while the water and soil are polluted with heavy metals and other toxic waste. All of this damages the ecological equilibrium of the natural environment and, in the long term, will cause severe degradation of vegetation and wildlife. Entirely or partially ignoring the proper use of necessary technologies worsens the negative effects of mining. Consequently, the impact of mining activities on community health occurs at various levels and is a potential danger to human health, both in the short term and in the long run.

Based on the literature review, the results of several investigations conducted in different countries and on different types of mining present real evidence that mining has serious public health hazards. When mining companies carefully follow safety regulations, often with help from regulatory oversight, these risks can be substantially reduced. However, many examples discussed above show that this is often not the case in Georgia. Polluted soil, water, and air have a direct impact on public health outcomes in nearby settlements. This often means that nearby residents will breathe, drink, and eat substances that can negatively affect their health.

Based on this expectation that mining activities will potentially expose members of the population to harmful substances, which is a public health concern, I develop the following hypothesis: Rates for certain diseases will be relatively higher in municipalities where toxic mining operations are held, as compared to municipalities that have semitoxic mines, in turn compared to municipalities that have no mining activities at all.

Data and Methods

To test this hypothesis, I compiled a mining activity and public health dataset for 63 municipalities in Georgia. These 63 municipalities include all of Georgia's municipalities except for Russian-occupied territories and the capital city Tbilisi (which is qualitatively unique and tends to be an outlier data point because of non-mining pollution levels and as a center for medical services in the country). The dependent variable in each model is the municipality-level disease rate, as reported by the National Centre for Disease Control and Public Health.[2] Based on different studies it is possible to define what kind of health problems could be detected in the mining site areas, taking into account the types of mines. These diseases are: blood and immune diseases, endocrine diseases, nervous system diseases, coronary circulation diseases, respiratory diseases, digestive diseases, urinary system diseases, oncological diseases, infectious diarrheas, hypertension, and chronic obstructive pulmonary disease.

The primary predictor variable is the presence of toxic or semitoxic mining.[3] Of the 63 municipalities, 5 have no mining activity, 10 have a toxic mine site(s), and the remaining 48 municipalities have some sort of semitoxic mining activity. Toxic mines are those that use cyanide, manganese particles, and other heavy metals, which often result in substantial generation of wastewater. Typically, these are mines for gold, copper, coal, or manganese. Examples of mining sites that use toxic substances include the gold mine in Kazreti and manganese mines in Tchiatura. Semitoxic mines are those that excavate sand, sandstone, gravel, marble, andesite, basalt, clay, limestone, and tufa.[4]

---

2 Source for municipality-level diseases rate information: National Centre for Disease Control and Public Health; https://www.ncdc.ge/.
3 Source for mining site information: National Environmental Agency; http://nea.gov.ge/.
4 Additional data were collected from an air quality portal about air pollution

To test the hypothesis, a Poisson regression model for count outcomes of interest is estimated over these data:

$$\ln(lamda) = \ln(P) + B0 + B1X1 + B2X2 + \text{error term}$$

In this model, *lambda* is the expected number of cases of the disease. P is the population number per municipality, and this offset term allows us to model the *rate* of a disease. X1 is an indicator for toxic mining. X2 is an indicator for semitoxic mining. These two dummy variables for mining activities indicate that *no mining* is the reference group for this nominal classification of mining activity. Hence, each coefficient shows how common a disease is, on average, relative to a municipality with no mining.

Empirical Results

I analyzed the rates of eleven diseases. For all eleven, municipalities with toxic mines, on average, had higher rates of the disease than municipalities with semitoxic mines. Relative to municipalities with no mining at all, however, places with semitoxic mines had higher disease rates for only three diseases (nervous system diseases, blood and immune system diseases, and hypertension). Municipalities with toxic mines had higher disease rates than places with no mining for five diseases, where in addition to nervous system diseases, blood and immune system diseases, and hypertension, two deceases chronic obstructive pulmonary disease (COPD) and coronary circulation diseases are added.

Substantively, three of the five diseases above relate to the blood circulatory system. For the other two, COPD is a lung disease, while the nervous system diseases can be caused by any number of factors. The fact that, close to toxic mining areas, blood and immune system diseases rates are very high, compared to non-mining or semitoxic mining areas was not surprising, as heavy metals affect

---

rates in the regions, more precisely about sulphur dioxide and nitrogen dioxide quantity in the air. Because of limitations, these data are not used further in research as air quality is measured only in thirteen municipalities out of sixty-three.

the circulatory, immune, and central nervous systems (Jan et al., 2015). Immediately, then, our analysis implies that for assessing public health costs from mining, cardio-vascular diseases would be the first place to look at.

To look more closely at this issue, I present in this section the findings from models of nervous system diseases, blood and immune system diseases, and COPD. (Analyses of the other eight diseases can be found in the appendix section.) Table 9.1 presents a model of nervous system diseases. In this table, each row represents a different predictor. The first numerical column shows the estimate of the parameter estimate, the second column shows the standard error, the third column shows the z-ratios, and the final column shows the two-tailed p-values.

Table 9.1 Nervous System Disease Rates in 63 Georgia Municipalities

Parameter	Estimate	Std. Error	z value	Pr (>|z|)
Intercept	-3.4423	0.0099	-348.07	0.0000
Toxic	0.9691	0.0114	85.38	0.0000
Semitoxic	0.3271	0.0104	31.34	0.0000

Notes: N = 63. AIC=60054. Poisson model with municipality population as an offset.

In Table 9.1, the dependent variable is the number of cases of nervous system diseases in a municipality, which is offset by the population of the municipality. Hence, each predictor speaks to the rate of nervous system diseases in the municipality. There are two predictors—an indicator for a toxic mine in the municipality and an indicator for a semitoxic mine in the municipality. These are coded exclusively, so the reference group is for a municipality to have no mining activity at all. The positive and significant coefficients for both toxic and semitoxic mining presence indicate that each have a higher rate of nervous system diseases, on average, compared to municipalities without any mining activity. Specifically, the rates in semitoxic mining areas are 39% higher than non-mining areas, and the rates in toxic mining municipalities are 164% higher than non-mining areas.[5] This statistical evidence therefore implies that the risk rates for nervous system diseases are elevated in the presence of both toxic and semitoxic mining activities.

Table 9.2 analyses the rates of blood and immune system diseases, with the same predictors and modeling form. Again, the coefficients for both the toxic and semitoxic mining indicators are positive and significant. In municipalities with a semitoxic mine, the rate of these diseases is 15% higher, on average, than in areas with no mining. Municipalities with toxic mines have an 89% higher rate relative to areas with no mining activity, on average.[6] Hence, blood and immune system diseases also appear to have elevated risk rates in areas with both toxic and semitoxic mining.

Table 9.2 Blood and Immune System Disease Rates in 63 Georgia Municipalities

Parameter	Estimate	Std. Error	z value	Pr (>|z|)
Intercept	-4.3994	0.0160	-275.66	0.0000
Toxic	0.6391	0.0192	33.36	0.0000
Semitoxic	0.1375	0.0170	8.08	0.0000

Notes: N = 63. AIC=12665. Poisson model with municipality population as an offset.

Table 9.3, finally, applies the same modeling approach to analyze COPD rates. In this case, municipalities with a semitoxic mine actually have lower rates of COPD on average relative to those with no mining at all. The rate is 32% lower for semitoxic mining

---

5   These ratios are computed based on the count ratios of exp(.3271)=1.39 and exp(.9691)=2.64 for semitoxic and toxic mines, respectively.
6   These ratios are computed based on the count ratios of exp(.1375)=1.15 and exp(.6391)=1.89 for semitoxic and toxic mines, respectively.

municipalities than it is for non-mining municipalities. Areas with toxic mines, however, do have the highest rates of COPD of all. Relative to non-mining areas, the rate of COPD is 29% higher on average in municipalities with a toxic mine.[7] For COPD, as well as coronary circulation diseases (reported in the appendix), municipalities with a toxic mine have the highest rate, followed by non-mining areas, and finally semitoxic mining areas.

Table 9.3   COPD Rates in 63 Georgia Municipalities

Parameter	Estimate	Std. Error	z value	Pr (>|z|)
Intercept	-4.8755	0.0202	-240.78	0.0000
Toxic	0.2575	0.0260	9.91	0.0000
Semitoxic	-0.3845	0.0225	-17.11	0.0000

Notes: N = 63. AIC=6750. Poisson model with municipality population as an offset.

Conclusion

An intriguing finding of this study is that several diseases appear to be less prominent in mining areas than in non-mining areas. Again, all eleven diseases studied in the chapter are more common in toxic mining areas than in semitoxic areas, but for six of these diseases the incidence rates were actually highest in non-mining areas. The rates of endocrine, digestive, urinary, diarrheal, and respiratory diseases are higher near toxic mining areas than semitoxic ones. But a subject for further research is the finding that in the non-mining areas the rates of these diseases are higher relative to both toxic and semitoxic areas. Particularly important is the finding that there is a similar result regarding oncological diseases. Proximity to a toxic mining site does not affect the rate of cancer relative to non-mining sites, and the rates are lowest near semitoxic mines. This would suggest that heavy metals and polluted air from mining are

---

7   These ratios are computed based on the count ratios of exp(-.3845)=0.68 and exp(.2575)=1.29 for semitoxic and toxic mines, respectively.

not the main factors in the increasing numbers of cancer cases in Georgia.

What I do find is, as expected, that there are higher rates of blood, immune system, and nervous system diseases close to toxic mining sites. This offers evidence that mining activities do affect public health in Georgia. Analysis of the ground and water near toxic and semitoxic mines shows elevated exposure of heavy metals, and heavy metal exposure can increase the risks of these kinds of diseases (Jan et al., 2015). From a public health perspective, then, safety concerns from mining might first focus on limiting exposure to heavy metals in hopes of reducing these disease rates.

References

Avkopashvili, Guranda, Avkopashvili, Marika, Gognadze, Alexander, and Gakhokidze, Ramaz. 2017. "Eco-Monitoring of Georgia's Contaminated Soil and Water with Heavy Metals." *Carpathian Journal of Earth and Environmental Sciences* 12(2): 595-604.

CENN. 2016. *Environmental and Socio-Economic Implications of the Mining Sector and Prospects of Responsible Mining in Georgia*. Caucasus Environmental NGO Network. Available at www.cenn.org.

Coelho, Patricia C.S., Teixeira, João Paulo F., and Gonçalves, O. 2011. "Mining Activities: Health Impacts." *Encyclopedia of Environmental Health* 788-802.

Hanauer, Thomas, Felix-Henningsen, Peter, Steffens, Diedrich, Kalandadze, Besik, Navrozashvili, Levan, and Urushadze, Tengiz. 2011. "In Situ Stabilization of Metals (Cu, Cd, and Zn) in Contaminated Soils in the Region of Bolnisi, Georgia." *Plant Soil* 341: 193-208.

Hendryx, Michael. 2008. "Mortality Rates in Appalachian Coal Mining Counties: 24 Years Behind the Nation." *Environmental Justice* 1(1): 5-11.

Hendryx, Michael, and Ahern, Melissa M. 2008. "Relations Between Health Indicators and Residential Proximity to Coal Mining in West Virginia." *American Journal of Public Health* 98(4): 669-671.

Hendryx, Michael, and Entwhistle, Jennifer. 2015. "Association Between Residence Near Surface Coal Mining and Blood Inflammation." *The Extractive Industries and Society* 2(2): 246-251.

International Atomic Energy Agency. 2005. *Guidebook on Environmental Impact Assessment for In Situ Leach Mining Projects*. Vienna: International Atomic Energy Agency.

Jan, Arif Tasleem, Azam, Mudsser, Siddiqui, Kehkashan, Ali, Arif, Choi, Inho, Mohd, Qazi, and Haq, Rizwanul. 2015. "Heavy Metals and Human Health: Mechanistic Insight into Toxicity and Counter Defense System of Antioxidants." *International Journal of Molecular Sciences* 16: 29592-29630.

Legislative Herald of Georgia. 2018. *Georgian Law about Mines (1996, with amendments in 2005 and 2013).* Document number 242. Available at https://matsne.gov.ge/en/document/view/33040.

Miranda, Marta, Blanco-Uribe, Alberto Q., Hernández, Lionel, Ochoa, José G., and Yerena, Edgard. 1998. *All That Glitters Is Not Gold: Balancing Conservation and Development in Venezuela's Frontier Forests.* Washington, DC: World Resources Institute.

Pyatt, F.B., and Grattan, J.P. 2001. "Some Consequences of Ancient Mining Activities on the Health of Ancient and Modern Human Populations." *Journal of Public Health Medicine* 23(3): 235-236.

Shavlishvili, L., Bakradze, E., Arabidze, M., and Kuchava, G. 2017. "Arsenic Pollution Study of the Rivers and Soils in Some of the Regions of Georgia." *International Journal of Current Research* 9(2): 47002-47008.

Timoney, Kevin P., and Lee, Peter. 2009. "Does the Alberta Tar Sands Industry Pollute? The Scientific Evidence." *The Open Conservation Biology Journal* 3: 65-81.

Appendix

Additional Background on Environmental Policy

Two major sources of environmental policy mandates are important to consider on the topic of mining regulations in Georgia. After Georgia signed an Association Agreement with the EU in 2014, which entered into force since July 1, 2016 — the first source is related to legislation stipulating that all companies must improve the quality and standards of their products and activities.

Second source is the Constitution of Georgia mandating that environmental protection and human health must be a priority. Article 37, states the following (Constitutional Law of Georgia No 3710 of 15 October 2010 - LHG I, No 62, 5.11.2010, Art. 379):

"3. Everyone shall have the right to live in a healthy environment and to use the natural and cultural environment. Everyone shall be obliged to protect the natural and cultural environment."

"4. Taking into account the interests of current and future generations, the State shall guarantee environmental protection and rational use of nature in order to ensure a safe environment for human health and maintain sustainable development of the country in line with the ecological and economic interests of society."

"5. Everyone shall have the right to complete, objective, and timely information about environmental conditions."

Additional Models for Disease Rates

Table A9.1 Hypertension Rates in 63 Georgia Municipalities

Parameter	Estimate	Std. Error	z value	Pr (>|z|)
Intercept	-2.8718	0.0074	-386.2360	0.0000
Toxic	0.9848	0.0085	115.6265	0.0000
Semitoxic	0.1266	0.0079	15.9601	0.0000

Notes: N = 63. AIC=59472. Poisson model with municipality population as an offset.

This appendix presents the results of models of eight diseases that were not reported in the main text of the paper. Tables A.1-A.8 present Poisson models of municipality-level disease rates that are just like those of the main text, including municipality population as an offset. As mentioned before, in all eight models, the disease rate is higher for the municipalities with toxic mines than it is for semitoxic mines. In Table A.1, we see that hypertension rates are higher in both toxic and in semitoxic mining areas than in areas with neither kind of mine. In Table A.2, we see that toxic mining areas have the highest rates of coronary and circulation diseases. However, semitoxic mining areas actually have lower rates than municipalities with no mining at all.

In Tables A.3 and A.4, we see that toxic mining areas show no significant differences from non-mining areas in terms of cancer rates or respiratory disease rates. However, both areas have higher rates of these diseases than municipalities with semitoxic mines, as the negative and significant coefficient for the *semitoxic* dummy indicates. Finally, in Tables A.5-A.8, we see negative and significant coefficients in each table for both the *toxic* and the *semitoxic* dummies. This means that areas with no mining at all actually have higher rates of infectious diarrhea, urinary system diseases, digestive system diseases, and endocrine system diseases. Note, though, that in each case there is a stronger negative effect for the *semitoxic* dummy, meaning that the rates of these diseases are still higher in toxic municipalities than in semitoxic municipalities.

Table A9.2 Coronary and Circulation Disease Rates in 63 Georgia Municipalities

Parameter	Estimate	Std. Error	z value	Pr (>|z|)
Intercept	-1.5391	0.0038	-403.0508	0.0000
Toxic	0.5795	0.0046	125.2449	0.0000
Semitoxic	-0.1683	0.0042	-40.3869	0.0000

Notes: N = 63. AIC=169782. Poisson model with municipality population as an offset.

Table A9.3 Cancer Rates in 63 Georgia Municipalities

Parameter	Estimate	Std. Error	z value	Pr (>|z|)
Intercept	-6.0548	0.0365	-165.8162	0.0000
Toxic	-0.0332	0.0499	-0.6658	0.5055
Semitoxic	-0.1603	0.0399	-4.0173	0.0001

Notes: N = 63. AIC=883. Poisson model with municipality population as an offset.

Table A9.4 Respiratory Disease Rates in 63 Georgia Municipalities

Parameter	Estimate	Std. Error	z value	Pr (>|z|)
Intercept	-0.8900	0.0028	-322.4257	0.0000
Toxic	-0.0035	0.0037	-0.9468	0.3437
Semitoxic	-0.1087	0.0030	-36.3283	0.0000

Notes: N = 63. AIC=212379. Poisson model with municipality population as an offset.

Table A9.5 Infectious Diarrhea Disease Rates in 63 Georgia Municipalities

Parameter	Estimate	Std. Error	z value	Pr (>|z|)
Intercept	-3.3172	0.0093	-357.0717	0.0000
Toxic	-1.2434	0.0183	-67.7900	0.0000
Semitoxic	-2.2125	0.0147	-150.2292	0.0000

Notes: N = 63. AIC=18481. Poisson model with municipality population as an offset.

Table A9.6 Urinary System Disease Rates in 63 Georgia Municipalities

Parameter	Estimate	Std. Error	z value	Pr (>|z|)
Intercept	-1.9484	0.0047	-415.8071	0.0000
Toxic	-0.3331	0.0069	-48.2985	0.0000
Semitoxic	-0.7147	0.0054	-132.6387	0.0000

Notes: N = 63. AIC=73023. Poisson model with municipality population as an offset.

Table A9.7 Digestive System Disease Rates in 63 Georgia Municipalities

Parameter	Estimate	Std. Error	z value	Pr (>|z|)
Intercept	-0.9168	0.0028	-327.7097	0.0000
Toxic	-0.1082	0.0039	-27.8304	0.0000
Semitoxic	-1.4838	0.0036	-407.3064	0.0000

Notes: N = 63. AIC=311958. Poisson model with municipality population as an offset.

Table A9.8 Endochrine System Disease Rates in 63 Georgia Municipalities

Parameter	Estimate	Std. Error	z value	Pr (>|z|)
Intercept	-2.0340	0.0049	-415.8886	0.0000
Toxic	-0.1503	0.0069	-21.8873	0.0000
Semitoxic	-0.6109	0.0056	-109.9492	0.0000

Notes: N = 63. AIC=78165. Poisson model with municipality population as an offset.

Part III

Georgia in the Context of Post-Soviet Transitions

10
Centralized versus Decentralized Human Resource Practices: The Cases of Georgia and Estonia

Sabina Alakbarova

Most governments around the world are constantly working to improve the performance of public sector organizations. Often, these efforts focus on reforms of the civil service. These endeavors began to receive considerable attention in the late 1970s when public employers and citizens came to believe that government was excessively bureaucratic and had become unresponsive and ineffective. In the United States, the Civil Service Reform Act of 1978 was a response to these concerns. In the 1980s and 90s, similar reforms designed to augment the flexibility of government managers and make government more efficient and more business-like were increasingly common (Pollitt and Bouckaert, 2017). These reforms were collectively known as the New Public Management (NPM), but some observers saw them as a neo-Taylorian approach to public management that "took no account of the distinctive properties of public sector organizations" (Hood, 1999). Nevertheless, public management reforms have remained a priority in political arenas into the Twenty First Century and have spread to numerous countries.

A central focus of the NPM was a drive for efficiency. There was an emphasis on financial control and enhancing financial accountability, increased power and flexibility for senior management, a concern for performance and the quality of services, the adoption of market-based approaches to public sector work including the implementation of pay for performance and contracting out many functions to the private sector, and a push to downsize and decentralize public organizations (Ferlie at al., 1996; Pollitt and Bouckaert, 2017).

In terms of civil service structure, this last concern led to expansive delegations of authority to line agencies and bureaus and away from government-wide centralization of human resources management policy. This poses an interesting dilemma. On one hand, civil service systems are built on the promulgation and enforcement of rules that structure hiring, promotion, compensation, and employee disciplinary processes. A central authority may be seen as necessary to ensure uniform compliance with these rules. On the other hand, however, centralized oversight can lead to bureaucratic delays and inefficiencies. The purpose of this chapter is to examine more closely the concepts of centralization and decentralization of authority for the operation of human resources policy within civil service systems. To this end, the research question of this study is: How do different degrees of human resources (HR) system centralization of recruitment and selection of public employees in the countries of Georgia and Estonia affect employee turnover?

One may ask, why study Georgia and Estonia? The answer is that these countries allow a meaningful comparison. Georgia is a democratizing former Soviet nation that overall is still highly centralized in its public administration. Estonia, like another post-Soviet nations, inherited a bureaucratic structure that was highly centralized and characterized by a top-down management system. But in contrast to Georgia, Estonia started decentralization reforms in the public sector at the time of its independence and has made tremendous progress in achieving the decentralization of government administration. Thus, Estonia is considered to have highly decentralized HR practices while Georgia's practices remain highly centralized. Consequently, this study focuses on two countries with similar backgrounds but different human resource management (HRM) systems. The objective is to see if employee turnover is lower in a system of recruitment and selection that is more decentralized than one that is centralized.

In this chapter, I first describe the theoretical background on HR practices, as established by the literature on this subject. Second, I contrast the HR practices in Georgia and Estonia, and, third,

I analyze empirical evidence about how hiring practices relate to turnover.

Theoretical Background

A centralized personnel system, in general, is defined as one in which central-government bodies, including central HR agencies, control the decision-making processes regarding personnel management activities associated with recruitment and selection. In centralized recruitment and selection, central HR units are responsible for testing applicants, placing announcements, and identifying small groups of applicants for further consideration. In a decentralized system, by contrast, the involvement of a government-wide operating body, or central HR agency, is substantially reduced, and responsibilities are shared with separate government departments or agencies. Decentralized recruitment and selection of government employees is done by allowing most of the needed procedures to take place within the organizations seeking to fill the position, therein giving managers in those organizations more flexibility in controlling the recruitment and selection process.

Meanwhile, recruitment itself is defined by the literature as a process of finding potentially qualified applicants for announced vacancies and enticing them to apply for jobs. Selection is the process where applicants are evaluated and interviewed for the specific jobs they have applied for and are ultimately chosen based on specified criteria. Employee turnover is defined by scholars as the rotation of employees among organizations, among jobs and occupations, and between the employment and unemployment conditions. In short, it occurs when employees leave their jobs. Again, the objective of this study is to compare the centralized and decentralized recruitment and selection processes in Estonian and Georgian public organizations and to assess which system has the higher rate of employee turnover.

So what does past research say about centralized versus decentralized hiring practices and why can that matter for employee turnover rates? One of the primary aims of administrative decentralization is to "let managers manage." The assumption is that the centralization of authority will deprive line managers of necessary flexibility in decision-making and in solving emerging problems. During the last three decades, many governments implemented practices designed to enhance managerial flexibility and offer line managers the freedom to decide what should be done in particular situations (Brewer and Kellough, 2016; Meyer and Hammerschmid 2010; Brewer, 2000; Pollitt and Bouckaert, 2011). These changes were part of the wave of NPM reforms, which were believed to improve public organizations' abilities to hire, manage, and retain civil servants. However, "as agency and managerial discretion increases and there is an absence of centralized oversight, opportunities for inconsistent or egregious personnel decisions will also increase" (Brewer and Kellough, 2016, 10).

In a centralized approach, the power is usually given to a Central Personnel Agency (CPA), which directs the HR system's policy decisions and implementation. Delegations of HR functions to separate agencies and their line managers is often limited (Tesemma et al., 2009). The focus is on centralized control and consistency in the treatment of job applicants and employees.

Some countries use a hybrid approach in delegating HR practices; hence, some of the HR functions are centralized and some decentralized. Strikwerda (2005) argues that centralized shared services might enhance the efficiency of the HR system without any negative effect on the responsiveness of the HR system. He also said that the central organization in this approach might have an influence on setting HR strategies and general policies but allows organizational actions to be done independently by relevant entities. According to Tesemma et al. (2009), civil service decentralization is not a panacea to improve the impact of HR practices, especially if decentralization of HR policies is not well administered. Shared or hybrid kinds of reforms are designed in many countries with the aim "to make refinements to personnel systems and processes, so that essential personnel management activities are performed more adequately" (Kellough et al., 2010, 407).

In general, however, reforms in public personnel management have focused on shifting from more centralized approaches towards more decentralized systems with the aim of increasing managerial flexibility to meet specific organizational needs. The primary reason for changing the centralized system is its perceived inefficiency (Kellough et al., 2010). But, on the other hand, centralized HR systems ensure the protection of employees against political abuse and coercion by ensuring administrative oversight of agency actions. It also contributes to fairness in equal treatment of employees and can ensure greater effectiveness because qualified HR experts are dealing with the evaluation and ranking job candidates (Coggburn, 2005; Meyer and Hammerschmid, 2010).

A decentralized approach with no central coordination mechanisms may cause conflicts among various government departments dealing with HR issues (Meyer and Hammerschmid, 2010). But Coggburn (2005) also claims that decentralized HR systems are believed to give flexibility and responsiveness required for effective management. Proponents of decentralized HRM argue that in this approach: 1) decisions can be faster, 2) recruitment can be less complicated, and 3) recruitment can be customized to the particular requirements of an organization (Meyer and Hammerschmid, 2010; Coggburn 2005). Nevertheless, decentralization to a high degree is considered to be dangerous because it may decrease professionalism in the public service and cause "fragmentation of policies from a strategic point of view" (Meyer and Hammerschmid, 2010, 457).

The effectiveness of centralized and decentralized recruitment and selection systems for public employees is evaluated here by examining variation in turnover of employees in contrasting systems. Hiring the right people and training them is one of the most vital tasks of any HRM structure. If the right persons are hired, they usually stay longer in the organization and perform their jobs effectively. Turnover will be reduced as a result. Therefore, selection and recruitment criteria should recognize the importance of a candidate's potential commitment to the organization. To avoid the high cost of turnover, managers must maintain an expert workforce with a consistent strategic vision. One of the costliest outcomes of poor management of recruitment and selection processes in an organization is high employee turnover. Managers who recruit and select the right people are likely to help organizations to avoid a high level of turnover, and managers in specific individual organizations are most likely to accomplish that task. To this extent, the decentralization of recruitment and selection processes should be associated with lower rates of turnover.

But in countries such as Georgia, where many administrative and political problems are still to be addressed, questions of nepotism, political influence, and corruption are still big issues. In this context, the decentralization of human resource practices, especially in hiring public employees, may not be the best solution. In such a context, the decentralization of recruitment may further increase corruption (Prud'Homme, 1995) and may also create inequality, favoritism, nepotism, and a lack of coordination in administrative processes (Wang et al., 2002). In essence, in some countries, effective recruitment and selection requires a robust central mechanism. According to Tesemma et al. (2009), the decentralization of human resource practices without serious control procedures is likely to stimulate nepotism and favoritism. In addition, decentralized systems are also seen as producing quicker results compared to more centralized systems. But as Kolehmainen-Aitken (2004) pointed out, decentralized recruitment can lead to an unequal distribution of high-quality employees across agencies, and decentralized approaches may lead to the growth of nepotism, favoritism, patronage, corruption, and inequality in the treatment of employees (for example, Berman et al., 2012, Parrado-Diez, 1997).

In the case of Georgia, the centralized system of recruitment may solve problems of inequality, corruption, nepotism, and favoritism. In 2014, Georgia initiated reforms in the field of public sector HRM, and a Civil Service Bureau (CSB) was established with primary authority over the recruitment and selection of public servants. The announcement of vacancies, the gathering applications, job analysis, and selection are all the responsibility of the Georgian CSB. This centralized approach is widely believed to have the advantage of offering protection against political coercion of employees. HR experts who are dealing with recruitment and selection processes within a centralized approach can work to ensure equal treatment of employees (Coggburn, 2005), achieve standardization in the application of HR practices, control the distribution of wages and salaries, and enhance national integration (Green, 2005).

But on the other hand, there are disadvantages to a centralized system. In the centralized approach, applicants must pass a standardized set of examinations, which may not be specific enough for separate and distinct organizations. For example, if an agency is seeking an employee with highly specialized skills unique to that agency, additional specific testing may be needed beyond that given by the central personnel authority to show the level of knowledge of the applicant in the designated field. Central HR bodies, especially in less developed countries, are not likely to have staff who can tailor HR procedures to the needs of specific government agencies (Tesemma et al., 2009).

Contrasting Processes in Georgia and Estonia

Estonia, like Georgia, has witnessed numerous major political and administrative reforms since 1991. While Estonia and Georgia gained independence from the Soviet Union in the same year (1991), the countries implemented different political and administrative changes since then. Estonia has been a Member State of the European Union since May 1, 2004. Georgia also emerged after the collapse of the Soviet Empire with promises of quick reforms, and while several administrative and economic reforms have been implemented, those reforms did not go as far as the reforms in Estonia. With the support of the European Union and other international organizations, Estonia achieved major political, economic, and administrative reforms. In Georgia's case, economic collapse, civil war, and Russian occupation of breakaway regions, have been significant obstacles for the development of the newly born country.

During the past two decades, all government units in Estonia have implemented structural reforms, which led to changes in the administrative systems and coordination mechanisms within those systems (Randma-Liiv et al., 2015). The Cabinet of Ministers is the highest coordinating power in Estonia. In Estonia the segmented administrative structure ensured a sharing of responsibility among ministries. Notwithstanding that ministries in Estonia are relatively small, they function as strong administrative bodies to deal with all issues in their areas of responsibility. Even though there have been several attempts towards the reinforcement of central coordination, they were unsuccessful and eventually failed.

Since 2003, Georgia started down the complicated road of conversion to a wholly developed democracy and free market economy. Though many challenges remain to be overcome, during the last two decades Georgia has achieved significant advancements in indicators of good governance (UNDP, 2015). The first law on civil service adopted by Georgia aimed to reform the civil service system through the development of a somewhat more decentralized management structure where power would be shared among ministers and other public administration entities. But in comparison with the Estonian fragmented administrative system, Georgian government created a central Civil Service Bureau (the CSB) to guide the implementation of the civil service reform concept across all public administration levels. Ironically, after the implementation of this law, the civil service system in Georgia became a highly centralized structure (Shundi and Mikelsons, 2014).

A survey conducted by the Georgian CSB of HR managers in 2011 shows that 50% of those practitioners confirmed the fact that their institutions followed HRM strategies mandated by the CSB. According to the survey, only 10 of 21 government departments have their own HRM policies defining strategic HRM directions and goals (Civil Service Bureau of Georgia, 2011). The CSB of Georgia was given the responsibility for ensuring the implementation of all established HR regulations in public institutions across the country (Shundi and Mikelsons, 2014).

Estonia decentralized HRM practices to separate Ministries and their manages to a very large degree immediately after independence. In fact, they went farther on this score than any other OECD country. The central HRM body focuses only on issuing legal framework guidelines. The administration of all issues concerning recruitment, pay, dismissal, and selection is the responsibility of separate government departments. In general, the delegation has produced a widely comparable employment framework within departments, but there are significant discrepancies across them (OECD, Estonia 2012). Estonia practices a position-based recruitment system, which is highly decentralized. All vacancies are published by the departments in which they occur, and those announcements are available for external and internal recruitment. To gain entry to public service, individuals apply via direct application and interview for specific positions in distinct departments, with entry feasible at all levels, even the highest (OECD, Estonia 2012).

In comparison with Estonia, Georgia utilizes a much more centralized HR system. According to Shundi and Mikelsons (2014), there are two stages in the employee selection process. In the first stage, the CSB is responsible for recruitment and initial assessment of a candidate's general skills and knowledge. This process is referred to as "Certification." The CSB is also responsible for the publication of the vacancies as well as organization and implementation of the recruitment processes. In the second stage, line institutions organize specific competitions for the vacancy, applying rules and standards, which are issued by the CSB. Generally, "the Law requires that procedures for the competitive process assess the candidate against the requirements of the position, ensure equal access for Georgian nationals, and be transparent in decision making on the selection of candidates and the making of appointments" (Article 4, Law of Georgia on Civil Service). The CSB in Georgia also has been given a new function called "waiting list management" involving control of a list of applicants deemed qualified by the CSB who are waiting for appointment (Shundi and Mikelsons, 2014). This is another example of a significant shift in HR practices in Georgia toward centralization.

Empirical Evaluation

Turning to the empirical comparison of these two countries, I proceed in two parts. First, I evaluate empirically how centralized or decentralized recruitment and examination procedures are in each country. For this analysis, data were collected by reviewing the Public Service statutes of Estonia and Georgia and by examining internal documents and reports of the Ministry of Education, Science, Culture and Sport of Georgia and the Ministry of Justice of Estonia. The objective was to determine how exactly recruitment and selection are done and by whom. I also conducted interviews to collect supplemental information. Second, I examine employee turnover in these two organizations. For this, I collected archived data on turnover from each country.

Centralization and decentralization of HR practices are concepts that can be hard to measure empirically (Donoghue and Castle, 2006). Coggburn argued that: "systematic inquiry into personnel deregulation has been impeded by lack of a dependent variable that measures the concept across units of government" (2001, 229). The core of the problem is that these concepts are not dichotomous, but rather, are largely present to a matter of degree. Therefore, to measure the level of centralization versus decentralization, I conducted semi-structured interviews with public managers in each country. In particular, I sought to determine through these interviews the extent of involvement of different actors such as those in central personnel agencies as well as managers from separate government departments. The interview questions addressed the extent to which managers from these different administrative locations in each country were involved in recruitment and selection processes and the effect of various degrees of centralization on the selection outcomes. The use of semi-structured interviews provided a coherent framework for discussion and allowed for clarification and follow-up questions (May 2011, 123; Johnson 2002, 90-91). Ten civil servants in various positions in the Ministry of Education, Science, Culture, and Sport of Georgia and in the Estonian Ministry of Education and Research were interviewed. Interviewees were asked how different degrees of centralization would influence recruitment and selection in each country.

Interview results in Estonia confirm that representatives of each separate department of government are usually highly involved in recruitment and selection processes. These interviews, conducted in the Estonian Ministry of Justice, show that central actors from each separate division of government have great responsibility in hiring processes. Importantly, there is only minor involvement of experts from the central government HR organization.

By contrast, in Georgia, HR managers and other representatives of the Ministry of Education, Science, Culture, and Sport of

Georgia indicated that recruitment and selection processes are controlled almost entirely by the Civil Service Bureau of Georgia (CSB). Final selection decisions are made by a board, which includes representatives of the CSB, the department that announced the position, independent experts, and a representative of the top administration level of the ministry. Furthermore, in the case of Georgia, responsibilities are rarely given to line management or lower hierarchical levels.

In sum, interview results verified that, in Estonia, the recruitment and selection of employees is segmented and decentralized. In the case of Georgia, recruitment and selection processes are highly centralized. In both countries, independent experts are usually invited during the selection (especially examination) processes, but the respondents marked their involvement as minor.

Since the interviews show such a clear contrast in hiring procedures, what does this mean for the issue of employee turnover? I gathered both voluntary and total turnover data from the ministries mentioned above in Estonia and Georgia. The Ministry of Justice in Estonia provided these numbers for 11 years from 2008-2018. For the Ministry of Education, Science, Culture, and Sport of Georgia, I received data for four years from 2014-2017. Figure 10.1 shows the total turnover rates (measured as the percentage of employees who leave employment) in these two government ministries. The horizontal axis represents each year, while the vertical axis represents the total turnover. The dashed line with triangle characters represents Georgia's Ministry of Education, Science, Culture, and Sport. The solid line with circle characters represents Estonia's Ministry of Justice.

As can be seen in Figure 10.1, Georgia's Ministry had an enormous 72% turnover rate in 2014. Fortunately, this dropped considerably over the four years observed to 39% in 2017. In contrast, the employee turnover rate in the Ministry of Justice of Estonia is consistently lower. Although it peaked in 2017 with a value of 37%, at no other time in this decade did Estonia's turnover exceed 24%. Thus, Georgia's Ministry of Education, Science, Culture, and Sport of Georgia experienced very high total turnover, but saw a significant decrease in that rate, while Estonia's Ministry of Justice consistently did a better job of retaining employees across the board.

Figure 10.1 Total Turnover Rates at Example Ministries in Georgia and Estonia

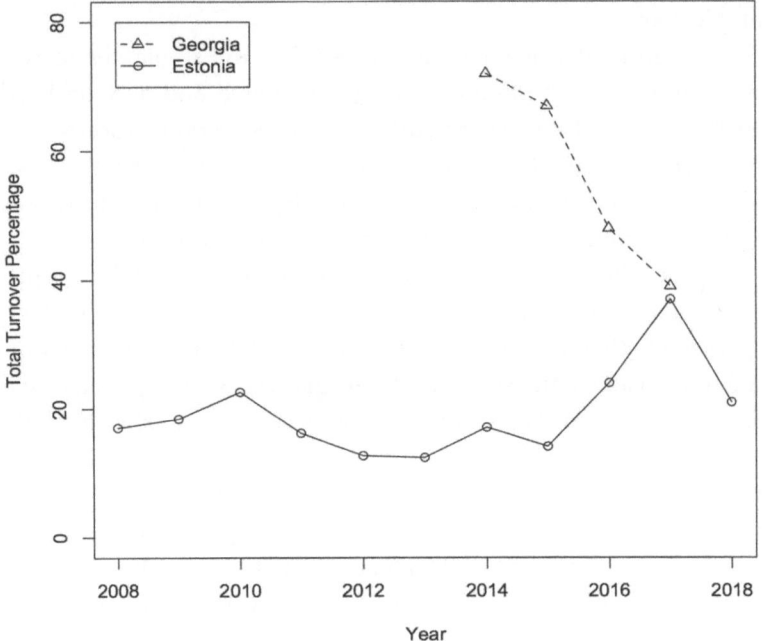

Turning to *voluntary* turnover, Figure 10.2 presents these rates by year. The vertical axis again presents the turnover rate, but note that the maximum on this scale is much lower than in the previous figure because voluntary turnover is just a portion of total turnover. The horizontal axis again represents years; Georgia again is represented with a dashed line, and Estonia is again represented with a solid line. While voluntary turnover is a much smaller part of turnover, presumably HR practices can have more of an impact in this area. The Ministry of Culture, Science, Sport, and Education of Georgia is at a high level of 37% in 2014 and 2015, and then it drops noticeably to 30% in 2016 and 31% in 2017. Meanwhile, the Ministry of Justice of Estonia peaked at 16.2% in 2011 and generally stays much lower. Examining the figures together, then it appears that both total and voluntary turnover rates are significantly higher in Georgia than in Estonia.

Figure 10.2 Voluntary Turnover Rates at Example Ministries in Georgia and Estonia

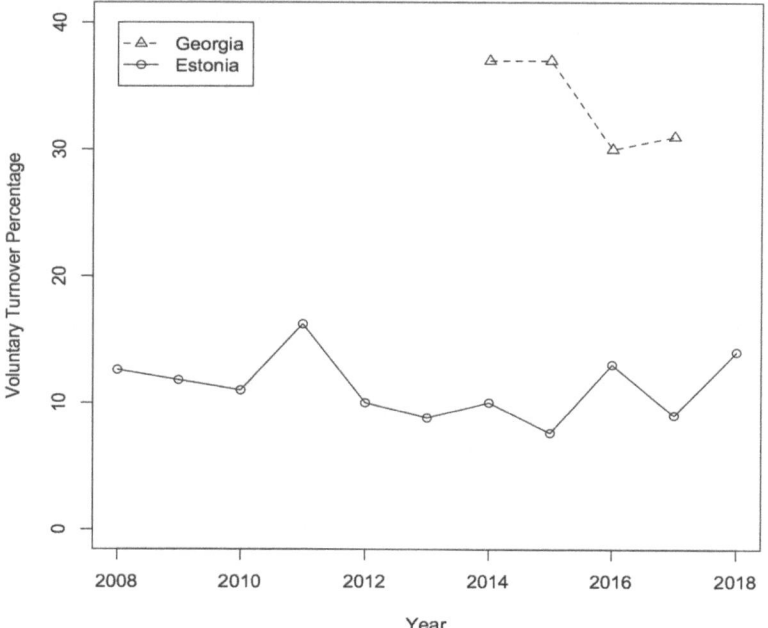

Conclusion

The goal of this study was to analyze the extent to which HR recruitment and selection practices are decentralized or centralized in Estonian and Georgian public organizations and to relate those patterns to public employee turnover. The study found out that in Estonia HR practices are highly decentralized. Recruitment and selection processes in Estonia's public sector are segmented; that is to say, each public organization is responsible for hiring its own employees. Typically, the period of time required for recruitment and selection processes to operate is not more than one month. In the case of Georgia, the recruitment and selection processes are considerably more centralized. In Georgia, the selection of employees is done by representatives of the central HR unit. In general, this chapter furthers the notion that the degree of centralization or decentralization reflects the involvement of multiple actors in the decision-making processes. Decentralization of decision-making is mostly delegation of authority to separate government organizations.

The Estonian public sector achieved a consistently lower level of employee total turnover compared to Georgia. With two cases, it is hard to isolate why exactly these turnover rates are so different, as many internal and external factors could be relevant to these differences. The different types of work in the two agencies may account for some of the difference. But, the contrast is so striking that one may question if the decentralized approach in Estonia finds employees who fit well with their organizations and as a result are less likely than the Georgian counterparts to leave their jobs.

A high turnover rate creates problems for organizations, such as higher recruitment, selection, and training costs. Managers must remember that employees are the major drivers of effective achievement of organizational goals. If employees are leaving an organization frequently, it will not only create financial problems for the organization but will also affect organizational performance. To this end, the government of Georgia may want to consider reforming the public sector recruitment and selection by decentralizing the process with the goal of reducing employee turnover. As a potential solution, however, decentralization often comes with negative consequences such as corruption, favoritism, and imbalances in staff quality. But if the Georgian government can prevent these issues in other ways, such as by giving separate government departments greater authority in recruitment and selection, there may well be a set of decentralization strategies worth considering for improving employee retention.

References

Article 4. 2018. "Competition Purposes and Tasks, Procedure for Conduct of an Open Competition as Prescribed by the Law of Georgia on Civil Service."

Berman, E.M., Bowman, J.S., West, J.P., and Van Wart, M.R. 2012. *Human Resource Management in Public Service: Paradoxes, Processes, and Problems*. Atlanta, GA: Sage.

Brewer, G.A. 2000. "Administrative Reform and Organizational Change in the Public Sector." *Democracy Project* AP 24/2000. Copenhagen, Denmark: University of Copenhagen.

Brewer, G.A., and Kellough, J.E. 2016. "Administrative Values and Public Personnel Management: Reflections on Civil Service Reform." *Public Personnel Management* 45(2): 171-189.

Civil Service Bureau of Georgia. 2011. "Survey on HRM Systems in the Civil Service Agencies." Civil Service reform and Development Department, Georgia.

Coggburn, J.D. 2001. "Personnel Deregulation: Exploring Differences in the American States." *Journal of Public Administration Research and Theory* 11(2): 223-44.

Coggburn, J.D. 2005. "The Benefits of Human Resource Centralization: Insights from a Survey of Human Resource Directors in a Decentralized State." *Public Administration Review* 65(4): 424-35.

Donoghue, C., and Castle, N.G. 2006. "Voluntary and Involuntary Nursing Home Staff Turnover." *Research on Aging* 28: 454-472.

Ferlie, E., Ashbumer, L., Fitzgerald, L., and Pettigrew, A. 1996. *New Public Management in Action* New York, NY: Oxford University Press.

Green, A. 2005. "Managing Human Resources in a Decentralized Context." In *East Asia Decentralizes: Making Local Governments Work*. Washington, DC: The World Bank.

Hood, C. .1999. "Public Service Bargains and Public Service Reform." *Working Paper, ECPR Joint Meetings*.

Johnson, G. 2002. *Research Methods for Public Administrators*. Westport, CT: Quorum Books.

Kellough, J.E., Nigro, G.L., and Brewer, G.A. 2010. "Civil Service Reform Under George W. Bush: Ideology, Politics, and Public Personnel Administration." *Review of Public Personnel Administration* 30(4): 404-422.

Kolehmainen-Aitken, R. 2004. "Decentralization and Human Resources: Implications and Impact." *Human Resources for Health* 2(5): 1-29.

May, T. 2011. *Social Research: Issues, Methods and Process*. 4th eds. Philadelphia, PA: Open University Press.

Meyer, E., and Hammerschmid, G. 2010. "The Degree of Decentralisation and Individual Decision Making in Central Government Human Resource Management: a European Comparative Perspective." *Public Administration* 88(2): 455-478.

OECD. 2012. "Human Resource Country Profile, Estonia."

Parrado-Díez, S. 1997. "Staffing and Human Resources Flexibilities in the Spanish Public Services." *Review of Public Personnel Administration* 17(3): 46-56.

Pollitt, C., and Bouckaert, G. 2011. *Public Management Reform: A Comparative Analysis: New Public Management, Governance, and the Neo-Weberian State*. 3rd eds. New York, NY: Oxford University Press.

Pollitt, C., and Bouckaert, G. 2017. *Public Management Reform: A Comparative Analysis-Into the Age of Austerity*. New York, NY: Oxford University Press.

Prud'Homme, R. 1995. "The Dangers of Decentralization." *The World Bank Research Observer* 10(2): 201-220.

Randma-Liiv, T., Uudelepp, A., and Sarapuu, K. 2015. "From Network to Hierarchy: The Evolution of the Estonian Senior Civil Service Development System." *International Review of Administrative Sciences* 81(2): 373-391.

Shundi, A., and Mikelsons, M. 2014. "Functional Review of the Civil Service Bureau in Georgia. Consultancy Assessment Report and Recommendations." USAID: Good Governance in Georgia (G3).

Strikwerda, J. 2005. "Shared Service Centers. From Cost Reduction to Value Creation." Netherlands: Van Gorcum.

Tesemma, T.T., Soeters, L.J., and Ngoma, A. 2009. "Decentralisation of HR Functions. Lessons from the Singapore Civil Service." *Review of Public Personnel Administration* 29(2): 168-188.

UNDP. 2015. "Governance Reform Fund."

Wang, Y., Collins, C., Tang, S., and Martineau, T. 2002. "Health Systems Decentralization and Human Resources Management in Low and Middle Income Countries." *Public Administration and Development* 22(5): 439-453.

11
Legal Institutions, Financial Liberalization and Financial Development in Transition Economies[1]

Ulrich Eydam
Irakli Gabriadze

The dissolution of the Soviet Union marked the breakdown of central planning in most former Soviet Union member countries and satellite states. The transition from a planned to a market-based economy required the realignment of political and economic institutions. One particularly important as well as challenging aspect of this realignment was the transformation of the system of financial intermediation. While during soviet times, banks were merely bookkeepers, after the dissolution, a system that promotes an efficient allocation of funds into investment projects had to develop. Thus, it is not surprising, that policy makers and international observers in transition economies repeatedly emphasized the important role of financial institutions and paid close attention to the process of financial development.

It is now a well-established consensus that an efficient financial system is an important determinant of economic growth and financial stability (see for example Beck, Levine, and Loayza (2000) or Loayza, Ouazad, and Ranciere (2017) for a discussion of the relevant literature), but there is ongoing debate about the role of financial structure, i.e. whether a bank-based or market-based system performs better. However, as discussed by Levine (2002), both systems are able to efficiently allocate funds into investment projects if a country has established functioning institutions. As argued

---

[1] This work was supported by the Shota Rustaveli National Science Foundation (SRNSF) [grant number: PhD-F-17-137, Project Title: The Role of Institutions in Economic Growth and Development Models (Lessons from the Post-Soviet Union Countries)].

by La Porta et al. (1998), in this context, the quality of legal institutions is particularly important. Therefore, it becomes apparent, that after the dissolution many post-Soviet transition economies were facing the challenge to reform both, their legal and financial institutions. In the study, we will focus on the determinants of financial institutions in transition economies. In particular, since most post-Soviet transition economies implemented a primarily bank-based system, the focus will be placed on bank-based financial institutions and only briefly discuss financial market institutions.

There are many reasons why the development of financial institutions in transition countries is particularly interesting. As discussed in Bonin, Hasan, and Wachtel (2012), the development was accompanied by repeated setbacks and proceeded unevenly across countries and across time. Thus, given that countries started the transformation process at about the same time, the sample is ideal to study aspects of financial development. Furthermore, as documented by Harper and McNulty (2008), compared to other transition economies, former Soviet Union member countries show a robust, below average performance in terms of financial development. While the gap has decreased since then, recently Kakhkharov and Akimov (2018), still document a substantial heterogeneity across transition countries. Finally, the high degree of foreign financial corporations is another defining feature of financial institutions in these countries. Weill (2003) argues that the entry of foreign financial institutions into markets led to a rapid increase in the development of financial sectors in transition economies that was mostly driven by the transfer of knowledge about banking practices. All the mentioned factors highlight the need to better understand the underlying determinants of financial development in transition economies.

In this chapter, we examine the development of financial institutions, which refers to all kinds of banking institutions, in transition economies. In particular, we want to shed light on the factors that determine the path of financial development and assess the relative importance of these factors in shaping it. We put particular emphasize on the interaction between financial and legal institutions. As discussed by Pistor, Raiser, and Gelfer (2000), the quality of legal institutions is an important determinant of financial development in the context of transition economies. Furthermore, as documented by Chinn and Ito (2006), legal institutions are particularly important for the effects of financial liberalization on financial development. Whereas, financial development in countries with a sound quality of legal institutions benefits from financial liberalization, in countries with poor legal institutions, this effect reverses and financial liberalization might undermine financial development.

To examine the financial institutions nexus, we use panel data for 25 former Soviet Union member and satellite states over the period 1996–2016. In the analysis we employ an index of financial development, developed by Sahay et al. (2015). Thus, in contrast to most other studies, we do not rely on single measures of financial development and can take into account several relevant dimensions of financial institutions jointly. In addition, the index also allows testing the different dimensions of financial institutions separately. In order to address the raised issues, we proceed in several steps. First, we take stock of the development process and highlight heterogeneity with respect to several indicators within the sample. Second, we examine the role of legal institutions and financial liberalization in a cross section. Third, to overcome problems with the sample size, we utilize the time dimension of the panel and conduct several panel regressions to draw an improved picture of the development process.

Overall, our results confirm the important role of legal institutions for financial development. Furthermore, we also find that financial liberalization can play an important role in this process. The descriptive statistics, as well as results of a comparison within a cross-section, point towards the important role of legal institutions and financial liberalization in explaining differences in the quality of financial institutions across the sample. Both factors are positively associated with financial institutions. The results of a fixed-effects panel estimation also suggest that the quality of legal institutions is significantly positively associated with financial development throughout the sample period. We find that the relationship between the efficiency of financial institutions and legal institutions is strong compared to other dimensions of financial development. Yet, in contrast to the cross-sectional analysis we do not find a statistically significant relationship between financial liberalization and financial development. However, when we take the interaction between legal institutions and financial liberalization explicitly into account, we find a statistically significant positive association between financial liberalization and financial development. Hence, overall our findings support the stand that a developed legal system is the prerequisite for a successful liberalization of financial markets.

Financial Development in post-Soviet Countries

The important role of financial intermediation for economic growth is widely acknowledged (see for example Levine, Loayza, and Beck (2000), or Beck and Levine (2004)). The key argument for the importance of financial system is to achieve and ensure an efficient allocation of funds into investment projects. Cihak et al. (2012), provide a brief account of the five key functions of these institutions. First, Financial Institutions help to produce and process information about investment projects and allocate the capital accordingly. Second, they play an important role in monitoring investment projects and in exerting corporate governance. Third, financial institutions enable investors to trade shares of corporations, diversify their portfolios and thereby provide the basis for an efficient risk management. Fourth, they lay the foundation for the mobilization and pooling of savings. Fifth, and more general, financial institutions ease the exchange of goods and services and provide a host of financial instruments for the private sector. Therefore, to sum up, functioning financial institutions help to overcome problems of asymmetric information, moral hazard and facilitate an efficient allocation of funds. Thus, a crucial aspect on the way to establish a stable macroeconomic environment and promote economic growth is the development of sound financial institutions.

A central question in the debate on financial development is whether a financial system that is based on financial institutions (e.g. banks) or a system that relies on financial markets (e.g. stock markets) performs better. In an early work on the question, Levine and Zervos (1998), find that both systems can promote economic growth and thus can provide an efficient allocation of funds. In a later work, Levine (2002), assesses the question in a broad cross-section of countries and argues, that there is no evidence that one of the systems is superior. This finding supports the *financial service view*, which defines the role of financial arrangements in overcoming market imperfections that impede an efficient allocation of funds. Moreover, it is argued, that the functioning of the legal system is particularly important in shaping an efficient allocation mechanism, which supports the idea of the *law and finance view* on financial systems.[2] Thus, the question of financial development is closely related to the institutional framework — in particular to the legal institutions — of a country.

The importance of legal institutions in defining and guaranteeing property rights to market participants has been stressed in the seminal paper of La Porta et al. (1998). They use a cross-section of 49 countries and examine the relationship between a country's legal origin, investor protection laws and other measures of institutional quality. Overall, they conclude that the legal origin of a country, i.e. whether a country has a *common law* or *civil law* legal system, is a good predictor for the development of a countries financial sector.[3] In La Porta et al. (2000), they argue that the law and finance view has direct implications for financial sector reforms. According to their discussion, increasing investor protection or more general property rights has a good potential to boost financial development.[4] For a more general overview on the relationship between

---

2 Note that, as argued by Levine (2002), the *financial service view* is in principle consistent with both, the market-based and bank-based views on financial structure. Furthermore, the law and finance view on financial systems can be regarded as a special case of the financial service view.
3 Common law refers to the legal code mostly implemented in Anglo-Saxon countries. There are different traditions in civil law, conditional on the origin of the legal code, La Porta et al. (1998), differentiate between German, Scandinavian and French legal origin.
4 A detailed discussion of the law and economics nexus, with a particular emphasize on differences in legal origin and their effects can be found in (La Porta, Lopez-de-Silanes, and Shleifer, 2008).

legal institutions and the financial system see Beck and Levine (2008). Beck, Demirgüç-Kunt, and Levine (2003) assess the question why legal origin matters for financial development. Their results suggest that common law is more flexible in adopting to the changing requirements of financial contracting and thus more favorable for financial development compared to civil law.

Another factor that has received considerable attention is financial liberalization. Financial liberalization can mitigate financial repression and allow for better diversification of portfolios and thus reduce the costs of capital for borrowers. Furthermore, financial liberalization is expected to lead to more intense competition in the financial sector, which will eventually cause less efficient financial corporations to leave the market, improving overall financial efficiency (Galindo, Schiantarelli, and Weiss, 2007; Abiad, Oomes, and Ueda, 2008; Levchenko, Rancière, and Thoenig, 2009). Chinn and Ito (2006), empirically examine the relationship between financial liberalization, legal institutions and financial development. They find that financial openness contributes to equity market development. However, their results suggest that the positive effect of liberalization is conditional on the legal environment, such that only countries that have acquired a sound legal system speed up financial development through financial liberalization. Ito (2006) confirms and refines this finding for a broad set of transition economies. More recently, Elkhuizen et al. (2018) argue that the positive effects of financial liberalization on financial institutions not necessarily require well developed legal institutions. Using panel data for a broad set of countries, they find that social capital can be a substitute for legal institutions and suffice to overcome setbacks resulting from financial liberalization.

Besides the importance of legal institutions and financial liberalization, other factors also have been found to contribute to financial development. One commonly considered factor is inflation rates. However, so far there is no consensus on the channels through which inflation rates and financial development are linked. Huybens and Smith (1999) provide a theoretical model that predicts a negative long-run relationship between inflation and financial development. Empirically, Boyd, Levine, and Smith (2001) find that there is a significant and economically meaningful negative relationship between inflation and financial development. According to their discussion, a likely explanation for the observed relationship is that high inflation rates impede financial development by exacerbating financial frictions. Besides inflation rates, trade openness is also expected to affect financial development. The argument is that countries that are better integrated into world trade also need to develop the necessary financial institutions to facilitate trade. Do and Levchenko (2004) examine the relationship between international trade and financial development, they find that a higher degree of trade openness is associated with larger and more developed financial sectors.

The experience of former Soviet Union member and satellite states in building up financial institutions has received particular attention. Scholtens (2000) gives a rather detailed account of the early years of transition, up to 1996, for a selected sample of central European countries, documenting a slow development of most financial indicators. He finds that countries tended to focus on the implementation of a bank-based system, nevertheless, he also documents that quickly after the dissolution capital markets started to develop. Furthermore, already the early stage of financial development reveals a high degree of heterogeneity among countries. In another assessment of the early transition period, Bonin and Wachtel (2003), find that financial sectors in most countries still do not provide all functions of a financial sector as discussed above. However, they argue that the majority of countries have made significant progress towards establishing a well-working financial sector within the first decade after the dissolution. In general, they confirm the tendency of the post-soviet transition economies to opt for a bank-based financial system, dominated by universal banks.

In a later work, Bonin, Hasan, and Wachtel (2012), argue that the experience of transition economies in establishing a working financial system can best be characterized by dividing it into three successive periods. In the early stage, roughly up to the end of the first decade after the dissolution, most countries were facing severe macroeconomic turmoil and repeated bankruptcies in the financial sector. This process has been fueled by a large amount of non-performing loans, which were either the result of long-standing borrower-lender relationships vis-à-vis large government owned companies or also the result of a lack of financial regulations. Overall, this period is characterized by frequent policy changes and a rather slow financial development. The second period (early 2000s), is then characterized by a rapid speed up of financial development and also by foreign entries into the banking sectors of many transition economies. Finally, in the third period, starting around 2005, they find that financial sectors in several transition economies show only small differences compared to financial sectors in more developed economies. However, as for example pointed out by Kakhkharov and Akimov (2018), more recently, there is still substantial heterogeneity in terms of financial development across post-soviet transition economies. In particular, they document that the former Soviet Union member states are lagging behind, compared to the other transition economies.

With respect to the relationship between financial development and legal institutions, former Soviet Union member states, in contrast to a broader sample of transition economies, faced the challenge to build up these structures jointly. Pistor, Raiser, and Gelfer (2000) provide a detailed examination of the relationship between legal institutions and financial institutions for post-soviet transition economies. They document that many of the countries have made good progress in improving the law on the books but were not successful in improving legal efficiency. Furthermore, they find that legal efficiency is a better predictor for financial development in transition economies than the law on the books. They conclude, that the implementation of good laws cannot overcome the deficiencies of bad institutions. In a later study, Harper and McNulty (2008) find that transition economies in general, and former member states of the Soviet Union in particular, have a significantly lower level of financial development, compared to developed economies. They assess how this is related to the legal origin of countries and find that Russian legal origin[5] has a strong negative effect on financial

---

5 Harper and McNulty (2008) consider a country to have a Russian legal origin if the legal system was imposed on the country by Czars, and by the expansion of

development. Overall, both studies confirm the important role of legal institutions for financial development in transition economies.

In light of the discussion on financial development in transition economies, the presence of foreign banks has received particular attention. As argued and documented by Weill (2003), in case of Poland and Czech Republic, foreign banks provided knowledge spillovers and thus contributed to overall financial development. For a larger sample of post-soviet transition economies, Naaborg et al. (2004) also document a high share of foreign banks. In addition, they find that foreign banks are more efficient, earn higher returns and are more likely to lend to the private sector, compared to domestic banks. Besides the positive effects of foreign entry on some dimensions of financial development, one concern about foreign entry into the banking system is a potential decrease in financial stability. In case of a crisis in the home country, a foreign bank might decrease lending in the host country, causing spillover effects of financial sector distress. de Haas and van Lelyveld (2006) examine a panel with individual bank data for transition economies over the 1990s. They find that during periods of economic downturn, domestic banks tend to contract their lending, while foreign banks rather stabilize the domestic financial system. However, they also find evidence, that foreign bank lending reacts strongly to the conditions of the parent bank. Nevertheless, by and large, the results point towards the stabilizing effects of international risk-sharing. Feyen et al. (2014) find evidence that, due to the high share of foreign financial institutions, bank lending in the group of transition economies is more susceptible to cross-border funding shocks. This markedly demonstrates one potential downside of financial integration, i.e. the increased exposure to global financial conditions, which can exert profound effects on domestic financial development.

---

communism afterwards. According to their reasoning, this kind of legal system (originally developed by Peter the Great and Alexander II) is characterized by vague principles and concepts, and is full with contradictions. Except of the three Baltic States, all former Soviet Union member states, Poland and Albania are classified as having Russian legal origin.

Overall, the above discussion reveals that the development of financial institutions depends on several factors, which might display differential effects conditional on other determinants. In particular, the legal environment seems to be a crucial precondition for financial development. From the discussion we expect that the quality of the legal system is positively related to financial development. Furthermore, we expect that financial liberalization has a positive effect on financial development in countries that have better developed legal institutions. Finally, we expect that trade openness is positively related to financial development and that inflation enters negatively. In the following section, we examine these hypotheses empirically.

Empirical Analysis

Data & Descriptive Statistics. To measure financial development, we employ the financial development index developed by Sahay et al. (2015). As Svirydzenka (2016) argues, traditional measures of financial development (e.g. the ratio of private credit to GDP or the ratio of stock market capitalization to GDP) are only taking into account the depth of the financial sector. However, over time financial markets are getting more complex, hence access and efficiency are as important as the depth of the market. Therefore, using a more comprehensive measure, which takes into account several dimensions of financial development is desirable. The index of financial development is divided into two main categories. One is measuring financial market development (FM) and the other measures the development of financial institutions (FI). Both of the measures are based on three sub-indexes separately measuring depth, access and efficiency of financial markets and institutions. This allows for a multi-dimensional assessment of financial development and still provides the basis for a more detailed analysis of these dimensions.

Since financial markets are not well developed in transition economies (cf. Bonin and Wachtel (2007), Kakhkharov and Akimov (2018)), in this chapter we will primarily concentrate on financial institutions. In order to measure the development of financial institutions (FI) the three different sub-indexes are aggregated and then normalized to vary from 0 to 1. All of the sub-indexes are normalized and vary in the same range. The first sub-index is financial institutions depth (FID), which is constructed based on credit to the private sector to GDP, pension and mutual fund assets to GDP, life and non-life insurance premiums to GDP. The measure is expected to capture the size of the financial system and its ability to channel the resources from savers to borrowers. In addition, large financial markets indicate that there is credit money available for investments.

The second sub index measures the degree of access to financial institutions (FIA) and is more bank specific. The index is based on the number of bank branches and ATMs per 100,000 adults. Access is an important measure of the provision of financial services. The potential of large financial systems will not be fully utilized if financial institutions are not accessible to wider public.

The third and final measure is the sub-index of financial institutions efficiency (FIE), which should capture how well financial institutions connect savings and investments. The index is based on the lending-deposit spread and net interest margin. In addition, operational efficiency is measured by overhead costs to total assets and non-interest income share in total income, and profitability of the sector is measured by return on equity (ROE) and return on assets (ROA). Efficiency is a particularly important aspect of financial institutions. Since, even if a country has a deep and accessible financial system, the extent of the positive influence of financial institutions on growth would be limited if the system is unable to channel the resources without waste and efficiency.[6]

To account for the quality of legal institutions we combine two measures, Rule of Law (ROL) and Regulatory Quality (RQ) from the Worldwide Governance Indicators (WGI) developed by Kaufmann et al. (2010). The index of Rule of Law is a general measure capturing the extent to which the public complies, and more importantly have confidence in the legal rules established in a country. It is based on several indicators measuring ease of contract

---

6 A detailed description of the construction of the index and the sub-measures can be found in Svirydzenka (2016).

enforcement, incidents of crime and perception towards criminal situation, as well as predictability and efficiency of the law enforcement and judiciary system. When combined, these indicators capture the extent to which property rights are guaranteed and fairness and predictability of an environment for social an economic interaction are ensured. Therefore, more generally, the measure accounts for the quality of the legal system.

On the other hand, the index of Regulatory Quality focuses on policies and measures the perception about the ability of the government to design, and more importantly, implement policies supporting private sector development. The index unites the measures about the perception of the regulatory burden on business sector and other market deterring policies such as weak banking supervision and price controls. Hence, the index measures overall quality of regulatory policies and the ability of executive bodies to implement these policies. By combining these two measures we expect to capture both aspects of the legal environment of the country. The data on the indexes for all countries in our sample is available from 1996 onward and ranges from -2.5 to 2.5.

To measure financial liberalization of a country we use the index of capital account liberalization originally developed by Chinn and Ito (2002) and extend by Chinn and Ito (2006). The measure is accounting for financial openness of a county and is based on several individual indicators including multiple exchange rates, restrictions on current account transactions, restrictions on capital account transactions and surrender of export proceedings. These individual indicators provide information on the external accounts and transactions of a country. As argued by Chinn and Ito (2006) the index is a good proxy to measure the extent of capital controls in a country. The index ranges between 0 and 1, where 1 indicates a fully open capital account.

Together with legal institutions and financial liberalization, we use different economic controls such as the level of economic development, openness and inflation. We control for the level of economic development by using real GDP per capita. To measure openness, trade share to GDP is used. All of these variables come from World Bank World Development Indicators. To control for inflation, we use consumer prices (annual %) as measured by the consumer price index. The data comes from International Monetary Fund.

Table 11.1 Descriptive Statistics

Indicator	Mean	SD	Min	Max	Obs.
FI	0.37	0.13	0.14	0.63	25
FID	0.15	0.09	0.03	0.29	24
FIA	0.38	0.19	0.08	0.77	24
FIE	0.59	0.13	0.31	0.76	25
FM	0.15	0.13	0.00	0.48	25
Legal	-0.10	0.83	-1.70	1.19	25
Financial Liberalization	0.51	0.31	0.09	0.99	25
Trade	98.98	26.54	53.55	146.72	25
Inflation	14.50	16.92	1.99	60.82	25
Real GDP	7384	5686	629	21351	25
FI in 2016	0.47	0.15	0.21	0.70	25

Notes: Trade denotes the trade share relative to GDP. Inflation is a measure of inflation based on CPI. Legal is the quality of legal institutions measured by an unweighted average of Rule of Law and Regulatory Quality. FI, FID, FIA, FIE, FM are measures of different dimensions of financial development of the country. Real GDP is real GDP per capita in constant 2010 prices. Data is averaged over the period 1996–2016. FI in 2016 is the level of the development of financial institutions in 2016.

Table 11.1 presents summary statistics for the cross section of the sample. If not indicated otherwise, the data is averaged over the period 1996–2016. Regarding trade openness, we find substantial variation across the sample. Slovakia is the most open economy in the sample with an average trade share of 146%, compared to Russia, which has the smallest trade share in the sample with roughly 53%. With respect to capital account openness, a similar pattern emerges. On average, over the sample period, Estonia had the most liberal capital account policies, in contrast to Ukraine and Turkmenistan, who had the most heavily regulated capital accounts across the sample. Also, with respect to the quality of legal institutions, we find substantial differences across countries. While

Estonia has the highest average score for legal institutions with a value of 1.19, Turkmenistan has an average score of -1.7. Regarding inflation, we find a quite high sample average. This is mostly driven by several countries. For example, Belarus experienced substantial inflation of more than 150% in 1999 and 2000. Furthermore, also Turkmenistan experienced an inflation rate of almost 1000% in 1996. In contrast, Estonia experienced an average inflation of 4.9% over the sample period.

With regards to the quality of financial institutions, Table 11.1 also highlights several noteworthy aspects. We find that in 2016, there are still large differences in terms of the quality of financial institutions. Bulgaria has the most developed banking sector, compared to Kyrgyz Republic, which has the lowest quality of financial institutions, as of 2016. Furthermore, from examining the averages across the different sub-indexes of financial institutions, we see that the efficiency of financial institutions is comparably high. In contrast, we find that the average depth of financial institutions remains at low levels. Moreover, as can be inferred from the standard deviation, there is quite important variation across all these measures.

Table 11.2 Correlations Statistics for the Sample Averages

	FI	FID	FIA	FIE	Legal	Fin.Lib.	Inflation	Trade
FI	1							
FID	0.904***	1						
FIA	0.931***	0.740***	1					
FIE	0.755***	0.799***	0.616**	1				
Legal	0.778***	0.767***	0.573**	0.688***	1			
Fin.Lib.	0.509**	0.37	0.427*	0.389	0.789***	1		
Inflation	−0.213	−0.2	0.0621	−0.115	−0.516**	−0.398*	1	
Trade	0.198	0.373	−0.0321	0.332	0.437*	0.242	−0.0421	1

Notes: * $p<0.05$; ** $p<0.01$; *** $p<0.001$.
Trade denotes the trade share relative to GDP. Inflation is a measure of inflation based on CPI. Fin.Lib. captures the level of financial liberalization of a country. Legal is the quality of legal institutions measured by an unweighted average of Rule of Law and Regulatory Quality. FI, FID, FIA, FIE, are measures of different dimensions of financial institutions.

Table 11.2 presents correlations for the sample averages. As expected, the measures of financial institutions are all highly correlated with each other. Only the correlation between access to financial institutions and efficiency of financial institutions is not significant on a 1 percent level. With respect to the quality of legal institutions we find significant positive correlations with all measures of financial institutions. This clearly points towards the important role of legal quality for financial institutions. Regarding financial liberalization, the pattern is less clear. While there is a significant positive correlation with overall financial institutions, the correlation with the sub measures is smaller. The relationship between inflation and the measures of financial institutions has the expected sign, however, the magnitude is small. Trade openness also possesses the expected positive association with financial institutions, but again, the correlation is weak.

Figure 11.1 Averages of Selected Indicators of the Development of Financial Institutions and Markets

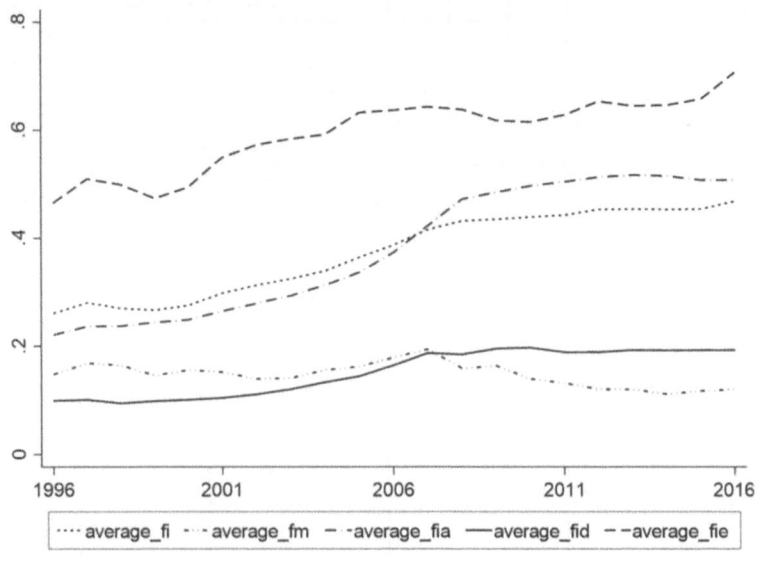

Figure 11.1 shows the development of several key indicators of financial development. First note, that for comparison, the

dashed double-dotted line shows the average financial market development. It is apparent, that in contrast to the indicators that reflect the development of financial institutions, financial markets remain rather underdeveloped and show only little improvements throughout the sample period or even a slight decline after 2007. The dotted line depicts the average overall quality of financial institutions. We find that, in line with the above discussion, the average quality of financial institutions improved between 1996 and 2016. From the sub-index that measures the efficiency of financial institutions, depicted by the dashed line, we see that also efficiency improved over the sample period. Furthermore, one finds that the average access to financial institutions, depicted by the dashed-dotted line, has also improved. Finally, only the average depth of financial institutions, given by the solid line, remains almost unchanged over the sample period. By and large, the graphs show that on average, financial institutions have shown substantial development since 1996. Furthermore, we see that efficiency is the dimension of financial institutions that has the highest average level across the sample.

Figure 11.2 Difference Between Financial Institutions in 1996 and 2016

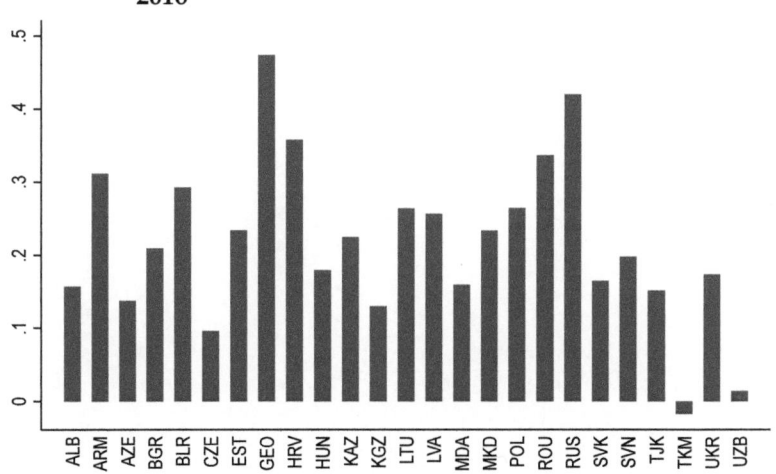

Next, we turn to the development of financial institutions across countries. Figure 11.2 depicts the difference in financial institutions between 1996 and 2016.[7] On average, the difference in financial institutions over the sample period is 0.22. But it is directly apparent that there are substantial differences across countries in terms of development. While Georgia and Russia saw the biggest improvements in financial institutions, development in Uzbekistan has almost stagnated over the period. Turkmenistan even saw a decline in the quality of financial institutions over the sample period. Furthermore, Czech Republic has seen a comparably small increase in the quality of financial institutions over the period. However, financial institutions were already more developed there, with a value of .46 in 1996, which corresponds roughly to the sample average in 2016. Overall, we see that the development was heterogeneous across countries, with a tendency of former Soviet republics to lag behind.

Figure 11.3 Quality of Legal Institutions and Financial Institutions

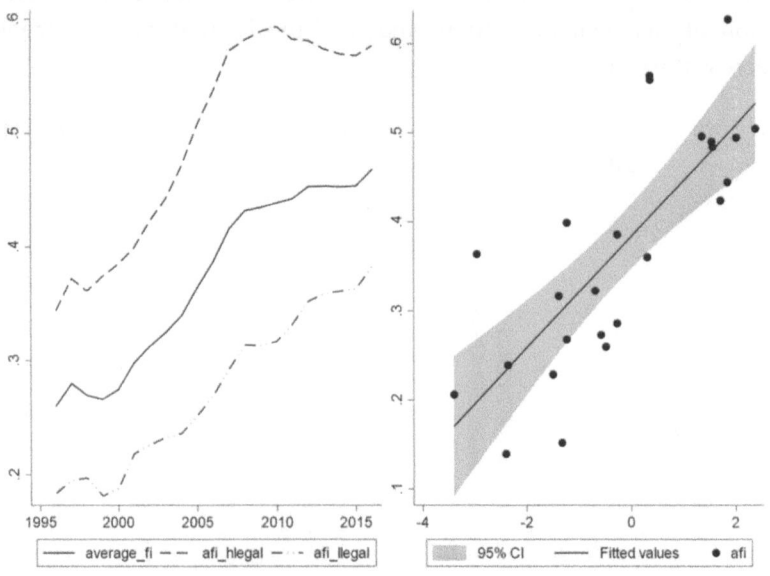

---

7. Note that due to missing data, the starting value for Turkmenistan and Tajikistan is 1998.

In order to assess the relationship between the quality of legal institutions and financial institutions, we divide the sample into two groups. The first group has above average quality of legal institutions (over the sample period), the other group is below the sample average. The left panel in Figure 11.3 depicts the average quality of financial institutions for both groups. As a reference, the solid line shows the average quality of financial institutions across the whole sample. The dashed line depicts the quality of financial institutions for countries with above average quality of legal institutions, while the dashed double-dotted line represents countries with below average quality of legal institutions. First, it is apparent that over the whole period the quality of financial institutions is higher in countries with better legal institutions. Second, while the development proceeds rather monotonically in countries with better legal institutions, the development path in countries with below average legal quality is characterized by repeated periods of stagnation. The right panel depicts a scatter plot for the average quality of financial institutions against the average quality of legal institutions. We find a statistically significant positive association between the two, supporting the law and finance view as stated in La Porta et al. (1998). Furthermore, there is no indication of severe outliers or other anomalies.

Next, we turn to the role of financial liberalization. The left panel in Figure 11.4 shows the development of average financial liberalization. We see that between 1995 and 2000 financial liberalization first accelerated and then reversed. However, as discussed above, from 2000 onward, we see a steep increase in financial liberalization that came first to a stop during the financial crisis in 2007. After the crisis, financial liberalization first declined and then more or less stabilized in the following years. The right panel depicts a scatter plot of the average quality of financial institutions against the averages of financial liberalization over the period. The association between both variables is positive and statistically significant. This finding supports the view that more financially liberalized countries tend to have more developed financial institutions.

Figure 11.4 Financial Liberalization and the Quality of Financial Institutions

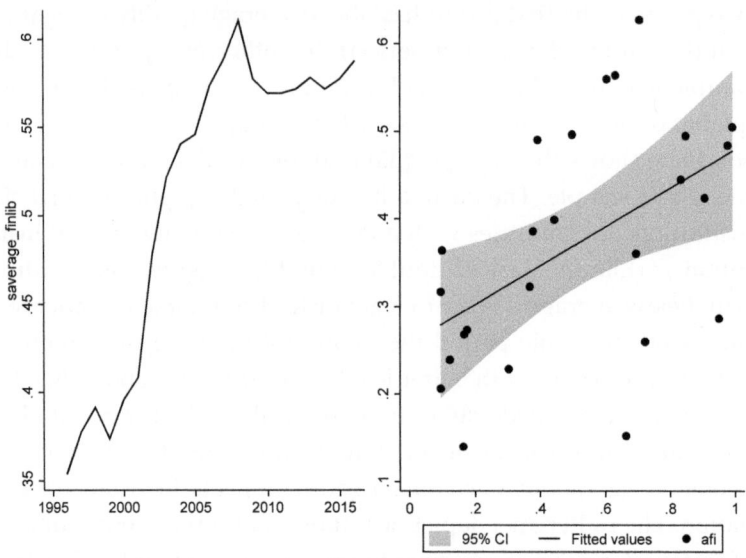

Finally, to evaluate the relationship between financial institutions and the other factors discussed above, Figure 11.5 presents two additional scatter plots. The left panel shows the relationship between the average inflation rate and financial institutions. We see the expected negative association between the two; however, the unconditional association between the two is not statistically significant. The right panel depicts the relationship between average trade openness and the average quality of financial institutions. Here we find a weak positive association between the two. So, while the relationship between both variables has the expected sign, the weak correlation might indicate that those factors did not matter much for financial development within the sample.

Figure 11.5 Scatter plot of the average inflation rate against the quality of financial institutions (left panel); Scatter plot of the average trade openness against the quality of financial institutions (right panel)

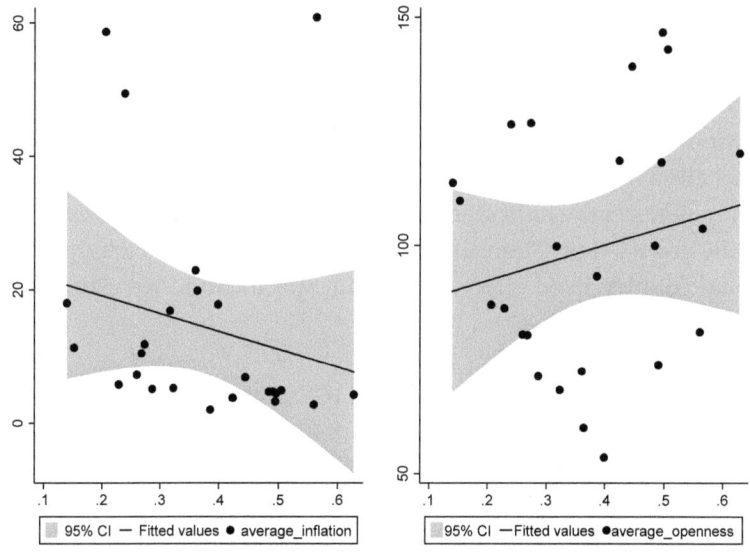

Overall, the inspection of the broader sample properties confirms the particular features of financial sectors in transition economies discussed above. Over the period 1996–2016, financial institutions in almost all transition economies have seen improvements. A striking feature of the countries in the sample is the low level of financial depth, which almost stagnates throughout the sample period. The same is true for the development of financial markets. Furthermore, we find that on average the quality of legal institutions is positively associated with the quality of financial institutions. The same holds for the measure of financial liberalization. With respect to the relationship of financial institutions vis-à-vis trade openness and inflation, the pattern is less clear-cut. In both cases, we find the expected sign, but the correlation is moderate.

Estimation

The preceding analysis has highlighted several factors that are related to financial institutions. In order to get an idea of the relative importance of these factors, and to overcome problems with the small sample size, we assess the factors jointly in a panel framework. To this end, we split the sample into non-overlapping 5-year intervals. This transformation is common and should eliminate business cycle fluctuations that might compromise yearly data, thus allowing us to focus more on medium-term to long-term developments of the indicators. The empirical model we use is similar to the one used by Chinn and Ito (2006); however, we include additional country fixed-effects.[8] The main specification we estimate is given by:

$$\delta(FI(t,t-5,i)) = B0 + B1 Legal(t,i) + B2 FinLib(t,i) \\ + B3(FinLib(t,i) * Legal(t,i)) + B4 FI(t-5,i) + X(t-5,i) \\ + \gamma(i) + \eta(t,i)$$

Where $\delta(FI(t,t-5,i))$ denotes the change in financial institutions over a 5-year interval, $X(t-5,i)$ denotes the vector of control variables, $\gamma(i)$ denotes country fixed-effects and $\eta(t,i)$ denotes an idiosyncratic error. We include the initial value $FI(t-5,i)$ to control for the level of financial development. The remaining variables represent period averages. The inclusion of country fixed-effects captures the time-invariant country characteristics, such as legal origin and geography. To overcome problems with heteroskedasticity, we cluster standard errors on the country level.

---

[8] For orientation and as a robustness check, we run the same specification with pooled OLS. The results of this exercise can be found in Appendix A11.2: Robustness. Qualitatively, the results do not change. However, for the specification presented in column 5, we do not find a statistically significant total effect of financial liberalization.

Table 11.3 Regression Results

VARIABLES	(1) Financial Inst.	(2) Financial Depth	(3) Financial Access	(4) Financial Efficiency	(5) Financial Inst.
Legal	0.142***	0.0486**	0.140**	0.205***	0.107**
	(0.0266)	(0.0230)	(0.0527)	(0.0535)	(0.0424)
Fin.Lib.	0.0746	0.0570	0.0939	0.0255	0.0572
	(0.0455)	(0.0377)	(0.0632)	(0.0955)	(0.0486)
Fin.Lib. × Legal					0.0665
					(0.0456)
FI_{t-5}	−0.452***	−0.246***	−0.362***	−0.748***	−0.445***
	(0.0653)	(0.0625)	(0.107)	(0.187)	(0.0714)
Inflation	−0.000215	−0.00128***	−0.000154	0.000276	−0.000242
	(0.000132)	(0.000340)	(0.000238)	(0.000525)	(0.000147)
Trade	0.000122	−0.000251	−0.000538	0.00130**	−2.20e-05
	(0.000329)	(0.000282)	(0.000614)	(0.000619)	(0.000317)
Growth	0.00198	−0.000105	0.00313	0.00189	0.00227
	(0.00224)	(0.00180)	(0.00270)	(0.00458)	(0.00224)
Constant	0.154***	0.120***	0.183***	0.157**	0.160***

	(0.0310)	(0.0357)	(0.0575)	(0.0761)	(0.0308)
Observations	100	96	96	100	100
R-squared	0.430	0.558	0.170	0.300	0.444
Number of cc	25	24	24	25	25
Standard Errors	Clustered	Clustered	Clustered	Clustered	Clustered

Notes: Robust standard errors in parentheses; *** $p<0.01$, ** $p<0.05$, * $p<0.1$ Financial Inst. is a measure of financial institutions development. Access, Depth and Efficiency are measures of financial institutions depth, access and efficiency respectively. Legal denotes the unweighted average of Rule of Law and Regulatory Quality. Fin.Lib. is a measure of financial liberalization. FI_{t-5} is a measure of initial values of financial development. Inflation stands for inflation rates calculated based on CPI. Trade is the trade share relative to GDP. Growth denotes the per capita growth rate.

Columns 1 to 4, in Table 11.3, present the results of the regressions without interaction term. It is apparent that when controlling for all the discussed factors, the quality of legal institutions enters statistically significant with a positive sign in all regressions. This indicates, that legal quality is significantly associated with financial development within the sample. Moreover, we find that the association between financial efficiency and legal institutions is stronger, compared to the other dimensions of financial development. Also note, that when controlling for the quality of legal institutions, financial liberalization is not statistically significant associated with financial development. However, as discussed by Chinn and Ito (2006), this finding might not be surprising since legal institutions are a necessary precondition for positive effects of financial liberalization on financial development.

To account for the conditional effect of financial liberalization on financial development we include the interaction term into the model. Thus, the specification in column 5 allows for a differential effect of financial liberalization on overall financial development, conditional on the quality of legal institutions. The overall effects of legal quality and financial liberalization on financial development are then taken into account. We find that both factors are statistically significant and possess a positive association with overall financial development.[9] Thus, as suggested by Chinn and Ito (2006), the effect of financial liberalization on financial development depends on the quality of legal institutions.

In order to provide a meaningful interpretation, we consider the effects of financial liberalization for different levels of legal quality. The average legal quality over the full period is -0.11, therefore, the average total effect of financial liberalization is 0.06. Given that the average difference in financial institutions over the sample period is 0.23, financial liberalization can explain a fair share of financial development over the period. Next, in order to assess the

---

9. We compute the significance of the linear combination of both coefficients and find that both are significant on a 5% level. Note that in the presence of the interaction term, legal quality remains significant for all sub-dimensions of financial institutions, however, financial liberalization is not significantly associated with the sub-dimensions.

differences in financial development between the group of former Soviet Union members and non-members, we split the sample accordingly. Over the sample period, former member states have an average legal quality of -0.46, this translates into a total effect of financial liberalization on financial development of 0.03. In contrast, non-members have a higher average legal quality of 0.42, which yields a total effect for financial liberalization of 0.09. Thus, on average, financial liberalization has a larger effect on financial development for non-members.

Moreover, considering the period 1996–2000, former member states had an average legal quality of -0.59, so that during this period, financial liberalization increased financial development only by 0.02. This finding is roughly in line with the findings of Chinn and Ito (2006), who report an average positive effect of financial liberalization on financial development for emerging market countries and a negative effect for less developed countries.[10]

Whereas, the group of former member states on average experiences positive effects for financial development through financial liberalization, this pattern changes if we consider specific countries. For example, Turkmenistan has an average legal quality of -1.69 over the sample period, which means that the total effect of financial liberalization on financial development for Turkmenistan amounts to -0.06. Compared to the average financial development of the sample, this is a substantial negative effect.

Georgia is another interesting case, because the country liberalized capital accounts early on, but was still lacking a sound legal system. According to our estimates, the early liberalization led to a small decline in financial development during the period 1996 to 2000. However, since then legal institutions in Georgia have improved, such that the overall effect of financial liberalization on financial institutions turns positive in later periods. This might, at least partly, explain the slow financial development observed for

---

10. Clearly, the group of former member states is itself quite heterogeneous and, as a group, does not fit the definition of less developed countries as stated by the International Financial Corporation's indices. Nevertheless, our results support the idea of a dichotomous effect of financial liberalization between the two groups.

Georgia between 1996 and 2000 and the subsequent acceleration. Overall, the results, with regards to the group of former member states, can contribute to explain the findings of Kakhkharov and Akimov (2018), who document, that many of these countries are lagging behind in terms of financial development.

With respect to the control variables, we find that inflation has no statistically significant association with overall financial development. However, inflation has a statistically significant negative association with financial depth. This finding could highlight an important channel through which inflation rates affect financial development. High inflation rates, as experienced by several countries within the sample, could undermine incentives of the private sector to hold funds at financial institutions. Less confidence in price stability could therefore negatively affect financial depth. With respect to trade openness we also find no statistically significant association with overall financial development. Nevertheless, trade openness has a statistically significant association with financial efficiency. This finding would at least support the theory of positive spillovers from trade openness towards financial development.

When it comes to policy advice, our findings suggest that in order to promote financial development countries should place particular emphasis on the quality of legal institutions. In addition, financial liberalization should be pursued carefully, while it is on average beneficial, the effect will heavily depend on the quality of legal institutions. Thus, countries that are at a stage where they need to develop legal institutions and increase financial liberalization, should do this sequentially and need to implement sound legal institutions before they opt for financial liberalization.

Conclusion

In this chapter we have examined financial development in post-Soviet transition economies. Over 25 years after the dissolution, several countries were able to implement a well-functioning financial system, mostly based on financial institutions. However, as documented in the descriptive parts and in the cross-sectional analysis of the chapter, several countries still lack sound financial institutions. Furthermore, the depth of financial institutions is comparably low in the sample of post-soviet transition economies. This might indicate a lack of available funds for investments. The cross-sectional comparison of the determinants of financial institutions has shown that the quality of legal institutions, as well as financial liberalization are positively associated with financial institutions. In contrast, inflation rates and trade openness show no significant association with the quality of financial institutions.

By and large, the panel analysis confirms the importance of legal institutions for financial development. Countries that have better developed legal systems also see a faster development of financial institutions. Importantly, legal quality seems to be pivotal for all dimensions of financial institutions. In contrast to the cross-section, in the panel, when controlling for the other determinants of financial institutions, we find no statistically significant association between financial liberalization and financial development. However, taking into account the interaction between financial liberalization and legal institutions, we find a statistically significant total effect of financial liberalization. This finding is in line with previous research on the subject, which argues that well developed legal institutions are a precondition for positive effects of financial liberalization on financial development. In addition, the panel analysis shows that inflation rates and trade openness are significantly associated with specific dimensions of financial development, which could explain previous findings for broader samples and might indicate channels through which both factors affect financial development. We also find indication of conditional convergence, in terms of financial development, within the sample.

Overall, the present chapter shows that financial development crucially requires a sound legal system. This finding highlights the difficult situation of many transition economies, which face a situation where they must implement both, financial and legal institutions jointly. However, we see that other factors, such as financial liberalization, inflation and trade openness might also matter for financial development and future research might shed more light on this.

References

Abiad, Abdul, Nienke Oomes, and Kenichi Ueda. 2008. 'The Quality Effect: Does Financial Liberalization Improve the Allocation of Capital?' *Journal of Development Economics* 87 (2): 270–82. https://doi.org/10.1016/J.JDEVECO.2007.12.002.

Beck, Thorsten, Asli Demirgüç-Kunt, and Ross Levine. 2003. 'Law and Finance: Why Does Legal Origin Matter?' *Journal of Comparative Economics*. https://doi.org/10.1016/j.jce.2003.08.001.

Beck, Thorsten, and Ross Levine. 2004. 'Stock Markets, Banks, and Growth: Panel Evidence'. *Journal of Banking and Finance*. https://doi.org/10.1016/S0378-4266(02)00408-9.

Beck, Thorsten, and Ross Levine. 2008. 'Legal Institutions and Financial Development'. In *Handbook of New Institutional Economics*. https://doi.org/10.1007/978-3-540-69305-5_12.

Beck, Thorsten, Ross Levine, and Norman Loayza. 2000. 'Finance and the Sources of Growth'. *Journal of Financial Economics* 58 (1–2): 261–300. https://doi.org/10.1016/S0304-405X(00)00072-6.

Bonin, John P., Iftekhar Hasan, and Paul Wachtel. 2012. 'Banking in Transition Countries'. In *The Oxford Handbook of Banking*. https://doi.org/10.1093/oxfordhb/9780199640935.013.0033.

Bonin, John, and Paul Wachtel. 2003. 'Financial Sector Development in Transition Economies: Lessons from the First Decade'. *Financial Markets, Institutions and Instruments* 12 (1): 1–66. https://doi.org/10.1111/1468-0416.t01-1-00001.

Bonin, John, and Paul Wachtel. 2007. 'Financial Sector Development in Transition Economies: Lessons from the First Decade'. *SSRN*. https://doi.org/10.2139/ssrn.1015704.

Boyd, John H., Ross Levine, and Bruce D. Smith. 2001. 'The Impact of Inflation on Financial Sector Performance'. *Journal of Monetary Economics*. https://doi.org/10.1016/S0304-3932(01)00049-6.

Chinn, Menzie D., and Hiro Ito. 2006. 'What Matters for Financial Development? Capital Controls, Institutions, and Interactions'. *Journal of Development Economics*. https://doi.org/10.1016/j.jdeveco.2005.05.010.

Chinn, Menzie David, and Hiro Ito. 2002. 'Capital Account Liberalization, Institutions and Financial Development: Cross Country Evidence'. *SSRN*. https://doi.org/10.2139/ssrn.315865.

Cihak, Martin, Asli Demirguc-Kunt, Erik Feyen, and Ross Levine. 2012. 'Benchmarking Financial Systems around the World'. http://documents.worldbank.org/curated/en/868131468326381955/Benchmarking-financial-systems-around-the-world.

Do, Quy-Toan, and Andrei Levchenko. 2004. 'Trade and Financial Development'. http://documents.worldbank.org/curated/en/39458146877 9413283/pdf/wps3347.pdf.

Elkhuizen, Luuk, Niels Hermes, Jan Jacobs, and Aljar Meesters. 2018. 'Financial Development, Financial Liberalization and Social Capital'. *Applied Economics* 50 (11): 1268–88. https://doi.org/10.1080/00036846.20 17.1358446.

Feyen, Erik, Letelier Raquel, Love Inessa, Samuel Munzele Maimbo, and Roberto Rocha. 2014. *The Impact of Funding Models and Foreign Bank Ownership on Bank Credit Growth: Is Central and Eastern Europe Different?* The World Bank. https://doi.org/10.1596/1813-9450-6783.

Galindo, Arturo, Fabio Schiantarelli, and Andrew Weiss. 2007. 'Does Financial Liberalization Improve the Allocation of Investment?: Micro-Evidence from Developing Countries'. *Journal of Development Economics* 83 (2): 562–87. https://doi.org/10.1016/J.JDEVECO.2005.09.008.

Haas, Ralph de, and Iman van Lelyveld. 2006. 'Foreign Banks and Credit Stability in Central and Eastern Europe. A Panel Data Analysis'. *Journal of Banking & Finance* 30 (7): 1927–52. https://doi.org/10.1016/J.J BANKFIN.2005.07.007.

Harper, Joel T., and James E. McNulty. 2008. 'Financial System Size in Transition Economies: The Effect of Legal Origin'. *Journal of Money, Credit and Banking*. https://doi.org/10.1111/j.1538-4616.2008.00156.x.

Huybens, Elisabeth, and Bruce D. Smith. 1999. 'Inflation, Financial Markets and Long-Run Real Activity'. *Journal of Monetary Economics*. https://doi.org/10.1016/S0304-3932(98)00060-9.

Ito, Hiro. 2006. 'Financial Development and Financial Liberalization in Asia: Thresholds, Institutions and the Sequence of Liberalization'. *North American Journal of Economics and Finance*. https://doi.org/10.10 16/j.najef.2006.06.008.

Kakhkharov, Jakhongir, and Alexandr Akimov. 2018. 'Financial Development in Less-Developed Post-Communist Economies'. *Problems of Economic Transition* 60 (7): 483–513. https://doi.org/10.1080/10611991.20 18.1551031.

Kaufmann, Daniel, Aart Kraay, and Massimo Mastruzzi. 2010. 'The Worldwide Governance Indicators: Methodology and Analytical Issues'. *World Bank Policy Research Working Paper*, no. 5430.

Levchenko, Andrei A., Romain Rancière, and Mathias Thoenig. 2009. 'Growth and Risk at the Industry Level: The Real Effects of Financial Liberalization'. *Journal of Development Economics* 89 (2): 210–22. https://doi.org/10.1016/J.JDEVECO.2008.06.003.

Levine, Ross. 2002. 'Bank-Based or Market-Based Financial Systems: Which Is Better?' *Journal of Financial Intermediation* 11 (4): 398–428. https://doi.org/10.1006/JFIN.2002.0341.

Levine, Ross, Norman Loayza, and Thorsten Beck. 2000. 'Financial Intermediation and Growth: Causality and Causes'. *Journal of Monetary Economics.* https://doi.org/10.1016/S0304-3932(00)00017-9.

Levine, Ross, and Sara Zervos. 1998. 'Stock Markets, Banks, and Economic Growth'. *The American Economic Review.* American Economic Association. https://doi.org/10.2307/116848.

Loayza, Norman, Amine Ouazad, and Romain Ranciere. 2017. *Financial Development, Growth, and Crisis: Is There a Trade-Off?* Policy Research Working Papers. The World Bank. https://doi.org/10.1596/1813-9450-8237.

Naaborg, Ilko, Bert Scholtens, Jakob de Haan, Hanneke Bol, and Ralph de Haas. 2004. 'How Important Are Foreign Banks in the Financial Development of European Transition Countries?' *Journal of Emerging Market Finance* 3 (2): 99–123. https://doi.org/10.1177/097265270400300202.

Pistor, Katharina, Martin Raiser, and Stanislaw Gelfer. 2000. 'Law and Finance in Transition Economies'. *Economics of Transition.* https://doi.org/10.1111/1468-0351.00047.

Porta, Rafael La, Florencio Lopez-de-Silanes, and Andrei Shleifer. 2008. 'The Economic Consequences of Legal Origins'. *Journal of Economic Literature.* https://doi.org/10.1257/jel.46.2.285.

Porta, Rafael La, Florencio Lopez-de-Silanes, Andrei Shleifer, and Robert Vishny. 2000. 'Investor Protection and Corporate Governance'. *Journal of Financial Economics* 58 (1–2): 3–27. https://doi.org/10.1016/S0304-405X(00)00065-9.

Porta, Rafael La, Florencio Lopez-de-SIlanes, Andrei Shleifer, and Robert W Vishny. 1998. 'Law and Finance'. *Journal of Political Economy* 106 (6): 1113–55. https://doi.org/10.1086/250042.

Sahay, Ratna, Martin Čihák, Adolfo Barajas, Ran Bi, Diana Ayala, Yuan Gao, Annette Kyobe, et al. 2015. 'Rethinking Financial Deepening: Stability and Growth in Emerging Markets'. https://www.imf.org/external/pubs/ft/sdn/2015/sdn1508.pdf.

Scholtens, Bert. 2000. 'Financial Regulation and Financial System Architecture in Central Europe'. *Journal of Banking and Finance.* https://doi.org/10.1016/S0378-4266(99)00079-5.

Svirydzenka, Katsiaryna. 2016. 'Introducing a New Broad-Based Index of Financial Development'. https://www.imf.org/external/pubs/ft/wp/2016/wp1605.pdf.

Weill, Laurent. 2003. 'Banking Efficiency in Transition Economies'. *Economics of Transition*. https://doi.org/10.1111/1468-0351.00155.

Appendix

Table A11.1 Data and Sources

Variable	Description	Source
FI	Index measuring the development of financial institutions. The three sub-indexes (FID, FIA, FIE) are aggregated and normalized. Taking values from 0 to 1.	IMF Financial development index database
FID	Index measuring the depth of financial institutions. Taking values from 0 to 1.	IMF Financial development index database
FIA	Index measuring the accessibility of financial institutions. Taking values from 0 to 1.	IMF Financial development index database
FIE	Index measuring the efficiency of financial institutions. Taking values from 0 to 1.	IMF Financial development index database
FM	Index measuring the overall development of financial markets. Taking values from 0 to 1.	IMF Financial development index database
Legal	Unweighted average of Rule of Law and Regulatory Quality	World Bank Worldwide Governance Indicators
Real GDP	GDP per capita in constant 2010 prices	World Bank World Development Indicators
Growth	Per capita GDP growth rate	World Bank World Development Indicators
Trade	Trade share to GDP	World Bank World Development Indicators
Inflation	Consumer prices (annual %) as measured by the consumer price index	International Monetary Fund
Fin.Lib.	Financial liberalization of a country	Chinn and Ito (2002)

Table A11.2　Robustness Models

VARIABLES	(1) Financial Inst.	(2) Financial Depth	(3) Financial Access	(4) Financial Efficiency	(5) Financial Inst.
Legal	0.0394***	0.0321**	0.0141*	0.0713***	0.0404***
	(0.00863)	(0.0143)	(0.00750)	(0.0175)	(0.00954)
Fin.Lib.	0.00319	0.0132	-0.00341	-0.0111	0.00352
	(0.0158)	(0.0194)	(0.0138)	(0.0386)	(0.0171)
Fin.Lib. × Legal					-0.00327
					(0.0204)
FI_{t-5}	-0.167***	-0.125*	-0.0766**	-0.306***	-0.165***
	(0.0322)	(0.0615)	(0.0306)	(0.0844)	(0.0347)
Inflation	-9.40e-05	-0.000138*	-0.00112***	0.000715	-9.13e-05
	(9.70e-05)	(7.91e-05)	(0.000383)	(0.000466)	(9.96e-05)
Trade	-0.000125	-0.000778***	-8.25e-05	0.000676	-0.000114
	(0.000197)	(0.000223)	(0.000131)	(0.000413)	(0.000201)
Growth	0.00280*	0.00284	0.000806	0.00458	0.00283*
	(0.00155)	(0.00200)	(0.00170)	(0.00316)	(0.00160)
Constant	0.0998***	0.163***	0.0687**	0.0519	0.0983***
	(0.0255)	(0.0391)	(0.0265)	(0.0645)	(0.0281)

Observations	100	96	96	100	100
R-squared	0.252	0.135	0.452	0.238	0.252
Standard Errors	Clustered	Clustered	Clustered	Clustered	Clustered

Notes: Robust standard errors in parentheses; *** $p<0.01$; ** $p<0.05$; * $p<0.1$.
Financial Inst. is a measure of financial institutions development. Access, Depth and Efficiency are measures of financial institutions depth, access and efficiency respectively. Legal denotes the unweighted average of Rule of Law and Regulatory Quality. Fin.Lib. is a measure of financial liberalization. FI_{t-5} is a measure of initial values of financial development. Inflation stands for inflation rates calculated based on CPI. Trade is the trade share relative to GDP. Growth denotes the per capita growth rate.

12
Estimation of the Government Spending Multiplier for Countries in Transition[1]

Lasha Arevadze

The main purpose of this chapter is to investigate evidence with regards to fiscal policy (spending side) efficiency in a group of countries that is largely comprised of CIS member countries (Commonwealth of Independent States: Armenia, Azerbaijan, Belarus, Georgia, Kazakhstan, Kyrgyz Republic, Moldova, Russia, Tajikistan, Turkmenistan, Ukraine, and Uzbekistan), hereafter CIS countries or economies. To this date, a limited number of publications is available for developing countries on fiscal multipliers, including the CIS region. The shortage of empirical studies from developing countries generally stems from data availability and data quality issues. Moreover, the relatively shorter time series for key macroeconomic variables are often nonstationary and serial correlation remains a serious problem.

Briefly, the article is focused on the effects of government spending within CIS economies and how this effect depends on economic and financial conditions, such as public debt levels, crisis periods and exchange rate regimes. The definition of a fiscal multiplier is that "it [spending multiplier] is the change in output due to a change in fiscal policy instrument" Chinn (2013). In order to properly evaluate the effects of spending shocks within these economies, a two-stage model is applied to estimate fiscal multipliers. In the first stage, an exogenous spending shock is identified,

---

[1] The article is prepared with the financial support from Shota Rustaveli National Science Foundation of Georgia through grant agreement PhDF2016_226. I would like to extend my appreciation to Professor Iuri Ananiashvili, my supervisor in the Department of Econometrics at Tbilisi State University. Also, I wish to express my thanks to the faculty from the University of Georgia (USA) for their comments on previous drafts of the chapter.

whereas in the second stage we assess its effect on the economy using a fixed effects panel data estimation model. Briefly, a spending multiplier for the CIS countries is not constant and it varies across policy environments. This spending effect is stronger in crisis times; however, there are non-confirming cases as well. Weak fiscal environments, measured as GDP to debt ratio, negatively impact the multiplier effect, and the impact is stronger in currency peg regimes. The chapter contributes to the literature on fiscal policy by identifying government spending multiplier effects for different policy instruments across diverging policy environments.

After the global financial crisis in 2008-2009 and the burst of the bubble in the capital asset markets, we face an increased level of interest regarding fiscal policy efficiency in the literature. Interest among economists is due to unprecedented sizes of fiscal stimulation packages continually proposed by national governments in support of their economies. In principle, the total amount of anti-crisis packages around the world, even with conservative estimates, was $2.18 trillion or 3.5% of the world's GDP. Existing literature from developed countries shows high levels of efficiency of fiscal policy presenting empirical evidence in support of high multipliers. In contrast, developing countries, including the CIS countries, still remain peripheral to researches and the relationship between government spending and its multiplier effects is not properly studied.

There is no single measure for "the multiplier" universally because the effect of government spending varies with economic conditions. The size of the multiplier is affected by crowding out the effects of private consumption and investment. If such effects are dominant, then a multiplier is small, and sometimes, it may turn negative. Therefore, the effect varies in response to the economic realities within any given economy. During economic and financial crises, fiscal policy is more efficient than in expansionary times, as there is scarce liquidity during recessions, which government spending policy aims to address. In addition, existing literature shows that spending multipliers can be high in environments with fixed exchange regimes. Government spending decisions (spending shocks) may result in higher interest rates if the financial market is open, which in turn can result in an appreciation of local currency. Currency appreciation could mean that exports in floating exchange regime decline. However, in fixed exchange regimes, a government may purchase foreign currency to prevent the appreciation of a local currency, thus limiting the negative effects on exports.

One of the stylized facts on multipliers is that they are smaller in developing countries. This may point at crowding out effect of government spending in less developed countries. Also, in advanced economies, there is no, or limited, difference between government consumption and investment multipliers, but the multiplier effect of government investment is higher in developing countries. Another stylized fact is that in countries with high public debt levels fiscal policy can be contractionary for the economy, while fiscal consolidation can be expansionary. This happens as fiscal discipline results in lower risk premiums for a country because of the lower debt burden.

To sum up, the size of government spending multiplier is not a unique number for a particular economy; moreover, its size is affected by various economic conditions.

Post-soviet countries have experienced one of the most turbulent economic environments after the collapse of the Soviet Union, on the way from a command-and-control system to market economy. The size of government declined substantially, and they have experienced financial and currency crises in 1998 and 2008, in addition to a wave of currency devaluations in CIS countries from 2014. Therefore, we seek to understand the effect of government spending in CIS countries and show how it contributes to their Gross Domestic Products (GDP) under such turbulent economic environments in transition. The literature applies various econometric models for identifying government spending multipliers, among which are a VAR model as in Ilzetzki and Mendosa (2013) and a Dynamic Stochastic General Equilibrium model (DSGE) by Blanchard and Perotti (2002). The chapter builds on these econometric applications in the literature when identifying macro-economic multipliers.

Literature Review

To this date, a limited number of publications are available for developing countries on fiscal multipliers, especially the CIS economies. Nevertheless, there exists a nascent and growing set of empirical studies on developing countries, with applications of various econometric models. A key feature is that researchers must work out new solutions to isolate fiscal policy shock measures in developing countries. This policy shock should be unanticipated and unrelated to ongoing economic processes. Otherwise private agents, who internalize a government's budget constraint in their intertemporal constraint, may change their behavior, thus rendering estimations of the effects biased.

One of the contemporary studies for a sample of 102 developing countries, which tackles the measure of government spending multiplier, was extended by (Kraay 2012). This is the largest panel of countries evaluated in applied macroeconomic research. Because of data limitations, Kraay (2012) uses an instrumental variable procedure for determining fiscal shocks. In particular, he uses a debt reimbursement measure as an instrument of government spending shock. Kraay (2012) addresses problems related to policy anticipation and independence from the economy by assuming that a debt reimbursement is scheduled in advance, and therefore, it is unrelated to current economic conditions. As long as debt remains one of the important sources to finance current expenditures in developing countries, it becomes a relevant instrument for government spending shocks. In this group of countries, Kraay (2012) applies an instrumental variable approach and finds that, on average, 16% of expenditures are financed at the expense of loans originating from multilateral and bilateral creditors. But this strategy cannot be adopted without a careful judgment. Because Kraay (2012) conducts this analysis on 102 developing countries, where approximately 84% of countries use foreign debt as a significant source for financing government expenditures, the estimates can be biased toward conditional multipliers in high debt states.

The multiplier identified by Kraay (2012) varies from 0.38 to 0.42; which is fairly lower than the multiplier estimated for developed countries. However, there is a question about these calculated multipliers as to whether they are really unconditional (i.e. multiplier in "normal", non-fiscal crisis times). If we take into account that most of the countries use loans to finance their expenditures in this his analysis, the measure does become a conditional multiplier due to levels of indebtedness. At the same time, as studies show, fiscal policy is less efficient in cases of higher debt, which may suggest that Kraay's estimated multipliers are context specific. Moreover, the size of a spending multiplier is affected not only by debt levels but also, the sources of debt financing.

Public Debt Level (and Its Composition) and Spending Multiplier. The indebtedness level of a country has an impact on the size of a fiscal multiplier, which is generally higher for countries with low levels of debt (Corsetti, Meier and Muller 2012). Initially, when public debt is not high, government spending and private consumption tend to be positively correlated. But when public debt reaches a critical level, they move in opposite directions. The motivation of this argument is that a high level of debt is accompanied by a high interest rate environment because of higher risk premiums, especially in developing countries. Consequently, the crowding out effect dominates, and fiscal policy efficiency is small. Furthermore, if the debt to GDP ratio is above 50%, then fiscal policy is unproductive; the long run multiplier in this case is -2 (Ilzetzki and Vegh 2008). This, once again, means that to finance government consumption at the expense of taking debt is not a good policy solution. It is obvious that we face a strong crowding out effect, which can be a result of expected future fiscal consolidations and higher taxes (i.e., Ricardian equivalence holds).

There exists evidence of a strong crowding out effect on private investment due to public expenditures financed with domestic bank loans. For instance, Shahe and Farazi (2008) show that if governments in developing countries take loans from the banking sector, then each $1 taken from a bank resulted in a reduction of private investment by $0.8. This evidence emphasizes the liquidity constraint in developing countries. Moreover, Sanjeev et al. (2005) argue that a 1 percentage point increase of expenditures financed through domestic loans results in a reduction of the potential growth rate by 0.75 percentage points. The argument is that if deficit is financed through domestic debt, then it amplifies inflation, which negatively effects economic growth.

It should be mentioned that the source of financing matters for the size of a multiplier. In particular, debt financed expenditures cause an increase in private investments in developing countries; however, if such expenditures are financed through taxes, the policy has a negative effect Ahmed and Miller (2000). Miller and Ahmed (2000) analyze the effect of the source of spending on crowding out effect on investments and show that debt-financed expenditure crowds out investment if it is concentrated on social security and welfare spending. However, expenditures on communication and infrastructure projects crowd in investments. As for tax-financed infrastructure expenditures, the effect on private investments in negative. This idea is also supported by the analysis in Barro (1990). He states that tax-financed government expenditures result in a negative effect on GDP. Moreover, if it is productive spending, then it balances negative tax effects and yields a positive impact on the economy. A government also provides additional liquidity to the economy by taking loans (from abroad) instead of tax-based expansion. However, we should keep in mind the discussion about critical levels of debt and the negative impacts on (the effectiveness of) public expenditures.

Composition of Government Spending and Spending Multiplier. A determination of the size of a fiscal multiplier is equivalent to identifying whether it crowds in or crowds out private consumption and investment. Existing literature about the effect of fiscal policy on investment can be summarized as follows: government capital expenditure in developing countries crowds in investment, as private and public investment can be considered complementary, while government investment is not more effective than consumption in developed countries. The last finding fits the traditional view of crowding out effect of government spending due to higher interest rates. However, evidence from developing countries falls into a non-traditional view, where the relationship is more powerful under a non-full employment condition. However, the magnitude of this effect depends on the structure of spending. For example, Mahmoudzadeh, Sadeghi and Sadeghi (2013) in their panel analysis about developing and developed countries show that the elasticity of private investment with respect to public investment is positive and significant (0.31), while it is 0.18 in developed ones.

Moreover, private investment elasticity with respect to other type of expenditures is negative and lower than in developed countries, i.e. incidence of a crowding out effect. Sadeghi et al. (2013) conclude that in developing countries public investment is more efficient because private agents face a liquidity constraint, and interest rate differentials exist. However, there is evidence that does not support this idea. For example, Hasan (1960) states that in developing countries, public investment has a long run nature (infrastructure projects, irrigation system and so on); it has a low effect on current output and it contributes to inflation. While the paper by Parvez (1960) begins with a theoretical discussion, recent empirical evidence from the IMF suggests that public spending on investment has positive impact on the economy, not only in the short run, but also in the medium-run. Estevao and Samarke (2013) estimate an investment multiplier to be from 0.2 to 0.7 and from 0.42 to 0.92 in the short-run and in the medium-run, respectively. These coefficients are for Central American developing countries. They also show that non-productive expenditure has a negative impact in those countries. As for the type of expenditure, the empirical evidence about developing countries shows that cutting expenditures on investment can be more harmful in economic downturn relative to cuts to current expenditure.

Devarajan et al. (1996) show that in developing countries, current expenditures positively affect the GDP, while capital expenditures have a negative influence in a panel of 43 developing countries over 20 years. In their model, they also account for the total level of government spending; hence, in their model a one dollar increase of capital spending automatically means a dollar reduction in current expenditures. But in other models, which do not account for a total level of expenditures, as Devarajan et al. (1996) claim, the strong positive effect of capital expenditure can be a reflection of a level effect of expenditure and not the relative advantage of capital over current expenditures. Miller and Ahmed (2000) do not control the total level of expenditures in their linear fixed effects estimates for 23 developing and 16 developed countries. In principle, they show that if expenditures on transportation and communication are financed through either obtaining loans or taxation, there is a positive effect on investment for developing countries, but a zero or a negative impact on investment in developed countries. However, if the government spends money on social security and welfare, it crowds out private investment. The work by Miller and Ahmed (2000), however, does not say anything about the gross effects on GDP for different types of budget spending.

In developing countries, a full effect of government investment is not reflected in a multiplier. Kraay (2013) claims that a higher share of expenditure on investment does not mean that it automatically results in higher levels of asset accumulation in developing countries due to inefficiency and waste. This analysis is supported by Kneffer and Kanck (2007). Moreover, Gupta et al. (2011) numerically show that a significant part of public expenditures on investment are not reflected in productive investment categories in developing countries. For example, in low-income countries, the share of capital stock adjusted with efficiency criteria is 30.1% of GDP, while the raw share is 71%. This finding magnifies our intuition that, due to institutional rigidities, the spending on productive assets is not used effectively in those countries. Furthermore, the income share of adjusted public investment in GDP is lower (0.14 instead of 0.25), but because of a downward adjustment of public investment by efficiency criteria, the marginal productivity for low-income countries reaches 0.88, which is too high. Moreover, it is slightly higher than the marginal productivity of private investment (0.71). To sum up, consistent with the analysis by Ilzetzki and Mendosa (2013), the government investment multiplier is 0.6, which is significantly higher than a consumption multiplier (-0.19) in developing contexts.

Fixed Exchange Rate versus Flexible Exchange Rate Regimes. In their paper Corsetti, Meier and Muller (2012) identify a government spending multiplier to be 0.75 under a floating regime vs. 1.2 under a pegged exchange regime. The difference is significant but not as large as in other works. For example, Petrovic, Arsic and Nojkovic (2014), for a panel of 10 emerging European economies, show that the spending multiplier under a pegged regime is 1.31 versus 0.03 under a fixed exchange regime. Moreover, Muller, Jußen and Born (2012) find evidence against the traditional Mundel-Flaming channel; in this standard framework, government spending under a flexible exchange regime causes an appreciation of the domestic currency and an additional crowding out of net exports. This means that there are other channels for creating the gap between fiscal policy efficiency under fixed and flexible regimes.

There is no strong convention among economists about fiscal policy efficiency under fixed and flexible regimes. Corsetti, Meier and Muller (2012) claim that increasing spending from the budget causes an increase in the interest rate. As a result, it causes currency appreciation. If a monetary authority desires to fix the exchange rate, then it should increase money supply, which is an additional stimulus for an economy, and because of this, one would expect a higher multiplier. But as other studies show, the real world is not so simple and we should investigate the effect of a fiscal expansion under a fixed exchange regime and its interactions with a variety of conditions in the economic environment. For example, Lukkezen and Bonam (2013) show that as a country experiences high sovereign debt risk, the currency devaluation is expected to a response for fiscal expansion. As a result, the monetary authority will have to tighten monetary policy in a fixed exchange regime. Consequently, we face a higher interest rate and a stronger crowding out effect of investment and consumption; hence, a lower multiplier under a fixed exchange regime.

However, Lukkezen and Bonam (2013) argue that there is room for fiscal policy when its effect is higher under a pegged regime, even if we introduce sovereign risk in our analysis. For example, expansionary fiscal contraction holds only in the case of a fixed exchange regime only in the short run. Hence, if sovereign risk is high and fiscal authority consolidates finances, it reduces the risk premiums and stimulates an inflow of capital, which in turn causes an appreciation of the domestic currency. Under the peg, however, monetary authority intervenes and we do not face crowding out effects of exports. This last finding once again emphasizes the importance to account for existing economic environments during discussions on spending multipliers.

The difference between multipliers under fixed or flexible regimes is also determined by a degree of capital mobility. Riguzzi (2014) finds that the output multiplier is lower (0.71) if capital markets are well functioning, relative to cases when capital mobility is limited (1.44). The intuition is that, when capital mobility is limited, exchange rates appreciate in response to fiscal expansion. But if capital mobility is unlimited, the degree of possible appreciation is lower, and, as a result, crowding out effect of exports is minor and a multiplier is higher. If we account for imperfect capital markets in the developing countries, this factor would have a positive effect on the size of a spending multiplier. Moreover, Kraay (2012) shows that in developing countries, there is no difference between multipliers under fixed or flexible regime, because the financial markets are malfunctioning and no appreciation of domestic currency is expected to occur as a result. Hence, financial openness negatively affects a spending multiplier, while trade openness results in a lower multiplier as well.

Effect of Openness on the Size of Multiplier. There is abundant empirical evidence about the relationship between openness and the effectiveness of fiscal policy. Also, Karras (2014) conducts an analysis for 62 developed and developing countries and shows that a fiscal multiplier is a decreasing function of the degree of openness. For example, when openness is around 10%, the multiplier is high (1.39) for this group of countries, but if openness is 50%, the multiplier becomes 1.05, and in the very extreme case when openness is more than 100%, the multiplier reaches the lowest level of 0.61. If the degree of openness is high, then the significant part of purchases by government are concentrated on imported commodities and the impact of policy on the domestic economy is limited. To sum up, we face a significant variation of fiscal multipliers across various policy environments. Yet, this discussion supports the idea by Corsetti, Meier and Muller (2012) that there is no single estimate for "the multiplier". Consequently, in this chapter we seek to estimate the government spending multiplier, by accounting for fiscal policy environments of CIS counties. Table 12.1 presents a summary of findings with regards to a spending multiplier in existing research.

Table 12.1 Summary of the Literature on Fiscal Multipliers

Author	Country	Impact multiplier	Cumulative	Methodology	Shock
Developed countries					
Perotti (2005)	Australia	-0.1/0.4	1.4/0.7	VAR	Government spending
	Canada	1/-0.3	0.6/-1.1		
	Germany	0.6/0.5	-0.8/-1.1		
	UK	0.5/-0.3	0/-0.9		
	USA	1.3/0.4	1.7/0.1		
Romer and Romer (2008)	USA	1.2 (one year)	4 (cumulative)	Narrative	Tax
Ramey (2008)	USA	1.5	1.5	Narrative	Gov. spending
Johnson, Souleles, and Parker (2006)	USA	0.2/0.4	n.a.		Tax rebates
Ilzetzki and Vegh (2008)	High income	0.4	1.5	VAR	Government spending
Blanchard and Perotti (2002)	USA	0.9	1.3	VAR	Government spending
Cogan and others (2009)	USA	1.0	1.2-1.5	DSGE	Government spending
Dalsgraard, Andre, and Richardson (2001)	USA	1.1-1.5 (one year)	2.1-2.8	OECD INTER-LINK model	Government spending
	Japan	1.7-2.6 (one year)	2.8-4.5		

ESTIMATION OF THE GOVERNMENT SPENDING MULTIPLIER

		Euro Area	1.2-1.9 (one year)	2.1-3.4	
Elmendorf and Furman (2006)		USA	1	n.a.	DSGE	Government spending
Corsetti and others (2012)		OECD	0.7	n.a.	Two step model	Government spending
Developing and emerging economies						
Kraay (2012)		102 developing countries		0.38-0.42	IV estimation	Government spending
Ilzetzki and others (2009)			-0.19	0.38	VAR	Government spending
Ilzetzki (2011)			0.2		VAR	Government spending
Shen and S. Yang (2012)		Developing countries		0.39	DSGE	Government spending using domestic debt
				0.32	DSGE	Government spending using external debt
Petrovic and others (2014)		Emerging European economies	0.2	0.58	VAR	Government spending

Note: The sample of authors is based on IMF staff papers on fiscal multipliers (2009).

Theoretical Framework

In this section, I review different theoretical approaches to identifying fiscal multipliers; i.e. what they are and why they vary across different studies. Corsetti, Meier and Muller (2012) claim that there is no "the multiplier" as it varies across different policy environments. Therefore, I will review key drivers of the size of fiscal multipliers that emerge from different economic environments. Based on a theoretical discussion, I will formulate a two-stage procedure for estimating government spending multipliers, in line with the model developed by Corsetti, Meier and Muller (2012).

The simplest definition of a fiscal multiplier is that "it [spending multiplier] is the change in output due to a change in fiscal policy instrument" Chinn (2013). Algebraically, it is $\partial y/\partial x$, where y is output and x is a policy instrument. If we seek to assess the immediate impact of a policy, we should calculate the impact multiplier (i.e. $\Delta Y/\Delta G$), but in most cases, especially when we try to calculate fiscal multipliers based on quarterly data, we should calculate a cumulative multiplier.

Most of empirical evidence about multipliers use not only Y_t (GDP) as an endogenous variable, but also, investigate how a change in fiscal policy is reflected in changes in consumption, investment, current account balance, exchange rate and other macroeconomic variables (Corsetti, Meier, and Muller, 2012; Petrovic, Arsic, and Nojkovic, 2014).

This theoretical model is characterized by Keynesian properties in the short run and Classical properties in the long run. As a result, as prices are sticky and cannot adjust quickly in the short run, fiscal policy is efficient and the multiplier is larger. Nevertheless, we expect no permanent effect from the change of fiscal policy as we use properties of Classical theory in the long run (Chinn 2013). The government spending multiplier is close to zero in Neoclassicists' approaches, as they assume no nominal rigidities. Moreover, this theory predicts a negative fiscal multiplier if taxes are distortionary.

Finally, as a New Keynesian model uses inter temporal optimization, it is close to Classical approaches in its prediction, but additionally the model uses assumptions about nominal and real rigidities. Due to these extensions, fiscal policy has an effect on output in the short run (Chinn 2013). Fiscal policy is not secured itself from a negative spending multiplier if expenditure is expected to be financed at the expense of taxes in the future; this is a reflection of Ricardian equivalence (Capet 2004). An expectation that taxes will be higher in the future erodes consumption and investment today and output decreases subsequently; so, there is a negative spending multiplier.

In order to estimate a multiplier, in practice at least two conditions must be satisfied for government spending shocks it should be unanticipated by economic agents and contemporaneously exogenous. First, the cyclical nature of government spending matters. If government spending is acyclical, the requirement of contemporaneous exogeneity holds. But we still do not have a guarantee that fiscal policy is unanticipated. Empirical literature about the cyclical nature of fiscal policy can be summarized as follows: fiscal policy is acyclical or counter cyclical in developed countries and mostly procyclical in developing ones (Ilzetzki and Vegh 2008). For example, the measure of the cyclical nature of government spending is 0.61 for developing countries and -0.11 for developed ones based on GMM estimation.

Kraay (2012) makes a distinction between discretionary fiscal policy and automatic stabilizers and claims that in developing countries, both of these are procyclical; automatic stabilizers are ineffective in those countries to smoothen fluctuations of output. Moreover, he states that the procyclical fiscal policy is a reflection of constraints on financial resources, and also, such policy is sometimes politically motivated. Kraay points out that during the post crisis in 2008, the developing world and their governments had a better fiscal stance and they had a tendency to utilize a more counter cyclical fiscal policy than in the pre-crisis period.

Theoretically, counter cyclical policy is optimal, as increases in government spending relax liquidity constraints in the economy during a recession. Hence, a recommendation is that governments increase spending in crisis times and reduce it in boom times. In contrast, Mahfouz, Hemming and Kell (2002) advocate that contractionary fiscal policy can be expansionary. Hence, fiscal consolidation causes a positive response from the private sector. The basic reasoning is that fiscal consolidation causes reductions of risk premiums if a country faces high public debt. Moreover, if a low and negative fiscal multiplier is typical in developing countries, then a pro-cyclical fiscal policy seems rational for those economies. For example, if a particular country increases its expenditure in bad times and the multiplier is negative, then it causes an additional reduction in GDP due to counter cyclical fiscal policy. Based on this discussion, procyclical fiscal policy is advantageous in developing countries, mainly during recessions.

Debt levels are the main reason why counter cyclical fiscal policy may not be optimal in developing countries as high debt levels bear high-risk premiums from investors' point of view. Hence, if public debt is high, the better strategy is to reduce government expenditure. In addition to low multipliers in high public debt environments, debt financed through domestic loans lowers the multiplier compared to debt financed with foreign loans. The intuition is that when financial resources are scarce within a country, additional financial resources from abroad provide liquidity to the economy, making the crowding in effect of government spending larger.

Furthermore, not only debt composition matters for the size of a multiplier but also spending composition is important. In developing countries, public investments are more efficient then government consumption, as public investment has a complimentary effect and crowds in private investment, making the aggregate fiscal effect even stronger. In fixed exchange rate regimes, a multiplier is higher, as expansionary fiscal policy generates expansionary monetary policy. However, the situation changes if capital market mobility is low. Higher government spending financed with debt may result in higher interest rates that can positively affect the inflow of financial resources from abroad. This results in exchange rate appreciation and the monetary authority has to increase the supply of money to reduce the interest rate differential. When capital mobility is low, on the other hand, there is no pressure on exchange rates and no necessity for monetary expansion exists.

Empirical Strategy

The existing literature on government spending (or consumption) multipliers are mostly concentrated on identification issues of discretionary fiscal policy shocks, i.e. the unanticipated part of government expenditure and its effect on output, private consumption, exports, and many other macroeconomic variables. An identification of the unanticipated part of government spending is a principal requirement for precise estimations. This is true especially for research on deriving government spending multipliers based on VAR (vector autoregressive) models. In order to identify the unexpected part of government consumption SVAR (stochastic specification of VAR model), models make several linear assumptions about fiscal policy rules, while the government spending can be considered as the unanticipated part. But as Ilzetzki and Mendosa (2013) point out, there is no guarantee that the unexplained part derived in econometric models cannot be predicted by private agents; this is common across other papers based on the conventional VAR estimations developed by Blanchard and Perotti (2002). Should the fiscal shock be predicted by private agents, it may cause changes in their behavior and we cannot estimate the efficiency of fiscal policy precisely.

There are also other papers, for example, by Ramey (2011) who use extraordinary shocks in the economy that generally cannot be anticipated. For example, Ramey uses wartime expenditure in the USA to predict a government spending multiplier. Ramey (2011) argues that military expenditures in the USA were a properly exogenous shock. Other findings show us that the exogeneity assumption of war time spending is ambiguous. For example, Ilzetzki and Vegh (2008) in their paper argue that war-time spending can be predicted by individuals in advance. The reason why it is problematic is that, when one wants to predict exogenous fiscal shocks, there are two basic requirements.

First, fiscal shocks should be unanticipated, and second, shocks should not be related to current economic conditions. While it can be said that wartime requisition is unrelated to current economic conditions, it nevertheless can be anticipated by private agents. Moreover, the main reason why the model proposed by Ramey contains potential problems is that it requires a long time series. For example, the analysis by Ramey (2011) is applied over a long period of US history and it covers a war-times in Vietnam, as well as in Korea. Such long series data is often unavailable for most other countries. Moreover, those wars were outside of the USA, and they were not related to a significant reduction of capital assets domestically. Of course, this is not the case in other countries where the result of war was an extraordinary destruction of capital assets. Those are the main drawbacks of the model proposed by Ramey and it is not easy to apply to contexts outside of the USA.

The basic requirement is that a fiscal shock should be contemporaneously exogenous. That is, a fiscal stimulus should not be driven by a current economic situation. Because of this, researchers have to make an assumption about the lag in which fiscal policy can react to contemporaneous change in the economy. In normal times, of course, this lag is just one year; as the fiscal authority works out a new budget plan with one-year intervals. More problematic context is an economy with sudden and sharp downturn or boom periods. Most researchers who use quarterly data claim that a one quarter-lag is quite relevant in this case; i.e. fiscal authority needs at least one quarter to adjust its initial budget plan. The assumption that a fiscal shock is contemporaneously exogenous is difficult to apply in the analysis based on annual data; in this context contemporaneously exogeneity means that the fiscal authority does not make any adjustment in the budgetary plan during a subsequent year. As Corsetti, Meier and Muller (2012) claim, a year as an implementation lag is relevant if there are no extraordinary cases.

The second group in the literature is based on New-Keynesian DSGE models. Structural models are not sensitive to assumptions required by VAR models, but they still bear some restrictions. The main assumption is related to price setting behaviors. DSGE framework follows Calvo type price setting; according to this, one part of prices on intermediate goods are rigid in the short term period, but other parts of prices are free to optimize to changes in the economic situation. For example, Cristiano, Eichenbaum and Rabelo (2009) in their paper on multipliers, make an assumption that 0.85 of a unit price is rigid. And they conclude that only under such exaggerated assumptions the fiscal multiplier is 1.05. It is obvious that the size of the fiscal multiplier identified by DSGE models is sensitive with respect to the assumptions about Calvo type price setting. If prices are more rigid then DSGE identifies, the multiplier is close to a Keynesian multiplier. This is not a big surprise in cases of high price rigidity. Moreover, there is no convention among macroeconomists about fiscal policy rules, which is one of the basic factors in DSGE framework (Batini, Luc, and Weber, 2014). In principle, we observe different models of fiscal rules in different papers; which can be a potential source of variation of the fiscal multiplier estimate itself.

The problems related to conventional VAR and DSGE models are amplified by data limitations in developing countries. This is the main reason why we have little empirical evidence for this group of countries. However, Batini, Luc and Weber (2014) provide a new model for estimating multipliers under data limitation, which they called "the bucket approach". This model is basically an "analytic guess" about a fiscal multiplier. A multiplier under this model is a simple weighted average of scores assigned to a particular state of a country (openness, rigidity of the labor market, level of automatic stabilizers, fixed or flexible exchange regimes, levels of government debt, effective expenditure/revenue management), but the authors allocate this multiplier measure to three different intervals. Hence, their approach gives us interval estimations and not point estimates of fiscal multipliers. Unfortunately, despite its simplicity, this model has no reasonable theoretical grounding.

Finally, each model type (i.e. VAR and DSGE models) cannot be used without considerations for their pros and cons. We must seek a deeper analysis of their specific application to determine when the identified multiplier is obtained without any significant biases. As it is stated in many papers, for example Perotti (2007), the conventional VAR models proposed by Blanchard and Perotti (2002) are unable to predict fiscal shocks, which is perfectly discretionary or unanticipated. Perotti's argument is that many papers use a one-quarter implementation lag, which is too short for fiscal policy to be implemented, while in long implementation lags fiscal spending can be anticipated by private agents.

This idea is adopted in Corsetti, Meier, and Muller (2012). They propose to add predicted government spending levels in models of fiscal policy related multipliers. Due to this, we can reduce the risk of anticipation. This approach is implemented by Corsetti, Meier, and Muller (2012) for OECD countries, where they use composite leading indicators as a proxy for predicted GDP levels in their two-stage regressions. As long run time series for predicted GDP or government spending levels is not available in developing countries, the economists work out new ways for predicting unanticipated fiscal shocks. For example, Kraay (2012) uses an instrumental variable estimation approach (but as was discussed, his approach is not free from problems as well).

Corsetti, Meier, and Muller (2012) suggest a two-stage model to identify fiscal multipliers. This model tries to solve the omitted variable problem, which is the main deficiency in conventional VAR models. In principle, they put dummy variables, which describe the economic environment in the model, such as a currency peg dummy, a crisis dummy, the state of the primary balance of the budget, and public debt levels. The objective in the first stage is to identify fiscal shocks, which will be orthogonal to other developments in the economy, i.e. exogenous shock of government spending. At this stage this model assumes that the fiscal policy rule can be described with past information on the economic environment.

In principle, the explanatory variables at this stage are: a trend variable, two lagged values of government spending (gt-1, gt-2); two lagged values of real GDP per capita (Yt-1, Yt-2); a public debt/GDP ratio (bt-1); a peg dummy (pegt-1,i); a dummy variable showing deficit (straint-1,1), and a crisis dummy (crisist-1,i). But as it is pointed out in other papers, a fiscal shock generated through fiscal policy rules can be anticipated if the rule is based on past events. Public expenditures can be predictable by private agents in this case. Due to this, Corsetti, Meier and Muller (2012) seek to control for future developments in the economy by introducing a composite leading indicator (clit-1,i) which is used as a proxy of predicted GDP. The dependent variable is government spending per capita in period t. Table 12.2 contains details of first and second state estimation models for fiscal multipliers.

Table 12.2 Stage 1 and Stage 2 Estimation Models for Fiscal Multipliers

Stage (1)
$G_{t,I} = \theta_i + \delta_i {*}trend_t + \beta_{i,1} g_{t-1} + \beta_{i,2} g_{t-2} + \gamma_{i,1} Y_{t-1} + \gamma_{i,2} Y_{t-2} + \theta_i cli_{t-1,I} + \lambda_i b_{t-1} + \rho_{i,1} peg_{t-1,1} + \rho_{i,2} strain_{t-1,1} + \rho_{i,3} crisis_{t-1,1} + \mu_t$
In the second stage, the model uses fiscal shock and its lagged values as explanatory variables ($\mu hat_{t,I}, \mu hat_{t-1,I}, \mu hat_{t-2,I}, \mu hat_{t-3,i}$) generated from the first stage regression. Also, an interaction between fiscal shock and dummies representing economic context are applied ($\mu hat_{t,I}{*}d_{t,I}, \mu hat_{t-1,I}{*}d_{t-1,I}, \mu hat_{t-2,I}{*}d_{t-2,I}, \mu hat_{t-3,I}{*}d_{t-3,I}$), as well as direct effects of dummy variables on the dependent variable is considered ($d_{t,I}, d_{t-1,I}, dt, i-2, d_{t-3,I}$). The dependent variable can be GDP per capita, as well as consumption, investment, export, exchange rate, and many other relevant macroeconomic variables.
Stage (2)
$X_{t,i} = a_i + k_i trend_t + q_i X_{t-1,I} + \xi_i \mu hat_{t,I} + \xi_2 \mu hat_{t-1,I} + \xi_3 \mu hat_{t-2,I} + \xi_4 \mu hat_{t-3,I} + \tau_1(\mu hat_{t,I}{*}d_{t,I}) + \tau_2(\mu hat_{t-1,I}{*}d_{t-1,I}) + \tau_3(\mu hat_{t-2,I}{*}d_{t-2,I}) + \tau_4(\mu hat_{t-3,I}{*}d_{t-3,I}) + \omega_1 d_{t,i} + \omega_2 d_{t-1,i} + \omega_3 d_{t,i-2} + \omega_4 d_{t-3,I} + \varepsilon_t$

Corsetti, Meier, and Muller (2012) use this model to estimate the spending multiplier for OECD countries, based on annual data. In this study, I apply their model for CIS economies. I use annual data from 1991 to 2016 on GDP per capita (current USD), instead of a dummy variable for a weak fiscal time (which is defined based on a primary balance in the original paper) I use public debt to GDP threshold. In general, debt to GDP is driven by primary balance, but in addition its level temporarily can be affected by sudden deterioration of economic and financial conditions. Despite the fact that primary balance and debt comove even under such circumstances, in some cases the influence of shocks to debt can be higher. For example, debt levels suddenly shift up in cases of currency depreciation in countries with high foreign currency debt, but primary balance is less sensitive to this shock. Also, instead of composite leading indicators, I use a one-year forward value of the trend component of GDP.

Data and Sources

In this paper, a government spending multiplier is estimated in a two-stage linear model. In the first stage, a government spending shock is identified based on the fiscal policy rule. As it was described in the empirical strategy section, fiscal policy rule environment is tied to public debt, budget balance, currency peg regimes, and crises periods. Detailed descriptions of key variables and their sources are given in Table 12.3.

Table 12.3 List of Variables and Sources

Variable	Data source
Log of per capita GDP	World Bank database, World Development Indicators: GDP per capita (constant 2010 US$) World Development Indicators. Data is available from 1992 to 2015, N = 290 observations.
Log of real per capita government spending	World bank database: World Development Indicators, general government final consumption expenditure (% of GDP) is used together with per capita GDP to reconstruct per capita government expenditure, data are available from 1992 to 2015 N = 288 observations.
General government gross debt (as % of GDP)	IMF, Data is available from 1992 to 2015 only for Russia and Ukraine; also, data on debt is available from 1995 to 2015 for most CIS countries, N = 256 observations, for 12 countries
Financial crisis dummy	Takes on value of 1 during financial crises, and 0 otherwise, when one of them has a Systemic Banking Crisis (starting date), Currency Crisis, Sovereign Debt Crisis. The data comes from

	IMF Working Paper „Systemic Banking Crises Database: An Update" by Laeven and Valencia (2012), which is available from 1992 to 2012, N = 262 observations, for 12 countries.
Bad fiscal times dummy	Takes on a value of 1 when lagged public debt exceeds 100 percent of or alternatively time when General government net lending/borrowing (Percent of GDP) is less than -6%. Because of limited data availability on General government net lending/borrowing, we have to use public debt threshold for determining bed fiscal time. The 100% threshold is adopted in Corsetti, Meier and Muller (2012) for advanced economies, but 60% threshold is more prudent for CIS countries.
Peg dummy	Carmen M. Reinhart database: Exchange rate regime classification, annual, 1946-2016, (http://www.carmenrein hart.com/data/browse-by-country/) is used as a peg dummy variable. Data is available from 1992 to 2015, N = 288 observations.

Empirical Results

In the first stage, 12 individual regressions were run and residuals (spending shocks) were identified. Residuals from the first stage linear regressions are considered to be government spending shocks, i.e. part of government spending that cannot be explained by a fiscal policy rule. In the second stage, an unconditional multiplier was estimated initially, where the model was estimated without an inclusion of dummy variables on economic condition. In the second stage, a unit root test was applied to the logarithmic value of GDP. As ln(GDP) was predicted to be non-stationarity in the Im–Pesaran–Shin test, a first difference of ln(GDP) is generated, which tested to be stationary. Hence, on the left-hand side, a dependent variable in our model is a growth rate of GDP. The unconditional fixed effect model predicts that a coefficient of impact of government spending over growth rate of GDP is 0.045.

However, this cannot be interpreted as a multiplier, because a multiplier is a level of change in GDP for 1dollar change in government spending. As the average share of government spending is 15% in CIS countries, we can expect an 0.045/0.15 = 0.3 unconditional government spending multiplier for the CIS. Hence, a dollar of government spending shock results in a 0.3 dollar increase in GDP. This coefficient is quite close to a multiplier identified by Kraay (2012). First and second year lag multipliers are insignificant, while the third-year impact multiplier is negative and significant. As a result, a cumulative lagged multiplier is smaller than the main multiplier effect. This finding suggests that government spending is significant contemptuously, but close to neutral in the longer run. Results from the second stage regression are presented in Table 12.4.

Table 12.4 Second Stage Regression Analysis Results

Variables	Unconditional (model 1)		Debt level (model 2)		Fixed vs. flexible exchange regime (model 3)		Recession vs. expansion (model 4)	
	Coefficient	t-score	Coefficient	t-score	Coefficient	t-score	Coefficient	t-score
Spending shock	0.045	(3.78)	0.052**	(3.36)	0.049*	(2.50)	0.019*	(2.23)
Spending shock -1	-0.038	(-1.40)	0.012	(0.34)	-0.026	(-0.85)	-0.039	(-1.79)
Spending shock -2	0.029	(1.30)	-0.034	(-1.37)	-0.018	(-1.07)	0.030	(1.52)
Spending shock -3	-0.026*	(-2.97)	-0.046	(-0.83)	-0.000	(-0.09)	-0.034*	(-5.12)
Spending shock*debt dummy			-0.013	(-1.59)				
Spending shock1*debt dummy1			-0.066***	(-5.33)				
Spending shock2*debt dummy2			0.068***	(6.32)				
Spending shock3*debt dummy3			0.016	(0.30)				
Debt dummy			0.040**	(3.67)				
Debt dummy -1			-0.034	(-1.90)				

Debt dummy -2	-0.022*	(-2.29)				
Debt dummy -3	0.005	(0.69)				
Spending shock*peg dummy			-0.001	(-0.11)		
Spending shock1*peg dummy1			-0.034*	(-4.78)		
Spending shock2*peg dummy2			0.060*	(4.52)		
Spending shock3*peg dummy3			-0.020	(-0.96)		
Peg dummy			0.037*	(3.36)		
Peg dummy 1			0.001	(0.21)		
Peg dummy 2			-0.015	(-1.70)		
Peg dummy 3			0.004	(0.55)		
Crisis dummy (1= expansion)					0.046*	(6.12)
Crisis dummy 1					-0.037*	(-7.46)
Crisis dummy 2					-0.009	(-1.43)
Crisis dummy 3					-0.032*	(-3.98)
Spending shock* crisis dummy					0.007	(0.67)

Spending shock1* crisis dummy1					0.0363* (4.56)
Spending shock2* crisis dummy2					0.006 (0.57)
Spending shock3* crisis dummy3					-0.000 (-0.01)
Constant	0.0534* (104.52)		0.0621* (9.94)	0.0280* (2.82)	0.065* (21.46)
N	210		210	210	210

Notes: Robust standard errors in parentheses; *** p<0.001, ** p<0.01, * p<0.05

One of the key questions in the chapter was how economic environments affect the size of a multiplier. Below we discuss conditional multipliers with regards to three key fiscal factors.

Public debt and spending multiplier. 60%[2] of debt to GDP ratio was taken as a threshold to analyze the effect of government spending on GDP growth. When the debt to GDP ratio is less than 60% (low level) the fiscal multiplier is 0.35 (0.0529/0.15). The coefficient of interaction between government spending and debt dummy is not significant contemporaneously. Hence, a multiplier at high debt versus low debt levels is not significantly different. However, the coefficients of first- and second-year lags interaction with a spending measure are significant, but the signs of these coefficients are inconsistent. Hence, the model doesn't provide consistent and comprehensive evidence to conclude that fiscal multiplier is smaller in high debt versus low debt CIS countries. This is likely because of lower frequency of sovereign debt problems among the CIS countries.

Crisis and spending multiplier. I defined crisis (recession) as a negative deviation from the HP trend of GDP. The negative deviation is a recession, while the positive deviation is an expansion. A government spending multiplier in crises time is 0.13 (0.019/0.15). This is significantly smaller than the unconditional multiplier. The coefficient of an interaction variable for government spending and a crisis dummy is not significant; hence, a multiplier is not different across crises versus non crises conditions. However, a previous year's multiplier in expansionary times is positive and significant (0.036). This means that if a government increases spending in crises time, the expenditure will have a negative effect on GDP in the next year (negative multiplier is 0.24). This evidence supports the idea that in expansionary environments fiscal consolidation must be preferred. Consequently, when governments consolidate budgets in crises times, they will have an expansionary effect on GDP.

---

2 According to the debt sustainability framework for low income countries external public sector debt bears high risk when it exceeds 55% of GDP (Internationl Monetary Fund 2018); taking into account small share of domestic debt in CIS countries, we increase the threshold only up to 60%, we also have set higher threshold but have come up quantitatively same results.

At the same time, a multiplier in non-crises times is 0.28, while the coefficient for its interaction with the spending measures is insignificant.

Currency regime and spending multiplier. Based on Izetzki, Reinhart and Rogoff (2019) database on currency regimes, I have applied an interaction variable between currency peg dummy variable and government spending measure to assesses any variations in multipliers for flexible versus fixed exchange rate regimes. A multiplier in fixed exchange rate regimes is 0.33, but the model fails to identify a differential impact multiplier in flexible exchange rate regimes. However, government spending has a smaller effect in flexible regimes versus fixed regimes (a multiplier is smaller by 0.23) after a year of fiscal spending. This result likely means that, all else equal, a monetary expansion channel takes time to react to fiscal policy interventions.

Conclusion

There is dearth of research on government spending efficiency in developing countries, and CIS countries are not an exception. This chapter analyses the government spending multiplier in CIS countries. The main challenge for macroeconomists when measuring a government spending multiplier is to identify spending shocks, which will be unanticipated and contemporaneously exogenous. This study uses a two-stage linear regression model approach to estimate multipliers. In the first stage, a spending shock is identified in the models of a fiscal policy rule, and in the second stage, a resultant spending shock measure is used as a policy variable to estimate a multiplier for the panel of 12 CIS countries.

An unconditional government spending multiplier identified in this article is 0.3 for CIS countries. In principle, the multiplier is close to other estimates for developing countries. It shows that a 1 dollar unexpected increase in government expenditure increases GDP by 0.3 dollars. As a result, there is weak evidence of expansionary effect of government spending in CIS countries.

Together with an unconditional multiplier, the chapter identifies spending multipliers across different economic environments.

As the results suggest, there is evidence that in crisis time government expansion can lead to negative consequences to the economy. The finding supports the idea that in expansionary times fiscal consolidation must be preferred. Furthermore, there is no evidence that a multiplier varies across high vs. low public debt environments. The model produces smaller estimates for a multiplier in flexible exchange rate regimes versus fixed rate regime environments. Finally, there is no strong and consistent evidence that there are lagged effects of government spending on GDP. To sum up, based on the empirical results of two-stage models for CIS countries, fiscal authorities should not expect significant effects of government spending shocks in their economies. However, there is evidence that fiscal consolidation contributes to a positive response of CIS economies in crisis times.

References

Capet, Stéphane. 2004. "The Efficiency of Fiscal Policies: A Survey of the Literature." *CEPII Working Paper.*

Ahmed, Habib, and Miller, Stephen M. 2000. "Crowding-Out and Crowding-In Effects of the Components of Government Expenditure." *Contemporary Economic Policy* 124-133.

Barro, Robert. 1990. "Government Spending in a Simple Model of Endogenous Growth." *Journal of Political Economy* 98(S5): 103-125.

Batni, Nicoletta, Luc, Eyraud, and Weber, Anke. 2014. "A Simple Method to Compute Fiscal Multipliers." *IMF working peper.*

Blanchard, Olivier, and Perotti, Robert. 2002. "An Empirical Characterization of the Dynamic Effects of Changes in Government Spending and Taxes on Output." *Quarterly Journal of Economics* 1329-1368.

Bonam, Dennis, and Lukkezen, Jasper. 2014. "Government Spending Shocks, Sovereign Risk and the Exchange Rate Regime." *Tinbergen Institute Discussion Paper.*

Chinn, Menzie. 2013. "Fiscal Multipliers." *The New Palgrave Dictionary of Economics.*

Corsetti, Giancarlo, Meier, Andre, and Muller, J. Gernot. 2012. "What Determines Government Spending Multiplier?" *IMF Working Paper WP/12/150.*

Cristiano, Lawrence, Eichenbaum, Martin, and Rabelo, Sergio. 2009. "When Is the Government Spending Multiplier Large." *NBER Working Paper 15394.*

Devarajan, Shantayanan, Swaroop, Vinaya, and Zou, Heng-fu. 1996. "The Composition of Public Expenditure and Economic Growth." *Journal of Monetary Economics* 313-344.

Estevao, Marcello, and Samarke, Marcello. 2013. "The Economic Effect of Fiscal Consolidation with Debt Feedback." *IMF Working Paper WP/13/136.*

Ilzetzki, Ethan, and Vegh, A. Carlos. 2008. "Procyclical Fiscal Policy in Developing Countries: Truth or Fiction?" *NBER Working Paper No. 14191.*

Ilzetzki, Ethan, and Mendosa, Enrique G. 2013. "How Big (Small?) Are Fiscal Multipliers?" Journal of Monetary Economics 239-254.

Ilzetzki, Ethan, Reinhart, Carmen M., and Rogoff, Kenneth S. 2019. "Exchange Rate Arrangements Entering the 21st Century: Which Anchor Will Hold?" *The Quarterly Journal of Economics* 599-646.

International Monetary Fund. 2018. The Debt Sustainability Framework for Low-Income Countries. July 13. Last accessed June 19, 2019 at https://www.imf.org/external/pubs/ft/dsa/lic.htm.

Kraay, Aart. 2012. "Government Spending Multiplier in Developing Countries." *The World Bank Research Working Paper No. 609.*

Laeven, Luc, and Valencia, Fabián. 2012. "Systemic Banking Crises Database: An Update." *IMF Working Paper WP/12/163.*

Mahfouz, Salma, Hemming, Richard, and Kell, Michael. 2002. "The Effectiveness of Fiscal Policy in Stimulating Economic Activity: A Review of the Literature." *IMF working paper.*

Mahmoudzadeh, Mahmoud, Sadeghi, Somaye, and Sadeghi, Soraya. 2013. "Fiscal Spending and Crowding out Effect: A Comparison between Developed and Developing Countries." *Institutions and Economies* 31-40.

Parvez, Hasan. 1960. "The Investment Multiplier in an Underdeveloped Economy." *Economic Digest* 21-29.

Perotti, Roberto. 2007. "In Search of the Transmission Mechanism of Fiscal Policy." *NBER Working Paper 13143.*

Petrovic, Pavle, Arsic, Milojko, and Nojkovic, Aleksandra. 2014. "Fiscal Multiplier in Emerging European Economies." *Fiscal Council of Republic of Serbia Research Paper.*

Ramey, Valerie. 2011. "Identifying Government Spending Shocks It's All in the Timing." *The Quarterly Journal of Economics* 1-50.

Riguzzi, Marco. 2014. "Economic Openness and Fiscal Multipliers." Diskussionsschriften dp1406, Universitaet Bern.

Sanjeev, Gupta, Clements, Benedict, Baldacci, Emanuele, and Mulas-Granados, Carlos. 2005. "Fiscal Policy, Expenditure Composition, and Growth in Low-Income Countries." *Journal of International Money and Finance* 441-463.

Shahe, Emran, and Farazi, Subika. 2008. "Government Borrowing and Private Credit: Evidence from Developing." *World Bank Working Papers.*

Shen, W., Yang, Shu-chun, and Zanna, Luis Felipe. 2015. "Government Spending Effects in Low Income Countries." *IMF Working Paper WP/15/286.*

13
Geographical and Globalization Patterns in Georgian Trade

Davit Akhvlediani

Geographically and economically Georgia is a small country. The country is located in the Caucasus region, between Asia and Europe, between the Caspian and the Black Sea basins. Historically Georgia had tasted both the joy of independence and the bitterness of foreign rule. During the past seven centuries it was ruled by Mongols, Persians, and Ottomans. Georgia was occupied in the 19th Century by the Russian Empire and later in the 20th Century by the Soviet Union. In 1990, after regaining independence, the country fell into civil war and eventually lost around 20% of its territories to secessionist republics that currently remain under Russian control. In 2008 Georgia fought a brief but bloody war with Russia that has deepened its security and social challenges.

Georgia was one of richest republics in the Soviet Union. In 1990, its GDP was $3,700 in constant 2010 U.S. dollars (World Bank, 2020). After internal turmoil in the 1990s the country lost 65% of its GDP and did not regain its prior level until 2013 (World Bank, 2018). Currently Georgia is inhabited by 3.7 million people, has a GDP per capita of $4,770 (World Bank, 2020), and is labeled as an upper middle-income country. Despite moderate economic recovery during past years, poverty remains a huge challenge. The World Bank (2018) estimates that one fifth of the total population lives beyond the absolute poverty line. To pull its citizens from misery and open new horizons for development, Georgia needs fast and robust economic growth. The Government of Georgia, largely aware of internal weaknesses, undertook a number of structural reforms in almost all dimensions of public life and for its success was labeled as a number one reformer country by the World Bank in 2010. Today, Georgia has a simple and attractive tax system, and it scores seventh in the World Bank's famous easiness of doing business ranking. In the Human Development Index, a measurement that studies quality of human capital, Georgia is labeled highly with the 70th world ranking.

Economically small countries require investments and exports to increase their welfare. From 2014-2018 Georgia received on average $1.68 billion in foreign direct investment (FDI) (Geostat, 2020) that contributed to overall economic growth that averaged 3.8% during the same period. Structural weaknesses and the small size of the internal market forced the Georgian government to liberalize trade and seek export markets. In recent years Tbilisi has signed free trade agreements with the EU, China, and India in addition to already-existing similar treaties with Turkey and the Commonwealth of Independent States (CIS) countries. Yet, the efforts of the Government of Georgia to secure international markets were clouded by sheer export growth (expressed in absolute growth). From 2015-2018, Georgia's trade increased around 30%, from $9.5 billion in 2015 to $12.5 billion (Geostat, 2020). During the same period, Georgian exports increased around 52% from $2.2 billion to $3.35 billion, whereas imports marked a 25% increase from $7.3 billion to $9.13 billion. The export deficit, with minor fluctuation, averaged $5.3 billion per year during the same period (Geostat, 2020), consequently pressuring local currency to devaluate. According to Bloomberg, from January 2015 to January 2018, the Georgian lari depreciated 23%, and this trend has been largely continuing in 2019.

In addition to competitive industries overall, trade occurs when businesses have knowledge of the export markets, such as mutual awareness and cross-border contacts. In other words, trade occurs when businesses and people are *globalized*. Distance negatively affects trade. The further the export markets are, the harder it is to penetrate them due to higher trade costs and difficulty in managing overseas business activities. Although in recent years shipping costs have dropped, capturing distant markets remains costly. According to UNCTAD, the shipment cost of a 20 foot container from Shanghai to Northern Europe decreased from $1,789 to $822 between 2010-2018 and from Shanghai to the U.S. West Coast from $2,300 to $1,740 (UNCTAD, 2019).

In this chapter I aim to answer the question of whether distance and social globalization affect Georgia's trade. If they do, to what extent? In order to answer this question based on the findings of past literature, I develop a hypothesis. I expect that Georgia's trade grows proportionally to its GDP and that greater social globalization both at home and abroad contribute to greater trade. The chapter uses the *gravity equation* of international trade to derive a statistical model and tests its application in the Georgian context. Although the gravity equation remains a workhorse to analyze patterns in the literature on trade, the impact of social globalization on trade has never been tested. My study will fill this gap in the international trade literature. Additionally, my findings will provide statistically grounded results that the Government of Georgia can utilize in the process of shaping trade policy.

In order to test my hypotheses, I tabulate relevant data and estimate Poisson pseudo-maximum likelihood (PPML) regression models. As a robustness check, I verify that the findings are similar when using ordinary least squares (OLS) regression models. As mentioned above, my model uses GDP, physical distance, and social globalization levels as trade predictors and does not take into consideration other important factors that can have an effect. I estimate robust models using several strategies because omitted variables are extensive and, in theory depending on the context, they may or may not influence trade. Relevant economic variables may include exchange rate fluctuations, industrial competitive edge, tariffs, transportation costs. Relevant political variables may include the global financial crisis as well as Georgia's 5-day war with Russia, with its profound economic and social implications. Also, my research period covers the 2000-2015 timeframe and does not take into consideration the effects of the Georgia-EU rapprochement that is reflected in free trade and visa-free movement. As a final potential limit of this study, the social globalization index that this chapter uses still remains an arguable proxy to capture and quantify all aspects of cross-border connections. However, this measure has been extensively used in statistical analyses across different contexts. Having noted these potential limits, I now proceed to review the relevant literature on international trade.

Literature Review

Past literature reveals that the effect of distance on trade has been rather well-studied, whereas social globalization's effects have been largely left in the shade. The effect of distance and GDP size on trade has been captured by the *gravity model* of international trade. The gravity model found its way to the international trade literature from physics. Nobel Laureate Jan Tinbergen (1962) was the first scholar who used Newton's gravity model to analyze international trade. In the pioneering study *Shaping the World Economy*, he analyzed trade among 18 countries to conclude that the index of trade between two countries is positively linked to the GDP sizes and negatively to its resistance index, which is physical distance. Later scholarship revealed that the gravity model can be also derived from other international trade theories such as the Ricardian model, the Heksher-Ohlin model, and much earlier models of economies of scale (Kumar and Ahmed, 2015). The original gravity model is estimated as follows:

$$X(ij) = B0 + B1GDP(i) + B2GDP(j) + B3tau(ij) + eta(ij)$$

Where X_{ij} corresponds to the exports from country i to country j, GDP_i is the GDP of country i in the trading year, GDP_j is the GDP of country j, τ_{ij} represents the obstacles expressed in the physical distance between the countries, each b term is a partial regression coefficient (including an intercept), and e_{ij} is a random error term.

Further studies have strengthened the evidence that GDP and distance are relevant factors that affect trade. Daria Taglioni and Luca De Benedicts (2014) evaluated the 50-year progress of the model to conclude that, despite imperfections, it remains the best method to analyze trade. Seema Naryan and Tri Tung Nguyen (2016) retrieved the data from 54 trading partners over the period of 1986-2010 and concluded that Vietnam's trade with rich nations is more distance-sensitive than trade with low-income nations. Rebecca Freeman and Samuel Pienknagura (2018) used a gravity equation to analyze the role of the geographic distance on the trade of intermediate and non-intermediate goods among 185 counties covering the period between 1965-2010. They found that intermediary products are dependent on both distance and free trade agreements, whereas non-intermediary goods are not dependent on geography. The difference can be explained by the fact that intermediary products are used to produce final products, thus the time of transportation derived from the long geographic distance affects the trade, whereas non-intermediary products represent the final goods that are more sensitive to price and quality than to the timing of transportation. The only analysis using the gravity model for Georgian context was conducted by Azer Dilanchiev. Using panel data in 2000-2011, he analyzed Georgian trade and concluded that GDP, FDI, and common history are the factors influencing trade (Dilanchiev, 2012).

In order to export, companies require knowledge of the external markets. A lot has been written about the information frictions of trade. There exists a number of channels through which information and knowledge are transferred across the borders, such as interpersonal contacts and membership in international communities. Chetty and Holm (2000) utilized longitudinal research methods to study New Zealand's export characteristics and have concluded that membership in international business networks played a significant role in finding export partners. By analyzing French exports, Chaney (2014) observes that companies that start exporting in foreign markets through their subsidiaries acquire knowledge about the market situation, pricing, and other related opportunities, and these companies eventually export more.

Internet access is another channel that provides information about markets and contacts to businesspersons. Faqin Lin (2014), using a gravity model of international trade, finds that a 10% increase in internet penetration worldwide provides a 0.2% to 0.4% increase international trade. This finding was further strengthened by Lapatinas (2019), who studied the role of the internet access on the economic sophistication level of 100 economically developed and developing countries. He concluded that the level of internet penetration has a statistically significant positive effect on trade.

Empirical Framework and Hypothesis

The literature review shows that the gravity equation remains the best way to capture trade patterns. Also, I identified that exports require knowledge of the target country, business partnerships, and local contacts. The best method to capture knowledge sharing and contacts between the partners is a proxy of social globalization of the relevant countries. If a country is more globalized, then there is a better awareness of its products, and businesspersons have more information and awareness to find partners and markets around the globe. Globalization also drives a country to the knowledge and competition frontline. As more information about competitors and knowledge about markets is generated internally, there is a greater push for trade externally.

In line with the literature, I hypothesize that trade between Georgia and a relevant country will grow as the two nations' economies increase, but I also expect that growth of trade will occur in proximate territories. Additionally, I expect that counties that exhibit higher levels of globalization will trade with each other more. To test my hypotheses, I develop a statistical model that incorporates a globalization variable in the traditional gravity equation:

$$X(ij) = B0 + B1\log(GDP(i)) + B2\log(GDP(j)) + B3\log(tau(ij)) + B4\log(Glob(i)) + B5\log(Glob(j)) + eta(ij)$$

Where X_{ij} is the sum of exports between countries i (Georgia) and j in a given year, GDP_i is Georgia's gross domestic product in a given year, GDP_j is the GDP of relevant trading partner j in a given year, τ_{ij} represents the obstacles expressed in the physical distance between the countries, $Glob_i$ is the globalization index of Georgia in a given year, $Glob_j$ is the globalization index of trading partner country j, each b term is a partial regression coefficient (including an intercept), and e_{ij} is a random error term. Note that all GDP and globalization measures are included in logged form.

Based on the gravity equation, I also develop a separate model about Georgian exports. Although this model lacks prior theoretical justification, testing it in contrast with the gravity equation and comparing its results with the above-mentioned model can tell us characteristics about Georgian exports. In my second model I simply exchange the trade dependent variable with Georgia's exports to country j and leave the independent variables unchanged:

$$Y(ij) = c0 + c1\log(GDP(i)) + c2\log(GDP(j)) + c3\log(tau(ij)) + c4\log(Glob(i)) + c5\log(Glob(j)) + u(ij)$$

In this case Y_{ij} is the total of Georgia's exports to trading partner country j in a given year, and all other variables are the same. Because this is a new model, the coefficients are now denoted as c terms, and the error is denoted as u.

Data and Methods

To run these regressions, I constructed panel data of trade dyads between Georgia and 56 trading partners from 2000-2015, producing a total of 896 observations. The 56 world countries were randomly selected in Microsoft Excel. Table 13.1 reports the descriptive statistics of all variables to be included in the model: the number of observations, the mean, the standard deviation, the minimum, and the maximum. For simplicity, all statistics in the table are rounded to the nearest whole number. The first dependent variable of *trade* was constructed as the combined value of exports between the trading countries in a given year and is expressed in millions of dollars in current prices. The second dependent variable of *Georgian exports* stands for Georgian exports to a particular partner country. Exports were retrieved from Geostat (Geostat, 2020) and are expressed in thousands of dollars.

Continuing in Table 13.1 the independent variables of *GDP* of Georgia and relevant trading partners were retrieved from the World Development Indicators database, and GDP is expressed in millions of current dollars. The trade disturbance variable τ_{ij} calculates distances in kilometers between the Georgian capital of Tbilisi and the capital of its trading partner. The distance between the capitals was readily available and obtained from CEPPII (CEPPII, 2019). To estimate whether social globalization impacts trade, I retrieved the KOF index of social globalization for the years 2000-2014 (KOF Swiss Economic Institute, 2020). KOF uses multi-level analysis to measure social globalization of a country. The social globalization index consists of sub-indexes that measure information flows, personal contacts, and cultural proximities of that country in a given year. *Georgian globalization* is an independent variable that measures the social globalization index of Georgia in a given year, whereas *partner globalization* is the index for the trading partner country in that year.

Table 13.1 Summary Statistics for 56 Georgian Trade Relationship Pairs, 2000-2015

Variable	N	Mean	Std. Dev.	Min	Max
Trade	896	94	211	0	1968
Georgian exports	896	22237	58117	0	709919
Georgian GDP	896	7662	1959	4618	10718
Partner GDP	896	138256276	814132443	913	11414166528
Distance	896	2534	1548	173	9306
Georgian globalization	840	52	4	45	58
Partner globalization	840	67	20	7	93

In order to run the regression, I use Poisson pseudo-maximum likelihood (PPML) regression, which was developed by Santos Silva and Tenreyro (2006) and has been used in many studies afterwards (Westerlund & Wilhelmson, 2011; Siliverstovs & Schumacher, 2009; Liu, 2009; Shepherd & Wilson, 2009; and Martínez-Zarzoso, 2011). While there are many other methods of estimation, there is no universal solution: All of them have their advantages and shortcomings. PPML handles zeroes well in the statistical modeling, which is important because my panel includes several zero-valued trade and export flows. PPML also provides efficient estimates in the presence of heteroscedasticity that many other models lack, including fixed effects regression (Mátyás, 1998; Egger, 2003; Egger & Pfaffermayr, 2003; Andrews, Schank, & Upward, 2006; and

Henderson & Millimet, 2008). Also, PPML does not assume normality and is valid with the kinds of heteroskedasticity to a count variable: Given that trade and exports are measured with a count of how many dollars' worth of goods flow across borders, this is a logical choice.

The shortcoming of the PPML model is that it can censor a significant portion of the observations, resulting in a minor dependent variable bias. In order to check for these shortcomings, I run a robustness test with an OLS model. OLS was the workhorse to analyze the gravity equation before other methods were invented (Begeijk & Oldersma, 1990; Baldwin & Nino, 2006; and Wang & Winters, 113-136). OLS was regarded as an effective estimator, yet later it was shown to provide biased coefficients for this specification (Gomez-Herrera, 2012). Hence, international research moved towards more sophisticated methods of estimation. Nonetheless, if OLS estimates are used in parallel with PPML estimates, similar results imply that the findings are robust.

Empirical Analysis

Table 13.2 presents the results of the regression models that I describe in the prior section. Each column represents a different regression model fitted over the panel data of 56 Georgian trade relationships over the years 2000-2015. The first two numeric columns show the results from PPML estimation, first for the total trade between Georgia and each partner, and second for Georgia's exports to the partner country. The last two numeric columns show the robustness checks that result from re-estimating these models using OLS, again for combined trade and then for Georgia's outbound exports.[1] Each row represents another predictor in the model. Notably, the logged distance between the capitals varies only cross-

---

1 While not reported here, as an additional robustness check, I estimated models of trade and exports including random effects by dyad. This feasible generalized least squares (FGLS) model returns results that are similar to the last two columns of Table 14.2 both substantively and statistically, with one exception. The only difference is that, in the FGLS model of exports, Georgian globalization is statistically discernible instead of the trade partner's globalization.

sectionally and remains constant for each trade dyad over time. Meanwhile, logged Georgian GDP and logged Georgian globalization only vary over time, as these are features of Georgia itself and will not vary from trade partner to trade partner. However, the predictors about trade partners, logged partner GDP and logged partner globalization do vary over time and across dyads because partners do differ on these features and the partners' qualities evolve from year to year.

Table 13.2 Models of Georgian Trade and Exports with 56 Countries, 2000-2015

Estimator=	PPML	PPML	OLS	OLS
Outcome=	Trade	Exports	Trade	Exports
Log Georgian GDP	3.204***	2.244***	183.2***	25,141**
	(0.610)	(0.662)	(51.60)	(11,735)
Log partner GDP	0.103***	0.0256	10.07***	1,722***
	(0.0222)	(0.0304)	(1.818)	(524.2)
Log distance	-0.758***	-0.972***	-87.01***	-33,410***
	(0.100)	(0.0877)	(17.17)	(6,401)
Log Georgian globalization	-1.679	2.068	29.04	83,569
	(2.109)	(2.297)	(209.6)	(52,545)
Log partner globalization	1.005***	0.378**	57.26***	7,639***
	(0.198)	(0.168)	(11.39)	(2,431)
Constant	-17.48***	-13.05***	-1,357***	-330,302***
	(4.305)	(4.649)	(446.1)	(113,177)
Observations	840	840	840	840
R-squared	0.148	0.299	0.139	0.168

Notes: Robust standard errors in parentheses. *** $p<0.01$, ** $p<0.05$, * $p<0.1$

In Table 13.2, my findings reveal that for Georgian overall trade and exports my hypotheses have been supported. To start, across the four models, each predictor has the same sign and significance, with the one exception that the positive effect of the logarithm of a trade partner's GDP does not reach significance in the PPML model of Georgian exports. Breaking this pattern down: A

GDP increase in Georgia's trading partner has a statistically significant and positive influence on overall trade, regardless of whether we estimate with PPML or OLS. In terms of Georgia's exporting patterns, the OLS model implies that countries with a larger GDP import more from Georgia, but the preferred PPML model shows no discernible effect. Meanwhile, estimates show that both Georgian exports and overall trade with a given partner grows, on average and all else equal, with a GDP increase in Georgia's own economy. Hence, we conclude that both partners' GDP is important for the combined trade value, but Georgia's own GDP plays a bigger role in how much the nation exports than the GDP of the receiving country.

Continuing in Table 13.2, distance has a statistically strong negative impact both on overall trade with a partner as well as on outbound Georgian exports. A consistent null effect is that Georgia's social globalization index at home does not a have statistically significant influence on exports or combined trade with its partners. The variance over time on this variable is much smaller than the variance seen across partners, so there may have been limits to what could be seen in this time frame. By contrast, social globalization in the partner country has a strong, positive, and statistically significant impact both on combined trade with Georgia and on imports the country receives from Georgia. This final result implies that the more countries become globalized, the easier it is for them to become more globally aware and to establish business ties with Georgian businessmen or on the population level to acquire *Made in Georgia* products.

Conclusion

In this chapter I estimated geographical and social globalization patterns of Georgia's trade. By using PPML regression models I answered the question whether GDP, distance, and level of social globalization influence Georgia's trade and exports. My findings supported my hypotheses based on the gravity model: that Georgian trade grows with an increase of GDP both at home and abroad and that distance negatively affects Georgia's trade. For the exporting side of trade, a GDP rise for Georgia at home seems to matter more than a GDP increase in the destination country. This finding does not fit with the traditional gravity model assumptions but can be explained by the fact that Georgian exports are of smaller size relative to many countries, so they cannot be affected by minor changes of the GDP in the receiving country.

My model suggests that social globalization at home does not affect Georgia's trade and exports—or at least changes in globalization during the 2000-2015 time-frame did not have a noticeable effect. However, social globalization in the destination country has a statistically significant positive effect on both exports and combined trade. These findings allow us to suggest that Georgian companies should trade more with the socially globalized countries that exhibit high economic growth. Yet, I should also note that usually these markets are very competitive with high costs of entry. Once overcoming these barriers, though, a productive relationship is likely to flourish.

My chapter opens new horizons for further research. To start, it hopefully will stimulate further interest in the gravity model, which can be a useful tool for evaluating where potentially profitable trade relationships exist. Turning to a specific issue that can be further explored, recall that from 2015 to 2018 the Georgian lari depreciated by 23% against the U.S. dollar. Meanwhile, Georgian exports increased around 52% over the same period. The gravity equation also would allow us to check exchange rate fluctuation effects against trade effects, which could be another useful extension of this model. For now, countries that have large economies, that are geographically proximate, and that are globally well connected appear to be the best trade partners for Georgia.

References

Andrews, M., Schank, T., and Upward, R. 2006. "Practical Fixed-effects Estimation Methods." *The Stata Journal* 461-481.

Baldwin, R. E., and Nino, V. D. 2006. "Euros and Zeros: The Common Currency Effect on Trade in New Goods." *NBER Working papers*.

Begeijk, P. A., and Oldersma, H. 1990. "Détente, Market-oriented Reform and German Unification: Potential Consequences for the World Trade System." *Kyklos International Review for Social Sciences* 599-609.

CEPPII. 2019. "The Research and Expertise on World Economy." *Gravity*. http://www.cepii.fr/CEPII/en/bdd_modele/bdd_modele.asp.

Chaney, T. 2014. "The Networl Structure of International Trade." *The American Economic Review* 3600-3634.

Chetty, S., and Holm, D. B. 2000. "Internasiolasaion of Small to Medium Sized Manufacturing Firms: A Network Approach. *International Bussiness Review* 77-99.

Dilanchiev, A. 2012. "Empirical Analysis of Georgian Trade Pattern: Gravity Model." *Journal of Social Sciences* 75-78.

Egger, P. 2003. "A Note on the Proper Econometric Specification of the Gravity Equation. *Economic Letters* 25-31.

Egger, P., and Pfaffermayr, M. 2003. "The Proper Panel Econometric Specification of the Gravity Equation: A Threeway Model with Bilateral Interaction Effects. *Emperical Economics* 571-580.

Freeman, R., and Pienknagura, S. 2018. "Are All Trade Agreements Equal? The Role of Distance in Shaping the Effect of Economic Integration Agreements on Trade Flows." *Review of World Economics* 25-78.

Geostat. 2020, January 10. *Georgian Statistical Registry*. Foreign Direct Investment Module.

Gomez-Herrera, E. 2012. "Comparing Alternative Methods to Estimate Gravity Models of Bilateral Trade. *Emperical Economics* 1087-1111.

J.Henderson, D., and Millimet, D. L. 2008. "Is Gravity Linear?" *Journal of Applied Econometrics* 137-172.

KOF Swiss economic Institute. 2020, January 5. *KOF Globalisation Index*. https://kof.ethz.ch/en/forecasts-and-indicators/indicators/kof-globalisation-index.html.

Lapatinas, A. 2019. "The Effect of the Internet on Economic Sophistication: An Empirical Analysis. *Economic Letters* 35-45.

Lin, F. 2014. "Estimating the Effect of the Internet on International Trade." *Journal of International Trade and Economic Development* 409-428.

Liu, X. 2009. "GATT/WTO Promotes Trade Strongly: Sample Selection and Model Specification." *Review of International Economics* 428-446.

Mátyás, L. 1998. "The Gravity Model: Some Econometric Considerations." *The World Economy* 397-401.

Martínez-Zarzoso, I. 2011. "The log of Gravity Revisited." *Applied Economics* 311-327.

Narayan, S., and Nguyen, T. T. 2016. "Does the Trade Gravity Model Depend on Trading Partners? Some Evidence from Vietnam and Her 54 Trading Partners." *International Review of Economics and Finance* 220-237.

Santos, S. J., and Tenreyno, S. 2006. "log of Gravity." *The Review of Economics and Statistics* 641-658.

Shepherd, B., and Wilson, J. 2009. "Trade Facilitation in ASEAN Member Countries: Measuring Progress." *Journal of Asian Economics* 367-383.

Siliverstovs, B., and Schumacher, D. 2009. "Estimating Gravity Equations: To log or Not To log?" *Empirical Economics* 645-669.

Taglioni, D., and Benedictis, L. D. 2014. "The Gravity Model in International Trade." In L.D. Benedictis, and L. Salvatici eds., *The Trade Impact of European Union Preferencial Policies*. Berlin: Springer.

Tinbergen, J. 1962. *Shaping the World Economy*. New York: The Twentieth Century Fund.

UNCTAD. 2019. *Review of Maritime Transport*. New York: United Nations Publications.

Wang, Z. K., and Winters, A. 1992. "The Trading Potential of Eastern Europe." *Center for Economic Integration*.

Westerlund, J., and Wilhelmson, W. 2011. "Estimating the Gravity Model Without Gravity Using Panel Data." *Applied Economics* 641-649.

World Bank. 2018. *Georgia from Reformer to Performer*. The World Bank.

World Bank. 2020. *World Development Indicators. Georgia*. The World Bank

Contributors

Davit Akhvlediani is an MPA Program director at the Georgian Institute of Public Affairs (GIPA). His primary research interests are in international trade, development, entrepreneurship, and political economy. He can be reached at davitakhvlediani@gmail.com.

Sabina Alakbarova is a doctorate candidate in the Institute for European Studies at Tbilisi State University. Her primary research interests are public sector management, particularly human resource management, and public sector reforms. Sabina Alakbarova is the author of Your Ideal Career (in the Azerbaijani language). She is also a co-author of Why Relations with the EU are Significant for Georgia (published by the International Black Sea University). She can be reached at alekperova.sabina@gmail.com.

Lasha Arevadze is a doctorate candidate in the Department of Economics at Tbilisi State University and is a lead specialist in the Macroeconomic Research Division at National Bank of Georgia. His main research interests are in quantitative econometric modeling and applied macroeconomics. Arevadze publishes frequently on these issues for the working paper series of the National Bank of Georgia. He can be reached at l.arevadze@iset.ge.

Gene A. Brewer, Ph.D., is professor of public administration and policy in the University of Georgia School of Public and International Affairs. Dr. Brewer is an internationally recognized public administration scholar who specializes in politics, public management, and public policy. He frequently travels, consults, and conducts research in various regions of the world including the Americas, Asia, Europe, the Middle East, and Oceania. He currently holds several secondary appointments including Visiting Professor of Public Management at Utrecht University School of Governance in the Netherlands; Visiting Fellow at the KU-Leuven Public Governance Institute in Leuven, Belgium; and Global Professor of Public Management at the Georgian Institute of Public Affairs in Tbilisi,

Georgia. Dr. Brewer is an author/editor of Public Management and Performance: Research Directions (Cambridge University Press, 2012); Managing for Public Service Performance: How People and Values Make a Difference (Oxford University Press, 2020); and The Replication of Experimental Social Science Research (Routledge, 2021). He can be reached at geneabrewer@uga.edu.

Ulrich Eydam is a research associate at the University of Potsdam. His primary research interests are in macroeconomics, economic growth, institutional development and financial development. His recent article has been published by Journal of Evolutionary Economics. Eydam can be reached at ueydam@uni-potsdam.de.

Irakli Gabriadze is a doctorate student in the Department of Economics at Tbilisi State University. His primary research interests are in development economics, economic growth, transition countries and institutions, and political economy. Gabriadze served as a member of a consultancy group in the Ministry of Economy and Sustainable Development of Georgia, advising on various matters of economic policy. Currently, he is the head of Analysis, Monitoring, and Evaluation Department at Enterprise Georgia, which operates under the auspices of the Ministry of Economy and Sustainable Development and is tasked with supporting entrepreneurship activities in the country. Gabriadze is an invited lecturer of development economics and statistics at the Ilia State University. He can be reached at i.gabriadze@iset.ge.

Aytan M. Hajiyeva is a doctorate candidate in the Institute for European Studies at Tbilisi State University. Her primary research interests are in gender studies in social and political sciences. She is the author of articles on the views and attitudes of Azeris and Turks, in particular Muslim women from these communities, on key policy issues in Georgia and the Caucasus region. Hajieva can be reached at aytandilanchieva@yahoo.com.

Elene Jimshelishvili a doctorate student of social sciences in the Georgian Institute of Public Affairs (GIPA). Her primary research interests are in human capital development, employability, and lifelong career management. Jimsheleishvili has more than 15 years of experience in human resource management in public and private sector organizations. She is a member of the Society for Human Resource Management and is a senior certified professional of human resource management. She can be reached at: ljimsh@gmail.com.

J. Edward Kellough, Ph.D., is professor and PhD Program Director in the Department of Public Administration and Policy at the University of Georgia (UGA). He served previously for 6 years as the Head of the Department of Public Administration and Policy at UGA and as the UGA Master of Public Administration program director for 9 years. Dr. Kellough specializes in the field of public sector human resources management. He is an elected Fellow of the National Academy of Public Administration (NAPA) in the U.S., and is past President of NASPAA, the Network of Schools of Public Policy, Affairs, and Administration. He also served as a member of the NASPAA Executive Council and on the NASPAA Commission on Peer Review and Accreditation. Dr. Kellough was the 2019 recipient of the John Gaus Award and Lectureship, honoring a Lifetime of Excellence in Scholarship in the Joint Tradition of Political Science and Public Administration, given by the American Political Science Association. Previous books by Dr. Kellough include The New Public Personnel Administration, seventh edition, with Lloyd G. Nigro (Wadsworth, Cengage Learning, 2014); Understanding Affirmative Action: Politics, Discrimination, and the Search for Justice (Georgetown University Press, 2007); Civil Service Reform in the States: Personnel Policy and Politics at the Sub-National Level, edited with Lloyd G. Nigro (State University of New York Press, 2006); and Federal Equal Employment Opportunity and Numerical Goals and Timetables, (Praeger Publishers, 1989). His research has appeared also in numerous academic journals. He has lectured or made research presentations in Australia, Canada, China, Denmark, Germany, Italy, the Republic of Georgia, the Netherlands, Russian Federation, Saudi Arabia, South Korea, Ukraine, and the United Arab Emirates. He can be reached at kellough@uga.edu.

Ana Laitadze is a doctorate student in social sciences at the Georgian Institute of Public Affairs. She is also an invited lecturer at Ilia State University. Laitadze's research and teaching interests are in education management and policy, particularly interventions in early childhood education and student school performance. She can be reached at analaitadze@gmail.com.

Anna Menagharishvili is a doctorate student in the Department of Psychology and Educational Sciences at Tbilisi State University. Her primary research and teaching interests are in political and social psychology, voting behavior, and political culture. She can be reached at annamenagarishvili@gmail.com.

Marika Mkheidze is an advocacy expert at the Georgian office of Save the Children International and a guest lecturer at the University of Georgia. Her primary research interests are related to democratic policy-making process (with emphases on citizen participation, including child rights advocacy; and effects of disinformation or propaganda on public decision making). Mkheidze is a co-author of "The Juncker Commission: An Institutional Game Changer?" – published in 2015 by the Montesquieu Institute in the Hague. She can be reached at marika.mkheidze@savethechildren.org.

Tima T. Moldogaziev, Ph.D., is an associate professor in the School of Public Policy at the Pennsylvania State University. His primary research interests are in public sector management, regional and local governance, public sector infrastructure financing and fiscal policy. Dr. Moldogaziev is a co-author of Information Resolution and Subnational Capital Finance (Oxford University Press 2021) and State and Local Financial Instruments: Policy Changes and Management, 2nd Ed., (Edward Elgar Publishing 2021). His recent articles have been published by Governance, International Public Management Journal, Journal of Public Administration Research & Theory, Journal of Public Policy, Public Administration Review, Public Budgeting & Finance, and Urban Studies. He can be reached at timatm@psu.edu.

Nino Okhanashvili, Ph.D., is an assistant professor at David Aghmashenebeli National Defense Academy of Georgia. She also holds academic affiliations at Georgian National University, European University, and at East European University, as well as an invited lectureship at Tbilisi State University. Her primary research interests are in theories of international relations, international security, and conflicts in post-Soviet countries. Dr. Okhanashvili is the author of several articles on the causes and outcomes of conflicts in the Caucasus region. She can be reached at n.okhanashvili@seu.edu.ge.

Natia Tchigvaria, Ph.D., is an associate professor and head of the PhD Program in social sciences at the Georgian Institute of Public Affairs (GIPA). In the past, Dr. Tchigvaria worked as a researcher in the Russo-Georgian Conflict Centre. Her teaching and research interests are in education policy and management, social policy, and the role of public policy in social sciences. Dr. Tchigvaria is also the head of Policy Evaluation Center (GIPA) and serves as an external expert in the National Centre for Quality Educational Enhancement. She can be reached at n.tchigvaria@gipa.ge.

Giorgi Tchumburidze is an invited lecturer at the Tbilisi State University, where he teaches introductory psychology and research methods courses. He is also a national data manager and a co-project manager of OECD's Program for International Students Assessment (PISA) in the Republic of Georgia. His primary research and teaching interests are in social psychology. He can be reached at gtchumburidze@outlook.com.

SOVIET AND POST-SOVIET POLITICS AND SOCIETY
Edited by Dr. Andreas Umland | ISSN 1614-3515

1 *Андреас Умланд (ред.)* | Воплощение Европейской конвенции по правам человека в России. Философские, юридические и эмпирические исследования | ISBN 3-89821-387-0

2 *Christian Wipperfürth* | Russland – ein vertrauenswürdiger Partner? Grundlagen, Hintergründe und Praxis gegenwärtiger russischer Außenpolitik | Mit einem Vorwort von Heinz Timmermann | ISBN 3-89821-401-X

3 *Manja Hussner* | Die Übernahme internationalen Rechts in die russische und deutsche Rechtsordnung. Eine vergleichende Analyse zur Völkerrechtsfreundlichkeit der Verfassungen der Russländischen Föderation und der Bundesrepublik Deutschland | Mit einem Vorwort von Rainer Arnold | ISBN 3-89821-438-9

4 *Matthew Tejada* | Bulgaria's Democratic Consolidation and the Kozloduy Nuclear Power Plant (KNPP). The Unattainability of Closure | With a foreword by Richard J. Crampton | ISBN 3-89821-439-7

5 *Марк Григорьевич Меерович* | Квадратные метры, определяющие сознание. Государственная жилищная политика в СССР. 1921 – 1941 гг | ISBN 3-89821-474-5

6 *Andrei P. Tsygankov, Pavel A. Tsygankov (Eds.)* | New Directions in Russian International Studies | ISBN 3-89821-422-2

7 *Марк Григорьевич Меерович* | Как власть народ к труду приучала. Жилище в СССР – средство управления людьми. 1917 – 1941 гг. | С предисловием Елены Осокиной | ISBN 3-89821-495-8

8 *David J. Galbreath* | Nation-Building and Minority Politics in Post-Socialist States. Interests, Influence and Identities in Estonia and Latvia | With a foreword by David J. Smith | ISBN 3-89821-467-2

9 *Алексей Юрьевич Безугольный* | Народы Кавказа в Вооружённых силах СССР в годы Великой Отечественной войны 1941-1945 гг. | С предисловием Николая Бугая | ISBN 3-89821-475-3

10 *Вячеслав Лихачев и Владимир Прибыловский (ред.)* | Русское Национальное Единство, 1990-2000. В 2-х томах | ISBN 3-89821-523-7

11 *Николай Бугай (ред.)* | Народы стран Балтии в условиях сталинизма (1940-е – 1950-е годы). Документированная история | ISBN 3-89821-525-3

12 *Ingmar Bredies (Hrsg.)* | Zur Anatomie der Orange Revolution in der Ukraine. Wechsel des Elitenregimes oder Triumph des Parlamentarismus? | ISBN 3-89821-524-5

13 *Anastasia V. Mitrofanova* | The Politicization of Russian Orthodoxy. Actors and Ideas | With a foreword by William C. Gay | ISBN 3-89821-481-8

14 *Nathan D. Larson* | Alexander Solzhenitsyn and the Russo-Jewish Question | ISBN 3-89821-483-4

15 *Guido Houben* | Kulturpolitik und Ethnizität. Staatliche Kunstförderung im Russland der neunziger Jahre | Mit einem Vorwort von Gert Weisskirchen | ISBN 3-89821-542-3

16 *Leonid Luks* | Der russische „Sonderweg"? Aufsätze zur neuesten Geschichte Russlands im europäischen Kontext | ISBN 3-89821-496-6

17 *Евгений Мороз* | История «Мёртвой воды» – от страшной сказки к большой политике. Политическое неоязычество в постсоветской России | ISBN 3-89821-551-2

18 *Александр Верховский и Галина Кожевникова (ред.)* | Этническая и религиозная интолерантность в российских СМИ. Результаты мониторинга 2001-2004 гг. | ISBN 3-89821-569-5

19 *Christian Ganzer* | Sowjetisches Erbe und ukrainische Nation. Das Museum der Geschichte des Zaporoger Kosakentums auf der Insel Chortycja | Mit einem Vorwort von Frank Golczewski | ISBN 3-89821-504-0

20 *Эльза-Баир Гучинова* | Помнить нельзя забыть. Антропология депортационной травмы калмыков | С предисловием Кэролайн Хамфри | ISBN 3-89821-506-7

21 *Юлия Лидерман* | Мотивы «проверки» и «испытания» в постсоветской культуре. Советское прошлое в российском кинематографе 1990-х годов | С предисловием Евгения Марголита | ISBN 3-89821-511-3

22 *Tanya Lokshina, Ray Thomas, Mary Mayer (Eds.)* | The Imposition of a Fake Political Settlement in the Northern Caucasus. The 2003 Chechen Presidential Election | ISBN 3-89821-436-2

23 *Timothy McCajor Hall, Rosie Read (Eds.)* | Changes in the Heart of Europe. Recent Ethnographies of Czechs, Slovaks, Roma, and Sorbs | With an afterword by Zdeněk Salzmann | ISBN 3-89821-606-3

24 *Christian Autengruber* | Die politischen Parteien in Bulgarien und Rumänien. Eine vergleichende Analyse seit Beginn der 90er Jahre | Mit einem Vorwort von Dorothée de Nève | ISBN 3-89821-476-1

25 *Annette Freyberg-Inan with Radu Cristescu* | The Ghosts in Our Classrooms, or: John Dewey Meets Ceauşescu. The Promise and the Failures of Civic Education in Romania | ISBN 3-89821-416-8

26 *John B. Dunlop* | The 2002 Dubrovka and 2004 Beslan Hostage Crises. A Critique of Russian Counter-Terrorism | With a foreword by Donald N. Jensen | ISBN 3-89821-608-X

27 *Peter Koller* | Das touristische Potenzial von Kam"janec'–Podil's'kyj. Eine fremdenverkehrsgeographische Untersuchung der Zukunftsperspektiven und Maßnahmenplanung zur Destinationsentwicklung des „ukrainischen Rothenburg" | Mit einem Vorwort von Kristiane Klemm | ISBN 3-89821-640-3

28 *Françoise Daucé, Elisabeth Sieca-Kozlowski (Eds.)* | Dedovshchina in the Post-Soviet Military. Hazing of Russian Army Conscripts in a Comparative Perspective | With a foreword by Dale Herspring | ISBN 3-89821-616-0

29 *Florian Strasser* | Zivilgesellschaftliche Einflüsse auf die Orange Revolution. Die gewaltlose Massenbewegung und die ukrainische Wahlkrise 2004 | Mit einem Vorwort von Egbert Jahn | ISBN 3-89821-648-9

30 *Rebecca S. Katz* | The Georgian Regime Crisis of 2003-2004. A Case Study in Post-Soviet Media Representation of Politics, Crime and Corruption | ISBN 3-89821-413-3

31 *Vladimir Kantor* | Willkür oder Freiheit. Beiträge zur russischen Geschichtsphilosophie | Ediert von Dagmar Herrmann sowie mit einem Vorwort versehen von Leonid Luks | ISBN 3-89821-589-X

32 *Laura A. Victoir* | The Russian Land Estate Today. A Case Study of Cultural Politics in Post-Soviet Russia | With a foreword by Priscilla Roosevelt | ISBN 3-89821-426-5

33 *Ivan Katchanovski* | Cleft Countries. Regional Political Divisions and Cultures in Post-Soviet Ukraine and Moldova| With a foreword by Francis Fukuyama | ISBN 3-89821-558-X

34 *Florian Mühlfried* | Postsowjetische Feiern. Das Georgische Bankett im Wandel | Mit einem Vorwort von Kevin Tuite | ISBN 3-89821-601-2

35 *Roger Griffin, Werner Loh, Andreas Umland (Eds.)* | Fascism Past and Present, West and East. An International Debate on Concepts and Cases in the Comparative Study of the Extreme Right | With an afterword by Walter Laqueur | ISBN 3-89821-674-8

36 *Sebastian Schlegel* | Der „Weiße Archipel". Sowjetische Atomstädte 1945-1991 | Mit einem Geleitwort von Thomas Bohn | ISBN 3-89821-679-9

37 *Vyacheslav Likhachev* | Political Anti-Semitism in Post-Soviet Russia. Actors and Ideas in 1991-2003 | Edited and translated from Russian by Eugene Veklerov | ISBN 3-89821-529-6

38 *Josette Baer (Ed.)* | Preparing Liberty in Central Europe. Political Texts from the Spring of Nations 1848 to the Spring of Prague 1968 | With a foreword by Zdeněk V. David | ISBN 3-89821-546-6

39 *Михаил Лукьянов* | Российский консерватизм и реформа, 1907-1914 | С предисловием Марка Д. Стейнберга | ISBN 3-89821-503-2

40 *Nicola Melloni* | Market Without Economy. The 1998 Russian Financial Crisis | With a foreword by Eiji Furukawa | ISBN 3-89821-407-9

41 *Dmitrij Chmelnizki* | Die Architektur Stalins | Bd. 1: Studien zu Ideologie und Stil | Bd. 2: Bilddokumentation | Mit einem Vorwort von Bruno Flierl | ISBN 3-89821-515-6

42 *Katja Yafimava* | Post-Soviet Russian-Belarussian Relationships. The Role of Gas Transit Pipelines | With a foreword by Jonathan P. Stern | ISBN 3-89821-655-1

43 *Boris Chavkin* | Verflechtungen der deutschen und russischen Zeitgeschichte. Aufsätze und Archivfunde zu den Beziehungen Deutschlands und der Sowjetunion von 1917 bis 1991 | Ediert von Markus Edlinger sowie mit einem Vorwort versehen von Leonid Luks | ISBN 3-89821-756-6

44 *Anastasija Grynenko in Zusammenarbeit mit Claudia Dathe* | Die Terminologie des Gerichtswesens der Ukraine und Deutschlands im Vergleich. Eine übersetzungswissenschaftliche Analyse juristischer Fachbegriffe im Deutschen, Ukrainischen und Russischen | Mit einem Vorwort von Ulrich Hartmann | ISBN 3-89821-691-8

45 *Anton Burkov* | The Impact of the European Convention on Human Rights on Russian Law. Legislation and Application in 1996-2006 | With a foreword by Françoise Hampson | ISBN 978-3-89821-639-5

46 *Stina Torjesen, Indra Overland (Eds.)* | International Election Observers in Post-Soviet Azerbaijan. Geopolitical Pawns or Agents of Change? | ISBN 978-3-89821-743-9

47 *Taras Kuzio* | Ukraine – Crimea – Russia. Triangle of Conflict | ISBN 978-3-89821-761-3

48 *Claudia Šabić* | „Ich erinnere mich nicht, aber L'viv!" Zur Funktion kultureller Faktoren für die Institutionalisierung und Entwicklung einer ukrainischen Region | Mit einem Vorwort von Melanie Tatur | ISBN 978-3-89821-752-1

49 *Marlies Bilz* | Tatarstan in der Transformation. Nationaler Diskurs und Politische Praxis 1988-1994 | Mit einem Vorwort von Frank Golczewski | ISBN 978-3-89821-722-4

50 *Марлен Ларюэль (ред.)* | Современные интерпретации русского национализма | ISBN 978-3-89821-795-8

51 *Sonja Schüler* | Die ethnische Dimension der Armut. Roma im postsozialistischen Rumänien | Mit einem Vorwort von Anton Sterbling | ISBN 978-3-89821-776-7

52 *Галина Кожевникова* | Радикальный национализм в России и противодействие ему. Сборник докладов Центра «Сова» за 2004-2007 гг. | С предисловием Александра Верховского | ISBN 978-3-89821-721-7

53 *Галина Кожевникова и Владимир Прибыловский* | Российская власть в биографиях I. Высшие должностные лица РФ в 2004 г. | ISBN 978-3-89821-796-5

54 *Галина Кожевникова и Владимир Прибыловский* | Российская власть в биографиях II. Члены Правительства РФ в 2004 г. | ISBN 978-3-89821-797-2

55 *Галина Кожевникова и Владимир Прибыловский* | Российская власть в биографиях III. Руководители федеральных служб и агентств РФ в 2004 г. | ISBN 978-3-89821-798-9

56 *Ileana Petroniu* | Privatisierung in Transformationsökonomien. Determinanten der Restrukturierungs-Bereitschaft am Beispiel Polens, Rumäniens und der Ukraine | Mit einem Vorwort von Rainer W. Schäfer | ISBN 978-3-89821-790-3

57 *Christian Wipperfürth* | Russland und seine GUS-Nachbarn. Hintergründe, aktuelle Entwicklungen und Konflikte in einer ressourcenreichen Region| ISBN 978-3-89821-801-6

58 *Togzhan Kassenova* | From Antagonism to Partnership. The Uneasy Path of the U.S.-Russian Cooperative Threat Reduction | With a foreword by Christoph Bluth | ISBN 978-3-89821-707-1

59 *Alexander Höllwerth* | Das sakrale eurasische Imperium des Aleksandr Dugin. Eine Diskursanalyse zum postsowjetischen russischen Rechtsextremismus | Mit einem Vorwort von Dirk Uffelmann | ISBN 978-3-89821-813-9

60 *Олег Рябов* | «Россия-Матушка». Национализм, гендер и война в России XX века | С предисловием Елены Гощило | ISBN 978-3-89821-487-2

61 *Ivan Maistrenko* | Borot'bism. A Chapter in the History of the Ukrainian Revolution | With a new Introduction by Chris Ford | Translated by George S. N. Luckyj with the assistance of Ivan L. Rudnytsky | Second, Revised and Expanded Edition ISBN 978-3-8382-1107-7

62 *Maryna Romanets* | Anamorphosic Texts and Reconfigured Visions. Improvised Traditions in Contemporary Ukrainian and Irish Literature | ISBN 978-3-89821-576-3

63 *Paul D'Anieri and Taras Kuzio (Eds.)* | Aspects of the Orange Revolution I. Democratization and Elections in Post-Communist Ukraine | ISBN 978-3-89821-698-2

64 *Bohdan Harasymiw in collaboration with Oleh S. Ilnytzkyj (Eds.)* | Aspects of the Orange Revolution II. Information and Manipulation Strategies in the 2004 Ukrainian Presidential Elections | ISBN 978-3-89821-699-9

65 *Ingmar Bredies, Andreas Umland and Valentin Yakushik (Eds.)* | Aspects of the Orange Revolution III. The Context and Dynamics of the 2004 Ukrainian Presidential Elections | ISBN 978-3-89821-803-0

66 *Ingmar Bredies, Andreas Umland and Valentin Yakushik (Eds.)* | Aspects of the Orange Revolution IV. Foreign Assistance and Civic Action in the 2004 Ukrainian Presidential Elections | ISBN 978-3-89821-808-5

67 *Ingmar Bredies, Andreas Umland and Valentin Yakushik (Eds.)* | Aspects of the Orange Revolution V. Institutional Observation Reports on the 2004 Ukrainian Presidential Elections | ISBN 978-3-89821-809-2

68 *Taras Kuzio (Ed.)* | Aspects of the Orange Revolution VI. Post-Communist Democratic Revolutions in Comparative Perspective | ISBN 978-3-89821-820-7

69 *Tim Bohse* | Autoritarismus statt Selbstverwaltung. Die Transformation der kommunalen Politik in der Stadt Kaliningrad 1990-2005 | Mit einem Geleitwort von Stefan Troebst | ISBN 978-3-89821-782-8

70 *David Rupp* | Die Rußländische Föderation und die russischsprachige Minderheit in Lettland. Eine Fallstudie zur Anwaltspolitik Moskaus gegenüber den russophonen Minderheiten im „Nahen Ausland" von 1991 bis 2002 | Mit einem Vorwort von Helmut Wagner | ISBN 978-3-89821-778-1

71 *Taras Kuzio* | Theoretical and Comparative Perspectives on Nationalism. New Directions in Cross-Cultural and Post-Communist Studies | With a foreword by Paul Robert Magocsi | ISBN 978-3-89821-815-3

72 *Christine Teichmann* | Die Hochschultransformation im heutigen Osteuropa. Kontinuität und Wandel bei der Entwicklung des postkommunistischen Universitätswesens | Mit einem Vorwort von Oskar Anweiler | ISBN 978-3-89821-842-9

73 *Julia Kusznir* | Der politische Einfluss von Wirtschaftseliten in russischen Regionen. Eine Analyse am Beispiel der Erdöl- und Erdgasindustrie, 1992-2005 | Mit einem Vorwort von Wolfgang Eichwede | ISBN 978-3-89821-821-4

74　*Alena Vysotskaya* | Russland, Belarus und die EU-Osterweiterung. Zur Minderheitenfrage und zum Problem der Freizügigkeit des Personenverkehrs | Mit einem Vorwort von Katlijn Malfliet | ISBN 978-3-89821-822-1

75　*Heiko Pleines (Hrsg.)* | Corporate Governance in post-sozialistischen Volkswirtschaften | ISBN 978-3-89821-766-8

76　*Stefan Ihrig* | Wer sind die Moldawier? Rumänismus versus Moldowanismus in Historiographie und Schulbüchern der Republik Moldova, 1991-2006 | Mit einem Vorwort von Holm Sundhaussen | ISBN 978-3-89821-466-7

77　*Galina Kozhevnikova in collaboration with Alexander Verkhovsky and Eugene Veklerov* | Ultra-Nationalism and Hate Crimes in Contemporary Russia. The 2004-2006 Annual Reports of Moscow's SOVA Center | With a foreword by Stephen D. Shenfield | ISBN 978-3-89821-868-9

78　*Florian Küchler* | The Role of the European Union in Moldova's Transnistria Conflict | With a foreword by Christopher Hill | ISBN 978-3-89821-850-4

79　*Bernd Rechel* | The Long Way Back to Europe. Minority Protection in Bulgaria | With a foreword by Richard Crampton | ISBN 978-3-89821-863-4

80　*Peter W. Rodgers* | Nation, Region and History in Post-Communist Transitions. Identity Politics in Ukraine, 1991-2006 | With a foreword by Vera Tolz | ISBN 978-3-89821-903-7

81　*Stephanie Solywoda* | The Life and Work of Semen L. Frank. A Study of Russian Religious Philosophy | With a foreword by Philip Walters | ISBN 978-3-89821-457-5

82　*Vera Sokolova* | Cultural Politics of Ethnicity. Discourses on Roma in Communist Czechoslovakia | ISBN 978-3-89821-864-1

83　*Natalya Shevchik Ketenci* | Kazakhstani Enterprises in Transition. The Role of Historical Regional Development in Kazakhstan's Post-Soviet Economic Transformation | ISBN 978-3-89821-831-3

84　*Martin Malek, Anna Schor-Tschudnowskaja (Hgg.)* | Europa im Tschetschenienkrieg. Zwischen politischer Ohnmacht und Gleichgültigkeit | Mit einem Vorwort von Lipchan Basajewa | ISBN 978-3-89821-676-0

85　*Stefan Meister* | Das postsowjetische Universitätswesen zwischen nationalem und internationalem Wandel. Die Entwicklung der regionalen Hochschule in Russland als Gradmesser der Systemtransformation | Mit einem Vorwort von Joan DeBardeleben | ISBN 978-3-89821-891-7

86　*Konstantin Sheiko in collaboration with Stephen Brown* | Nationalist Imaginings of the Russian Past. Anatolii Fomenko and the Rise of Alternative History in Post-Communist Russia | With a foreword by Donald Ostrowski | ISBN 978-3-89821-915-0

87　*Sabine Jenni* | Wie stark ist das „Einige Russland"? Zur Parteibindung der Eliten und zum Wahlerfolg der Machtpartei im Dezember 2007 | Mit einem Vorwort von Klaus Armingeon | ISBN 978-3-89821-961-7

88　*Thomas Borén* | Meeting-Places of Transformation. Urban Identity, Spatial Representations and Local Politics in Post-Soviet St Petersburg | ISBN 978-3-89821-739-2

89　*Aygul Ashirova* | Stalinismus und Stalin-Kult in Zentralasien. Turkmenistan 1924-1953 | Mit einem Vorwort von Leonid Luks | ISBN 978-3-89821-987-7

90　*Leonid Luks* | Freiheit oder imperiale Größe? Essays zu einem russischen Dilemma | ISBN 978-3-8382-0011-8

91　*Christopher Gilley* | The 'Change of Signposts' in the Ukrainian Emigration. A Contribution to the History of Sovietophilism in the 1920s | With a foreword by Frank Golczewski | ISBN 978-3-89821-965-5

92　*Philipp Casula, Jeronim Perovic (Eds.)* | Identities and Politics During the Putin Presidency. The Discursive Foundations of Russia's Stability | With a foreword by Heiko Haumann | ISBN 978-3-8382-0015-6

93　*Marcel Viëtor* | Europa und die Frage nach seinen Grenzen im Osten. Zur Konstruktion ‚europäischer Identität' in Geschichte und Gegenwart | Mit einem Vorwort von Albrecht Lehmann | ISBN 978-3-8382-0045-3

94　*Ben Hellman, Andrei Rogachevskii* | Filming the Unfilmable. Casper Wrede's 'One Day in the Life of Ivan Denisovich' | Second, Revised and Expanded Edition | ISBN 978-3-8382-0044-6

95　*Eva Fuchslocher* | Vaterland, Sprache, Glaube. Orthodoxie und Nationenbildung am Beispiel Georgiens | Mit einem Vorwort von Christina von Braun | ISBN 978-3-89821-884-9

96　*Vladimir Kantor* | Das Westlertum und der Weg Russlands. Zur Entwicklung der russischen Literatur und Philosophie | Ediert von Dagmar Herrmann | Mit einem Beitrag von Nikolaus Lobkowicz | ISBN 978-3-8382-0102-3

97　*Kamran Musayev* | Die postsowjetische Transformation im Baltikum und Südkaukasus. Eine vergleichende Untersuchung der politischen Entwicklung Lettlands und Aserbaidschans 1985-2009 | Mit einem Vorwort von Leonid Luks | Ediert von Sandro Henschel | ISBN 978-3-8382-0103-0

98　*Tatiana Zhurzhenko* | Borderlands into Bordered Lands. Geopolitics of Identity in Post-Soviet Ukraine | With a foreword by Dieter Segert | ISBN 978-3-8382-0042-2

99   *Кирилл Галушко, Лидия Смола (ред.)* | Пределы падения – варианты украинского будущего. Аналитико-прогностические исследования | ISBN 978-3-8382-0148-1

100 *Michael Minkenberg (Ed.)* | Historical Legacies and the Radical Right in Post-Cold War Central and Eastern Europe | With an afterword by Sabrina P. Ramet | ISBN 978-3-8382-0124-5

101 *David-Emil Wickström* | Rocking St. Petersburg. Transcultural Flows and Identity Politics in the St. Petersburg Popular Music Scene | With a foreword by Yngvar B. Steinholt | Second, Revised and Expanded Edition | ISBN 978-3-8382-0100-9

102 *Eva Zabka* | Eine neue „Zeit der Wirren"? Der spät- und postsowjetische Systemwandel 1985-2000 im Spiegel russischer gesellschaftspolitischer Diskurse | Mit einem Vorwort von Margareta Mommsen | ISBN 978-3-8382-0161-0

103 *Ulrike Ziemer* | Ethnic Belonging, Gender and Cultural Practices. Youth Identitites in Contemporary Russia | With a foreword by Anoop Nayak | ISBN 978-3-8382-0152-8

104 *Ksenia Chepikova* | „Einiges Russland" - eine zweite KPdSU? Aspekte der Identitätskonstruktion einer postsowjetischen „Partei der Macht" | Mit einem Vorwort von Torsten Oppelland | ISBN 978-3-8382-0311-9

105 *Леонид Люкс* | Западничество или евразийство? Демократия или идеократия? Сборник статей об исторических дилеммах России | С предисловием Владимира Кантора | ISBN 978-3-8382-0211-2

106 *Anna Dost* | Das russische Verfassungsrecht auf dem Weg zum Föderalismus und zurück. Zum Konflikt von Rechtsnormen und -wirklichkeit in der Russländischen Föderation von 1991 bis 2009 | Mit einem Vorwort von Alexander Blankenagel | ISBN 978-3-8382-0292-1

107 *Philipp Herzog* | Sozialistische Völkerfreundschaft, nationaler Widerstand oder harmloser Zeitvertreib? Zur politischen Funktion der Volkskunst im sowjetischen Estland | Mit einem Vorwort von Andreas Kappeler | ISBN 978-3-8382-0216-7

108 *Marlène Laruelle (Ed.)* | Russian Nationalism, Foreign Policy, and Identity Debates in Putin's Russia. New Ideological Patterns after the Orange Revolution | ISBN 978-3-8382-0325-6

109 *Michail Logvinov* | Russlands Kampf gegen den internationalen Terrorismus. Eine kritische Bestandsaufnahme des Bekämpfungsansatzes | Mit einem Geleitwort von Hans-Henning Schröder und einem Vorwort von Eckhard Jesse | ISBN 978-3-8382-0329-4

110 *John B. Dunlop* | The Moscow Bombings of September 1999. Examinations of Russian Terrorist Attacks at the Onset of Vladimir Putin's Rule | Second, Revised and Expanded Edition | ISBN 978-3-8382-0388-1

111 *Андрей А. Ковалёв* | Свидетельство из-за кулис российской политики I. Можно ли делать добро из зла? (Воспоминания и размышления о последних советских и первых послесоветских годах) | With a foreword by Peter Reddaway | ISBN 978-3-8382-0302-7

112 *Андрей А. Ковалёв* | Свидетельство из-за кулис российской политики II. Угроза для себя и окружающих (Наблюдения и предостережения относительно происходящего после 2000 г.) | ISBN 978-3-8382-0303-4

113 *Bernd Kappenberg* | Zeichen setzen für Europa. Der Gebrauch europäischer lateinischer Sonderzeichen in der deutschen Öffentlichkeit | Mit einem Vorwort von Peter Schlobinski | ISBN 978-3-89821-749-1

114 *Ivo Mijnssen* | The Quest for an Ideal Youth in Putin's Russia I. Back to Our Future! History, Modernity, and Patriotism according to Nashi, 2005-2013 | With a foreword by Jeronim Perović | Second, Revised and Expanded Edition | ISBN 978-3-8382-0368-3

115 *Jussi Lassila* | The Quest for an Ideal Youth in Putin's Russia II. The Search for Distinctive Conformism in the Political Communication of Nashi, 2005-2009 | With a foreword by Kirill Postoutenko | Second, Revised and Expanded Edition | ISBN 978-3-8382-0415-4

116 *Valerio Trabandt* | Neue Nachbarn, gute Nachbarschaft? Die EU als internationaler Akteur am Beispiel ihrer Demokratieförderung in Belarus und der Ukraine 2004-2009 | Mit einem Vorwort von Jutta Joachim | ISBN 978-3-8382-0437-6

117 *Fabian Pfeiffer* | Estlands Außen- und Sicherheitspolitik I. Der estnische Atlantizismus nach der wiedererlangten Unabhängigkeit 1991-2004 | Mit einem Vorwort von Helmut Hubel | ISBN 978-3-8382-0127-6

118 *Jana Podßuweit* | Estlands Außen- und Sicherheitspolitik II. Handlungsoptionen eines Kleinstaates im Rahmen seiner EU-Mitgliedschaft (2004-2008) | Mit einem Vorwort von Helmut Hubel | ISBN 978-3-8382-0440-6

119 *Karin Pointner* | Estlands Außen- und Sicherheitspolitik III. Eine gedächtnispolitische Analyse estnischer Entwicklungskooperation 2006-2010 | Mit einem Vorwort von Karin Liebhart | ISBN 978-3-8382-0435-2

120 *Ruslana Vovk* | Die Offenheit der ukrainischen Verfassung für das Völkerrecht und die europäische Integration | Mit einem Vorwort von Alexander Blankenagel | ISBN 978-3-8382-0481-9

121 *Mykhaylo Banakh* | Die Relevanz der Zivilgesellschaft bei den postkommunistischen Transformationsprozessen in mittel- und osteuropäischen Ländern. Das Beispiel der spät- und postsowjetischen Ukraine 1986-2009 | Mit einem Vorwort von Gerhard Simon | ISBN 978-3-8382-0499-4

122 *Michael Moser* | Language Policy and the Discourse on Languages in Ukraine under President Viktor Yanukovych (25 February 2010–28 October 2012) | ISBN 978-3-8382-0497-0 (Paperback edition) | ISBN 978-3-8382-0507-6 (Hardcover edition)

123 *Nicole Krome* | Russischer Netzwerkkapitalismus Restrukturierungsprozesse in der Russischen Föderation am Beispiel des Luftfahrtunternehmens „Aviastar" | Mit einem Vorwort von Petra Stykow | ISBN 978-3-8382-0534-2

124 *David R. Marples* | 'Our Glorious Past'. Lukashenka's Belarus and the Great Patriotic War | ISBN 978-3-8382-0574-8 (Paperback edition) | ISBN 978-3-8382-0675-2 (Hardcover edition)

125 *Ulf Walther* | Russlands „neuer Adel". Die Macht des Geheimdienstes von Gorbatschow bis Putin | Mit einem Vorwort von Hans-Georg Wieck | ISBN 978-3-8382-0584-7

126 *Simon Geissbühler (Hrsg.)* | Kiew – Revolution 3.0. Der Euromaidan 2013/14 und die Zukunftsperspektiven der Ukraine | ISBN 978-3-8382-0581-6 (Paperback edition) | ISBN 978-3-8382-0681-3 (Hardcover edition)

127 *Andrey Makarychev* | Russia and the EU in a Multipolar World. Discourses, Identities, Norms | With a foreword by Klaus Segbers | ISBN 978-3-8382-0629-5

128 *Roland Scharff* | Kasachstan als postsowjetischer Wohlfahrtsstaat. Die Transformation des sozialen Schutzsystems | Mit einem Vorwort von Joachim Ahrens | ISBN 978-3-8382-0622-6

129 *Katja Grupp* | Bild Lücke Deutschland. Kaliningrader Studierende sprechen über Deutschland | Mit einem Vorwort von Martin Schulz | ISBN 978-3-8382-0552-6

130 *Konstantin Sheiko, Stephen Brown* | History as Therapy. Alternative History and Nationalist Imaginings in Russia, 1991-2014 | ISBN 978-3-8382-0665-3

131 *Elisa Kriza* | Alexander Solzhenitsyn: Cold War Icon, Gulag Author, Russian Nationalist? A Study of the Western Reception of his Literary Writings, Historical Interpretations, and Political Ideas | With a foreword by Andrei Rogatchevski | ISBN 978-3-8382-0589-2 (Paperback edition) | ISBN 978-3-8382-0690-5 (Hardcover edition)

132 *Serghei Golunov* | The Elephant in the Room. Corruption and Cheating in Russian Universities | ISBN 978-3-8382-0570-0

133 *Manja Hussner, Rainer Arnold (Hgg.)* | Verfassungsgerichtsbarkeit in Zentralasien I. Sammlung von Verfassungstexten | ISBN 978-3-8382-0595-3

134 *Nikolay Mitrokhin* | Die „Russische Partei". Die Bewegung der russischen Nationalisten in der UdSSR 1953-1985 | Aus dem Russischen übertragen von einem Übersetzerteam unter der Leitung von Larisa Schippel | ISBN 978-3-8382-0024-8

135 *Manja Hussner, Rainer Arnold (Hgg.)* | Verfassungsgerichtsbarkeit in Zentralasien II. Sammlung von Verfassungstexten | ISBN 978-3-8382-0597-7

136 *Manfred Zeller* | Das sowjetische Fieber. Fußballfans im poststalinistischen Vielvölkerreich | Mit einem Vorwort von Nikolaus Katzer | ISBN 978-3-8382-0757-5

137 *Kristin Schreiter* | Stellung und Entwicklungspotential zivilgesellschaftlicher Gruppen in Russland. Menschenrechtsorganisationen im Vergleich | ISBN 978-3-8382-0673-8

138 *David R. Marples, Frederick V. Mills (Eds.)* | Ukraine's Euromaidan. Analyses of a Civil Revolution | ISBN 978-3-8382-0660-8

139 *Bernd Kappenberg* | Setting Signs for Europe. Why Diacritics Matter for European Integration | With a foreword by Peter Schlobinski | ISBN 978-3-8382-0663-9

140 *René Lenz* | Internationalisierung, Kooperation und Transfer. Externe bildungspolitische Akteure in der Russischen Föderation | Mit einem Vorwort von Frank Ettrich | ISBN 978-3-8382-0751-3

141 *Juri Plusnin, Yana Zausaeva, Natalia Zhidkevich, Artemy Pozanenko* | Wandering Workers. Mores, Behavior, Way of Life, and Political Status of Domestic Russian Labor Migrants | Translated by Julia Kazantseva | ISBN 978-3-8382-0653-0

142 *David J. Smith (Eds.)* | Latvia – A Work in Progress? 100 Years of State- and Nation-Building | ISBN 978-3-8382-0648-6

143 *Инна Чувычкина (ред.)* | Экспортные нефти- и газопроводы на постсоветском пространстве. Анализ трубопроводной политики в свете теории международных отношений | ISBN 978-3-8382-0822-0

144 *Johann Zajaczkowski* | Russland – eine pragmatische Großmacht? Eine rollentheoretische Untersuchung russischer Außenpolitik am Beispiel der Zusammenarbeit mit den USA nach 9/11 und des Georgienkrieges von 2008 | Mit einem Vorwort von Siegfried Schieder | ISBN 978-3-8382-0837-4

145 *Boris Popivanov* | Changing Images of the Left in Bulgaria. The Challenge of Post-Communism in the Early 21st Century | ISBN 978-3-8382-0667-7

146 *Lenka Krátká* | A History of the Czechoslovak Ocean Shipping Company 1948-1989. How a Small, Landlocked Country Ran Maritime Business During the Cold War | ISBN 978-3-8382-0666-0

147 *Alexander Sergunin* | Explaining Russian Foreign Policy Behavior. Theory and Practice | ISBN 978-3-8382-0752-0

148 *Darya Malyutina* | Migrant Friendships in a Super-Diverse City. Russian-Speakers and their Social Relationships in London in the 21st Century | With a foreword by Claire Dwyer | ISBN 978-3-8382-0652-3

149 *Alexander Sergunin, Valery Konyshev* | Russia in the Arctic. Hard or Soft Power? | ISBN 978-3-8382-0753-7

150 *John J. Maresca* | Helsinki Revisited. A Key U.S. Negotiator's Memoirs on the Development of the CSCE into the OSCE | With a foreword by Hafiz Pashayev | ISBN 978-3-8382-0852-7

151 *Jardar Østbø* | The New Third Rome. Readings of a Russian Nationalist Myth | With a foreword by Pål Kolstø | ISBN 978-3-8382-0870-1

152 *Simon Kordonsky* | Socio-Economic Foundations of the Russian Post-Soviet Regime. The Resource-Based Economy and Estate-Based Social Structure of Contemporary Russia | With a foreword by Svetlana Barsukova | ISBN 978-3-8382-0775-9

153 *Duncan Leitch* | Assisting Reform in Post-Communist Ukraine 2000–2012. The Illusions of Donors and the Disillusion of Beneficiaries | With a foreword by Kataryna Wolczuk | ISBN 978-3-8382-0844-2

154 *Abel Polese* | Limits of a Post-Soviet State. How Informality Replaces, Renegotiates, and Reshapes Governance in Contemporary Ukraine | With a foreword by Colin Williams | ISBN 978-3-8382-0845-9

155 *Mikhail Suslov (Ed.)* | Digital Orthodoxy in the Post-Soviet World. The Russian Orthodox Church and Web 2.0 | With a foreword by Father Cyril Hovorun | ISBN 978-3-8382-0871-8

156 *Leonid Luks* | Zwei „Sonderwege"? Russisch-deutsche Parallelen und Kontraste (1917-2014). Vergleichende Essays | ISBN 978-3-8382-0823-7

157 *Vladimir V. Karacharovskiy, Ovsey I. Shkaratan, Gordey A. Yastrebov* | Towards a New Russian Work Culture. Can Western Companies and Expatriates Change Russian Society? | With a foreword by Elena N. Danilova | Translated by Julia Kazantseva | ISBN 978-3-8382-0902-9

158 *Edmund Griffiths* | Aleksandr Prokhanov and Post-Soviet Esotericism | ISBN 978-3-8382-0903-6

159 *Timm Beichelt, Susann Worschech (Eds.)* | Transnational Ukraine? Networks and Ties that Influence(d) Contemporary Ukraine | ISBN 978-3-8382-0944-9

160 *Mieste Hotopp-Riecke* | Die Tataren der Krim zwischen Assimilation und Selbstbehauptung. Der Aufbau des krimtatarischen Bildungswesens nach Deportation und Heimkehr (1990-2005) | Mit einem Vorwort von Swetlana Czerwonnaja | ISBN 978-3-89821-940-2

161 *Olga Bertelsen (Ed.)* | Revolution and War in Contemporary Ukraine. The Challenge of Change | ISBN 978-3-8382-1016-2

162 *Natalya Ryabinska* | Ukraine's Post-Communist Mass Media. Between Capture and Commercialization | With a foreword by Marta Dyczok | ISBN 978-3-8382-1011-7

163 *Alexandra Cotofana, James M. Nyce (Eds.)* | Religion and Magic in Socialist and Post-Socialist Contexts. Historic and Ethnographic Case Studies of Orthodoxy, Heterodoxy, and Alternative Spirituality | With a foreword by Patrick L. Michelson | ISBN 978-3-8382-0989-0

164 *Nozima Akhrarkhodjaeva* | The Instrumentalisation of Mass Media in Electoral Authoritarian Regimes. Evidence from Russia's Presidential Election Campaigns of 2000 and 2008 | ISBN 978-3-8382-1013-1

165 *Yulia Krasheninnikova* | Informal Healthcare in Contemporary Russia. Sociographic Essays on the Post-Soviet Infrastructure for Alternative Healing Practices | ISBN 978-3-8382-0970-8

166 *Peter Kaiser* | Das Schachbrett der Macht. Die Handlungsspielräume eines sowjetischen Funktionärs unter Stalin am Beispiel des Generalsekretärs des Komsomol Aleksandr Kosarev (1929-1938) | Mit einem Vorwort von Dietmar Neutatz | ISBN 978-3-8382-1052-0

167 *Oksana Kim* | The Effects and Implications of Kazakhstan's Adoption of International Financial Reporting Standards. A Resource Dependence Perspective | With a foreword by Svetlana Vlady | ISBN 978-3-8382-0987-6

168 *Anna Sanina* | Patriotic Education in Contemporary Russia. Sociological Studies in the Making of the Post-Soviet Citizen | With a foreword by Anna Oldfield | ISBN 978-3-8382-0993-7

169 *Rudolf Wolters* | Spezialist in Sibirien Faksimile der 1933 erschienenen ersten Ausgabe | Mit einem Vorwort von Dmitrij Chmelnizki | ISBN 978-3-8382-0515-1

170 *Michal Vít, Magdalena M. Baran (Eds.)* | Transregional versus National Perspectives on Contemporary Central European History. Studies on the Building of Nation-States and Their Cooperation in the 20th and 21st Century | With a foreword by Petr Vágner | ISBN 978-3-8382-1015-5

171 *Philip Gamaghelyan* | Conflict Resolution Beyond the International Relations Paradigm. Evolving Designs as a Transformative Practice in Nagorno-Karabakh and Syria | With a foreword by Susan Allen | ISBN 978-3-8382-1057-5

172 *Maria Shagina* | Joining a Prestigious Club. Cooperation with Europarties and Its Impact on Party Development in Georgia, Moldova, and Ukraine 2004–2015 | With a foreword by Kataryna Wolczuk | ISBN 978-3-8382-1084-1

173 *Alexandra Cotofana, James M. Nyce (Eds.)* | Religion and Magic in Socialist and Post-Socialist Contexts II. Baltic, Eastern European, and Post-USSR Case Studies | With a foreword by Anita Stasulane | ISBN 978-3-8382-0990-6

174 *Barbara Kunz* | Kind Words, Cruise Missiles, and Everything in Between. The Use of Power Resources in U.S. Policies towards Poland, Ukraine, and Belarus 1989–2008 | With a foreword by William Hill | ISBN 978-3-8382-1065-0

175 *Eduard Klein* | Bildungskorruption in Russland und der Ukraine. Eine komparative Analyse der Performanz staatlicher Antikorruptionsmaßnahmen im Hochschulsektor am Beispiel universitärer Aufnahmeprüfungen | Mit einem Vorwort von Heiko Pleines | ISBN 978-3-8382-0995-1

176 *Markus Soldner* | Politischer Kapitalismus im postsowjetischen Russland. Die politische, wirtschaftliche und mediale Transformation in den 1990er Jahren | Mit einem Vorwort von Wolfgang Ismayr | ISBN 978-3-8382-1222-7

177 *Anton Oleinik* | Building Ukraine from Within. A Sociological, Institutional, and Economic Analysis of a Nation-State in the Making | ISBN 978-3-8382-1150-3

178 *Peter Rollberg, Marlene Laruelle (Eds.)* | Mass Media in the Post-Soviet World. Market Forces, State Actors, and Political Manipulation in the Informational Environment after Communism | ISBN 978-3-8382-1116-9

179 *Mikhail Minakov* | Development and Dystopia. Studies in Post-Soviet Ukraine and Eastern Europe | With a foreword by Alexander Etkind | ISBN 978-3-8382-1112-1

180 *Aijan Sharshenova* | The European Union's Democracy Promotion in Central Asia. A Study of Political Interests, Influence, and Development in Kazakhstan and Kyrgyzstan in 2007–2013 | With a foreword by Gordon Crawford | ISBN 978-3-8382-1151-0

181 *Andrey Makarychev, Alexandra Yatsyk (Eds.)* | Boris Nemtsov and Russian Politics. Power and Resistance | With a foreword by Zhanna Nemtsova | ISBN 978-3-8382-1122-0

182 *Sophie Falsini* | The Euromaidan's Effect on Civil Society. Why and How Ukrainian Social Capital Increased after the Revolution of Dignity | With a foreword by Susann Worschech | ISBN 978-3-8382-1131-2

183 *Valentyna Romanova, Andreas Umland (Eds.)* | Ukraine's Decentralization. Challenges and Implications of the Local Governance Reform after the Euromaidan Revolution | ISBN 978-3-8382-1162-6

184 *Leonid Luks* | A Fateful Triangle. Essays on Contemporary Russian, German and Polish History | ISBN 978-3-8382-1143-5

185 *John B. Dunlop* | The February 2015 Assassination of Boris Nemtsov and the Flawed Trial of his Alleged Killers. An Exploration of Russia's "Crime of the 21st Century" | ISBN 978-3-8382-1188-6

186 *Vasile Rotaru* | Russia, the EU, and the Eastern Partnership. Building Bridges or Digging Trenches? | ISBN 978-3-8382-1134-3

187 *Marina Lebedeva* | Russian Studies of International Relations. From the Soviet Past to the Post-Cold-War Present | With a foreword by Andrei P. Tsygankov | ISBN 978-3-8382-0851-0

188 *Tomasz Stępniewski, George Soroka (Eds.)* | Ukraine after Maidan. Revisiting Domestic and Regional Security | ISBN 978-3-8382-1075-9

189 *Petar Cholakov* | Ethnic Entrepreneurs Unmasked. Political Institutions and Ethnic Conflicts in Contemporary Bulgaria | ISBN 978-3-8382-1189-3

190 *A. Salem, G. Hazeldine, D. Morgan (Eds.)* | Higher Education in Post-Communist States. Comparative and Sociological Perspectives | ISBN 978-3-8382-1183-1

191 *Igor Torbakov* | After Empire. Nationalist Imagination and Symbolic Politics in Russia and Eurasia in the Twentieth and Twenty-First Century | With a foreword by Serhii Plokhy | ISBN 978-3-8382-1217-3

192 *Aleksandr Burakovskiy* | Jewish-Ukrainian Relations in Late and Post-Soviet Ukraine. Articles, Lectures and Essays from 1986 to 2016 | ISBN 978-3-8382-1210-4

193 *Natalia Shapovalova, Olga Burlyuk (Eds.)* | Civil Society in Post-Euromaidan Ukraine. From Revolution to Consolidation | With a foreword by Richard Youngs | ISBN 978-3-8382-1216-6

194 *Franz Preissler* | Positionsverteidigung, Imperialismus oder Irredentismus? Russland und die „Russischsprachigen", 1991–2015 | ISBN 978-3-8382-1262-3

195 *Marian Madeła* | Der Reformprozess in der Ukraine 2014-2017. Eine Fallstudie zur Reform der öffentlichen Verwaltung | Mit einem Vorwort von Martin Malek | ISBN 978-3-8382-1266-1

196 *Anke Giesen* | „Wie kann denn der Sieger ein Verbrecher sein?" Eine diskursanalytische Untersuchung der russlandweiten Debatte über Konzept und Verstaatlichungsprozess der Lagergedenkstätte „Perm'-36" im Ural | ISBN 978-3-8382-1284-5

197 *Alla Leukavets* | The Integration Policies of Belarus and Ukraine vis-à-vis the EU and Russia. A Comparative Case Study Through the Prism of a Two-Level Game Approach | ISBN 978-3-8382-1247-0

198 *Oksana Kim* | The Development and Challenges of Russian Corporate Governance I. The Roles and Functions of Boards of Directors | With a foreword by Sheila M. Puffer | ISBN 978-3-8382-1287-6

199 *Thomas D. Grant* | International Law and the Post-Soviet Space I. Essays on Chechnya and the Baltic States | With a foreword by Stephen M. Schwebel | ISBN 978-3-8382-1279-1

200 *Thomas D. Grant* | International Law and the Post-Soviet Space II. Essays on Ukraine, Intervention, and Non-Proliferation | ISBN 978-3-8382-1280-7

201 *Slavomír Michálek, Michal Štefansky* | The Age of Fear. The Cold War and Its Influence on Czechoslovakia 1945–1968 | ISBN 978-3-8382-1285-2

202 *Iulia-Sabina Joja* | Romania's Strategic Culture 1990–2014. Continuity and Change in a Post-Communist Country's Evolution of National Interests and Security Policies | With a foreword by Heiko Biehl | ISBN 978-3-8382-1286-9

203 *Andrei Rogatchevski, Yngvar B. Steinholt, Arve Hansen, David-Emil Wickström* | War of Songs. Popular Music and Recent Russia-Ukraine Relations | With a foreword by Artemy Troitsky | ISBN 978-3-8382-1173-2

204 *Maria Lipman (Ed.)* | Russian Voices on Post-Crimea Russia. An Almanac of Counterpoint Essays from 2015–2018 | ISBN 978-3-8382-1251-7

205 *Ksenia Maksimovtsova* | Language Conflicts in Contemporary Estonia, Latvia, and Ukraine. A Comparative Exploration of Discourses in Post-Soviet Russian-Language Digital Media | With a foreword by Ammon Cheskin | ISBN 978-3-8382-1282-1

206 *Michal Vít* | The EU's Impact on Identity Formation in East-Central Europe between 2004 and 2013. Perceptions of the Nation and Europe in Political Parties of the Czech Republic, Poland, and Slovakia | With a foreword by Andrea Pető | ISBN 978-3-8382-1275-3

207 *Per A. Rudling* | Tarnished Heroes. The Organization of Ukrainian Nationalists in the Memory Politics of Post-Soviet Ukraine | ISBN 978-3-8382-0999-9

208 *Kaja Gadowska, Peter Solomon (Eds.)* | Legal Change in Post-Communist States. Progress, Reversions, Explanations | ISBN 978-3-8382-1312-5

209 *Paweł Kowal, Georges Mink, Iwona Reichardt (Eds.)* | Three Revolutions: Mobilization and Change in Contemporary Ukraine I. Theoretical Aspects and Analyses on Religion, Memory, and Identity | ISBN 978-3-8382-1321-7

210 *Paweł Kowal, Georges Mink, Adam Reichardt, Iwona Reichardt (Eds.)* | Three Revolutions: Mobilization and Change in Contemporary Ukraine II. An Oral History of the Revolution on Granite, Orange Revolution, and Revolution of Dignity | ISBN 978-3-8382-1323-1

211 *Li Bennich-Björkman, Sergiy Kurbatov (Eds.)* | When the Future Came. The Collapse of the USSR and the Emergence of National Memory in Post-Soviet History Textbooks | ISBN 978-3-8382-1335-4

212 *Olga R. Gulina* | Migration as a (Geo-)Political Challenge in the Post-Soviet Space. Border Regimes, Policy Choices, Visa Agendas | With a foreword by Nils Muižnieks | ISBN 978-3-8382-1338-5

213 *Sanna Turoma, Kaarina Aitamurto, Slobodanka Vladiv-Glover (Eds.)* | Religion, Expression, and Patriotism in Russia. Essays on Post-Soviet Society and the State. ISBN 978-3-8382-1346-0

214 *Vasif Huseynov* | Geopolitical Rivalries in the "Common Neighborhood". Russia's Conflict with the West, Soft Power, and Neoclassical Realism | With a foreword by Nicholas Ross Smith | ISBN 978-3-8382-1277-7

215 *Mikhail Suslov* | Geopolitical Imagination. Ideology and Utopia in Post-Soviet Russia | With a foreword by Mark Bassin | ISBN 978-3-8382-1361-3

216 *Alexander Etkind, Mikhail Minakov (Eds.)* | Ideology after Union. Political Doctrines, Discourses, and Debates in Post-Soviet Societies | ISBN 978-3-8382-1388-0

217 *Jakob Mischke, Oleksandr Zabirko (Hgg.)* | Protestbewegungen im langen Schatten des Kreml. Aufbruch und Resignation in Russland und der Ukraine | ISBN 978-3-8382-0926-5

218 *Oksana Huss* | How Corruption and Anti-Corruption Policies Sustain Hybrid Regimes. Strategies of Political Domination under Ukraine's Presidents in 1994-2014. With a foreword by Tobias Debiel and Andrea Gawrich | ISBN 978-3-8382-1430-6

219 *Dmitry Travin, Vladimir Gel'man, Otar Marganiya* | The Russian Path. Ideas, Interests, Institutions, Illusions. With a foreword by Vladimir Ryzhkov | ISBN 978-3-8382-1421-4

220 *Gergana Dimova* | Political Uncertainty. A Comparative Exploration. With a foreword by Todor Yalamov and Rumena Filipova | ISBN 978-3-8382-1385-9

221 *Torben Waschke* | Russland in Transition. Geopolitik zwischen Raum, Identität und Machtinteressen. Mit einem Vorwort von Andreas Dittmann | ISBN 978-3-8382-1480-1

222 *Steven Jobbitt, Zsolt Bottlik, Marton Berki (Eds.)* | Power and Identity in the Post-Soviet Realm. Geographies of Ethnicity and Nationality after 1991 | ISBN 978-3-8382-1399-6

223 *Daria Buteiko* | Erinnerungsort. Ort des Gedenkens, der Erholung oder der Einkehr? Kommunismus-Erinnerung am Beispiel der Gedenkstätte Berliner Mauer sowie des Soloveckij-Klosters und -Museumsparks | ISBN 978-3-8382-1367-5

224 *Olga Bertelsen (Ed.)* | Russian Active Measures. Yesterday, Today, Tomorrow | With a foreword by Jan Goldman | ISBN 978-3-8382-1529-7

225 *David Mandel* | "Optimizing" Higher Education in Russia. University Teachers and their Union "Universitetskaya solidarnost'" | ISBN 978-3-8382-1519-8

226 *Mikhail Minakov, Gwendolyn Sasse, Daria Isachenko (Eds.)* | Post-Soviet Secessionism. Nation-Building and State-Failure after Communism | ISBN 978-3-8382-1538-9

227 *Jakob Hauter (Ed.)* | Civil War? Interstate War? Hybrid War? Dimensions and Interpretations of the Donbas Conflict in 2014–2020 | With a foreword by Andrew Wilson | ISBN 978-3-8382-1383-5

228 *Tima T. Moldogaziev, Gene A. Brewer, J. Edward Kellough (Eds.)* | Public Policy and Politics in Georgia. Lessons from Post-Soviet Transition | With a foreword by Dan Durning | ISBN 978-3-8382-1535-8

229 *Oxana Schmies (Ed.)* | NATO's Enlargement and Russia. A Strategic Challenge in the Past and Future | With a foreword by Vladimir Kara-Murza | ISBN 978-3-8382-1478-8

230 *Christopher Ford* | Ukapisme – Une Gauche perdue. Le marxisme anti-colonial dans la révolution ukrainienne 1917-1925 | Avec une préface de Vincent Présumey | ISBN 978-3-8382-0899-2

231 *Anna Kutkina* | Between Lenin and Bandera. Decommunization and Multivocality in Post-Euromaidan Ukraine | With a foreword by Juri Mykkänen | ISBN 978-3-8382-1506-8

232 *Lincoln E. Flake* | Defending the Faith. The Russian Orthodox Church and the Demise of Religious Pluralism | With a foreword by Peter Martland | ISBN 978-3-8382-1378-1

233 *Nikoloz Samkharadze* | Russia's Recognition of the Independence of Abkhazia and South Ossetia. Analysis of a Deviant Case in Moscow's Foreign Policy Behavior | With a foreword by Neil MacFarlane | ISBN 978-3-8382-1414-6

ibidem.eu